Yeats

& the Poetry of Death

ELEGY, SELF-ELEGY,

AND THE SUBLIME

Jahan Ramazani

Yale University Press   New Haven & London

This book may not be reproduced, in whole or in part, including illustrations, in any form (beyond that copying permitted by Sections 107 and 108 of the U.S. Copyright Law and except by reviewers for the public press), without written permission from the publishers. Acknowledgment is made for permission by Macmillan Publishing Company to reprint the following poems from *The Poems of W. B. Yeats: A New Edition*, edited by Richard J. Finneran (New York, 1983): "The friends that have it I do wrong," copyright © 1983 by Anne Yeats; "Beautiful Lofty Things" and "The Spur," copyright 1940 by Georgie Yeats, renewed 1968 by Bertha Georgie Yeats, Michael Butler Yeats, and Anne Yeats; "Death," copyright 1933 by Macmillan Publishing Company, renewed 1961 by Bertha Georgie Yeats; "To Be Carved on a Stone at Thoor Ballylee," copyright 1924 by Macmillan Publishing Company, renewed 1952 by Bertha Georgie Yeats; "The End of Day," "Her Friends Bring Her a Christmas Tree," and "Lines Written in Dejection," copyright 1919 by Macmillan Publishing Company, renewed 1947 by Bertha Georgie Yeats; "The Magi" and "A Coat," copyright 1916 by Macmillan Publishing Company, renewed 1944 by Bertha Georgie Yeats.

Designed by Sonia Scanlon. Set in Galliard type by Keystone Typesetting, Inc., Orwigsburg, Pennsylvania. Printed in the United States of America by Book-Crafters, Inc., Chelsea, Michigan.

Library of Congress Cataloging-in-Publication Data
Ramazani, Jahan, 1960–
   Yeats and the poetry of death : elegy, self-elegy, and the sublime /
Jahan Ramazani.
     p. cm.
   Includes bibliographical references (p.).
   ISBN 0-300-04804-1 (alk. paper)
   1. Yeats, W. B. (William Butler), 1865–1939–Criticism and interpretation.
2. Elegiac poetry, English—History and criticism. 3. Sublime, The,
in literature. 4. Death in literature. 5. Self in literature. I. Title.
PR5908.D4R36   1990
821'.8—dc20
                                                        90-12255
                                                           CIP

10   9   8   7   6   5   4   3   2   1

For My Parents,
Nesta and Ruhi

CONTENTS

Acknowledgments   ix

Abbreviations   xi

Introduction   1

ONE   "Breathless Faces": The Elegy   14

TWO   "Laughing to the Tomb":

            Tragic Joy and the Sublime   79

THREE   "Man's Dirty Slate": The Self-Elegy   134

            Coda   200

            Notes   207

            Index   237

ACKNOWLEDGMENTS

I would like to thank the Yeats scholars with whom I have had the good fortune to work, since they have guided and shaped my thinking about this project: Thomas Whitaker, Harold Bloom, Hillis Miller, Otto Bohlmann, John Kelly, Terry Eagleton, and, if only it were possible to thank him, the late, ever generous Richard Ellmann.

Among these critics, Thomas Whitaker was the most extensively involved with the evolution of this book. In commenting on the manuscript, he asked tough and insightful questions at every turn, yet patiently granted me the space to develop nascent ideas.

Paul Fry also read the manuscript as it emerged. He contributed a great deal through his close attention to the argument and through his vigorous responses to the readings and theory.

Marie Borroff, Stephen Cushman, Richard Finneran, Margaret Homans, Paul Morrison, Austin Quigley, and George Wright read separate chapters and sections, kindly bringing to my notice theses and details that needed shoring up.

Later, Harold Bloom, Otto Bohlmann, Thomas Greene, and Geoffrey Hartman read the manuscript in its entirety and offered valuable suggestions for revision. As it approached its final form, Herbert Tucker and Eleanor Cook commented on the book with precision, lending me their meticulous scrutiny.

At the earliest stage of this project, Ayşe Agiş, Paul Armstrong, Ian Duncan, Julia Lupton, James Murphy, William Rushton, David Wyatt, and my brother Vaheed helped me to formulate the overall plan with the supportive criticism and trust that only such fine friends can provide.

In an earlier state, the second part of chapter 2 appeared in *PMLA*; my thanks to the editor for permission to reprint some of this material. I am grateful for support from the Research Committee at the University of Virginia and from the Whiting Foundation.

ABBREVIATIONS

The following abbreviations are used throughout. Unless otherwise specified by context, parenthetical references without abbreviations are to Finneran's revised edition of the *Poems* (abbreviated *P* where necessary).

Au   *The Autobiography of William Butler Yeats*. 1935. New York: Macmillan, 1965.

AV   *A Vision*. 1937. London: Macmillan, 1962.

CL1   *The Collected Letters of W. B. Yeats*. Vol. 1. Ed. John Kelly and Eric Domville. New York: Oxford University Press, 1986.

E&I   *Essays and Introductions*. London: Macmillan, 1961.

Ex   *Explorations*. New York: Macmillan, 1962.

L   *The Letters of W. B. Yeats*. Ed. Allan Wade. London: Rupert Hart-Davis, 1954.

Mem *Memoirs*. Ed. Denis Donoghue. New York: Macmillan, 1973.

Myth *Mythologies*. New York: Macmillan, 1959.

Ox   *The Oxford Book of Modern Verse*. Ed. W. B. Yeats. Oxford: Clarendon Press, 1936.

P   *The Poems*. Ed. Richard J. Finneran. Rev. ed. Vol. 1 of *The Collected Works of W. B. Yeats*. New York: Macmillan, 1989.

UP1   *Uncollected Prose*. Vol. 1. Ed. John P. Thrayne. New York: Columbia University Press, 1970.

UP2   *Uncollected Prose*. Vol. 2. Ed. John P. Thrayne and Colton Johnson. New York: Columbia University Press, 1976.

VP   *The Variorum Edition of the Poems of W. B. Yeats*. Ed. Peter Allt and Russell K. Alspach. Corrected ed. New York: Macmillan, 1966.

VPl   *The Variorum Edition of the Plays of W. B. Yeats*. Ed. Russell K. Alspach. New York: Macmillan, 1965.

INTRODUCTION

So far as this world of our positive experience is con-
cerned, death can only be an idea, not something
known by us as we know our bodily sensations. In fact,
its ideality is probably one element that recommends it
to the use of poets, whose trade is to deal exclusively in
symbols. . . . Moreover, since no poet can write of
death from an immediate experience of it, the imag-
ining of death necessarily involves images not directly
belonging to it. It lies beyond the realm of images—or
at least beyond the realm of such images as the living
body knows.
—Kenneth Burke
  "Thanatopsis for Critics"

As in death, too, the world does not change,
  but ceases.
Death is not an event of life. Death is
  not lived through.
—Ludwig Wittgenstein
  Tractatus Logico-Philosophicus

    Why Yeats and death? After all, many other writers
seem more obsessed with death—Dickinson, Poe, and Rilke, to
name only a few. And hardly any corpses rot or skulls rattle in
Yeats's lyrics. Worms spire about a dead man's bones only in "The
Man who dreamed of Faeryland," and in "The Black Tower"
alone do some old bones shake. If crossbones and maggots are
one's idea of death, then Yeats is disappointing. At the opposite
end of the representational spectrum from such physicality, a
handful of lyrics indulge fantasies of death as heaven, from the
dancing-place of "The Happy Townland" to the drowsy paradise

of "News for the Delphic Oracle"; but other poets give us more compelling visions of an afterlife. As bodily putrefaction or bodiless bliss, death in Yeats's lyrics is a meager and unilluminating topic. These concepts of death can tell us little about the finest poems in Yeats's oeuvre, his vexed meditations on loss, ruin, and oblivion: elegies such as "Easter, 1916," self-elegies such as "Man and the Echo," and poems of the sublime such as "Lapis Lazuli." And yet, death is the occasion of these poems and of most of Yeats's enduring lyrics—however irreducible to moldering bones or gilded angels.

The pressure of death on such poems may baffle us, since Yeats asserts in *Per Amica Silentia Lunae* and *A Vision* that, in effect, there is no death as absence or nothingness but only a recurrence of life in other bodies and other states. No doubt this elaborate myth of reincarnation is an important element of his "system," but an acceptance of it as his definitive view of death would lead us down several interpretive blind alleys. If there is no annihilation of self, then how can we explain the effort of lyric after lyric to summon up heroic energy in the face of death? One of Yeats's models for the lyric, as we shall see in our discussion of the poems of tragic joy, is the utterance of the hero upon encountering destruction: "The heroes of Shakespeare convey to us through their looks, or through the metaphorical patterns of their speech, the sudden enlargement of their vision, their ecstasy at the approach of death: 'She should have died hereafter,' 'Of many thousand kisses, the poor last,' 'Absent thee from felicity awhile'" (*E&I*, 522–23). Yeats tirelessly varies this idea in his essays, not hinting in these passages that there might be an afterlife, for such is not the kind of death that would make "our minds expand convulsively" and our speech blaze into lyric extravagance (*E&I*, 245). Moreover, Yeats rarely obtrudes the concept of reincarnation into his elegies for dead friends, relatives, and political figures. And it is impossible to explain the rhetorical strains and excesses in such self-elegies as "The Tower" and "Under Ben Bulben," their relentless struggle to work up courage, if we take at face value their assurance about reincarnation—about the

"Translunar Paradise" that follows our "brief parting from those dear" (198, 325). The system's displacement of death onto subsequent lives should not blinker our reading of the poems, since the strongest lyrics seldom ratify this view of death.[1] In "Man and the Echo" Yeats literally puts the system into question, intimating that death is irrevocably beyond his cognitive reach:

> O rocky voice
> Shall we in that great night rejoice?
> What do we know but that we face
> One another in this place? [346]

Death in Yeats's major poetry, then, cannot be understood in terms of presence—the rotting body or the later incarnation—but must be seen as a mode of absence, an absence that may be interpreted psychologically as the absence of libidinal objects, ontologically as the anticipated absence of one's own being, and linguistically as the absence of which the sign is a trace. Present only in representation and yet exceeding the compass of all representation, death for Yeats is an absence that elicits abundant imaginings and marks the limits of the imagination. In each of the broad generic groups that are the focus of this book's successive chapters, Yeats contemplates his dependence on the muse of death for the aesthetic life of his poetry. In the elegy "In Memory of Major Robert Gregory," he suggests that he may be able to make poetry of his companions only in their death: "All, all are in my thoughts to-night being dead" (132). In the anti-elegiac lyric "The Gyres," a poem of tragic joy and the sublime, he welcomes blood, ruin, and death as spur to his heroic countersong: "We that look on but laugh in tragic joy" (293). The imagination dwells the most, he implies in "The Tower," not upon a woman won but on a "woman lost"; while dwelling on men and women lost, he also declares in this self-elegy, "It is time that I wrote my will," thus making poetry out of his expectations of ultimate loss (197–98).

To make the void fruitful with lyrics, Yeats knows he must understand not only that friends or civilizations are subject to death but also that his own existence is founded on absence: "I shall find the dark grow luminous, the void fruitful when I understand I have nothing, that the ringers in the tower have appointed for the hymen of the soul a passing bell" (*Myth*, 332). He even goes so far as to suggest that when writing, poets announce death within themselves. Discussing Lady Gregory's death, Yeats shifts easily from it to his own poetic death: "A writer must die every day he lives, be reborn, as it is said in the Burial Service, an incorruptible self, that self opposite of all that he has named 'himself'" (*Au*, 307). Every day, in every act of writing, a poet rehearses death, dying to the biographical self and assuming a "mask" or "phantasmagoria." Thus, the daughters of the Sidhe sentence Yeats's surrogate, the bard Hanrahan, to the death of poetry: "It is death he has chosen; let him die, let him die, let him die" (*Myth*, 233). No wonder old men crowd Yeats's verse, from Oisin and the "Old Pensioner" to "The Old Men admiring Themselves in the Water"—withered Narcissi fixated on images of themselves:

> They had hands like claws, and their knees
> Were twisted like the old thorn-tree
> By the waters.   [82]

For Yeats, death is both the human absence that generates the anticipatory or retrospective mourning of poetry and the absence within poetry itself.[2]

In tracing Yeats's dialogue with death, I am chiefly concerned with the lyrics, because the lyrics are the most splendid outcome of Yeats's intimations of mortality. But it may be useful at the outset to recall that in the story Yeats tells about himself, particularly in his *Reveries over Childhood and Youth,* death is interwoven with his earliest memories. In *The Anxiety of Influence,* Harold Bloom makes a general assertion that has a special relevance to Yeats: "Every poet begins (however 'unconsciously') by rebelling more strongly against the consciousness of death's necessity than all other men and women do."[3] Yeats claims that his "realisation of death came" when his younger brother died, a "realisation" that would make him refuse to go see "old bedrid-den people because they would soon die" (*Au,* 16). But the opening pages of the *Autobiography* show that long before this encounter with another's death, he would continually ruminate over his own. His first memory is of looking at "a wall covered with cracked and falling plaster," a premature harbinger of decay; and this memory bleeds into another, in which a servant reports that a boy in uniform "is going to blow the town up, and I go to sleep in terror" (*Au,* 1). Much like Wordsworth in the "spots of time" of *The Prelude,* Yeats in *Reveries* stumbles from one fright-ening confrontation with death to another—though nothing so literal as a drowned man's face bolts upright amid Yeats's sub-limations of mortality. There soon follows the description of another "night of misery when, having prayed for several days that I might die, I began to be afraid that I was dying and prayed that I might live" (*Au,* 1–2). This vacillation between a mental flight toward death and a countermovement toward life is charac-teristic of Yeats, almost as if consciousness were for him the battlefield of Eros and the death drive.

Another characteristic vacillation that Yeats maps onto his early memories is between passive and active stances before death, or between elegiac pathos and anti-elegiac ethos. In his "attacks of melancholy," the boy would pray for punishment to a confused composite of God and his grandfather Pollexfen (*Au,* 3). His habitual sorrow always exceeded the immediate loss, especially once he had begun to nurse his "melancholy" disposition by reading Shelley (*Au,* 42). The outward emblem of Yeats's pathos was his dark complexion, which provoked the observation that he "could not live more than a year" and the repeated taunt of some boys, "Oh, here is King Death again" (*Au,* 18, 55). But Yeats admits to shame at his lack of courage, and a contrary impulse governs his youthful fantasies of heroism. In dream, the boy longed to "die fighting": "there was to be a big battle on the seashore near Rosses and I was to be killed" (*Au,* 7–8). For years, the only wish that competed with this one was the desire to turn magician; both are dreams of mastering death, whether by heroically willing or magically overriding it (*Au*, 30). From the start, representation was for Yeats a way to practice death and regulate anxieties about fragmentation and loss. After his brother's death, Yeats remembers himself "very happy" in drawing ships with their flags at half-mast, and at other times he would cover his table "with pen and ink pictures of myself, doing all kinds of courageous things" (*Au*, 16, 25). Yeats's concepts of the mask, Unity of Being, and the phantasmagoria evolve from these early enactments of heroic self-overcoming, for Yeats spun his aesthetic theory out of his youthful desire to master dread and melancholia.

Yeats universalizes his death anxiety as the generative principle of all truth and poetry. "I think profound philosophy must come from terror," he writes, adding that an "abyss opens under our feet," much as Schopenhauer had claimed death for the muse of philosophy (*E&I*, 502).[4] Close to dying, the newly enlightened Wise Man of *The Hour-Glass* proclaims with excitement:

> —I can explain all now.
> Only when all our hold on life is troubled,
> Only in spiritual terror can the Truth
> Come through the broken mind—as the pease burst
> Out of a broken pease-cod.   [*VPl*, 625]

Such statements about terror and the abyss would seem to be incommensurable with Yeats's *Vision*, his "belief" in reincarnation, and his heroic histrionics; but some brief quotations show that Yeats himself diagnosed all three as symptoms of a profound anxiety:

> When I was writing *A Vision* I had constantly the word 'terror' impressed upon me. [*Ex*, 425]

> Belief comes from shock and is not desired. . . . Belief is renewed continually in the ordeal of death. [*AV*, 53]

> And have I not sung in describing guests at Coole—"There one that ruffled in a manly pose, For all his timid heart"— that one myself? [*Au*, 307]

The system, the myth of reincarnation, and the heroic pose are all what the psychoanalyst calls "reaction-formations," representing the frightening thought of death by its opposite. Such an argument may invite the charge of nonfalsifiability, but this argument alone, in my view, can account for such apparent contradictions as the violence with which Yeats denies death and yet his need to rehearse it in one poem after another; his "belief" in an afterlife and yet his refusal of this consolation in the pained prose elegies of the *Autobiography;* his belittling of the fear of death and yet his assertions that terror alone begets knowledge. Indeed, the glory of Yeats's oeuvre lies precisely in this to-and-fro movement between the repression of death and the avowal of its finality. Unlike poets who write more deliberately about their anxiety, Yeats usually aestheticizes and sublimates it, and so his poetry, suffused with death, comments upon it pervasively—though evasively. "Man has created death," Yeats proclaims, and throughout his poetry he creates and recreates it ("Death," 234).

In spite of these special complexities, Yeats is not alone, of course, in taking death as his muse. In terms of cultural history, he could be seen as participating in a broad intensification of the perennial imaginative interest in death, which historians often trace to the eighteenth century; witness such scattered cultural phenomena as the tombstone ruminations of the Graveyard School, *Clarissa,* Burke on the sublime, the Gothic novel, Wordsworth's Lucy poems, and then in the nineteenth century, the poetic meditations of Keats, Beddoes, Tennyson, both Rossettis, Swinburne, and other late Romantics. Yeats considers himself one of "the last romantics," and nowhere is this more evident than in his elegiac and self-elegiac inheritance from Shelley (245).[5] He singles out for special praise the end of *Adonais,* in which Shelley "sees his own soon-coming death in a rapture of prophecy" (*E&I,* 72). The model poet for the youthful Yeats was the poet-figure of *Alastor*—"a Poet whose untimely tomb" is the poem itself. "I have made my bed / In charnels and on coffins," says the speaker, literalizing the intimacy of the Romantic poet with "black death."[6]

But the "Romantic Agony," as Mario Praz terms the aesthetic that paired beauty and death, would obviously outlive the nineteenth century.[7] Appropriating Pater's evocation of a mind enlarged by the apprehension of its own finitude, Yeats ascribes to the lyric in particular just such death-quickened and impassioned consciousness.[8] From Yeats, Eliot, and Stevens to Lowell, Plath, Hill, and Heaney, death often seems to be the raison d'être of the modern lyric. For these writers, as for their Romantic predecessors, "Death is the mother of beauty."[9] Some of the early modernists even cast poetry as a kind of death rite—a rite, that is, which enacts death and resurrection, much like the fertility myths that they culled from comparative anthropologists. In the absence of stable religious codes for mourning and self-mourning, Yeats, Eliot, and Pound sometimes represent their poetry on the analogue of planting corpses and slaying gods—essentially ways of practicing loss and one's own death. His "simple-minded" Protestantism spoiled by Huxley and Tyndall, Yeats "made a new religion, almost an infallible church of poetic tradition" (*Au*, 77). The young Yeats anticipates the modernist nostalgia for religious defenses against death: he scurries about the Irish countryside, collecting stories about the afterlife, the Sidhe, and ghosts; he undergoes ritual death in hermetic societies like the Golden Dawn; and he invents in his poetry what Eliot calls "the mythical method."[10]

Recuperating myth and ritual for his contests with death, Yeats also shares with such writers as Nietzsche, Hemingway, and Stevens the historical project of reconstructing a literary heroism. In his lyrics of tragic joy, the speakers laugh into the face of death; in his plays, Cuchulain, Seanchan, and Naoise bravely encounter their own destruction. During Yeats's lifetime the escalation of mass death made codes of personal heroism increasingly problematic; but the subversion of heroism, like the weakening of mourning ritual, helped to stimulate its reconstitution in poetry as an aesthetic construct. Modern warfare, Yeats knew, was incompatible with the code he was trying to salvage: "Deductions" from science "make possible the stimulation and condonation of revolutionary massacre and the multiplication of murderous weapons by substituting for the old humanity with its unique irreplaceable individuals something that can be chopped and measured like a piece of cheese" (*Ex,* 436). We shall later explore the political difficulties of Yeats's poetry, but suffice it to say that, as a reactionary, Yeats denounced such poets as Owen, Auden, and Spender; they seemed less intent than himself on preserving the lyric as a space in which the last warriors could duel with death (*Ox,* xxxiv–xxxv; *L,* 837). The pity and fear of these poets represented the powerful tendencies within his own mind that he tried so hard to stem, tendencies represented as the "hysterical women" in "Lapis Lazuli" and the sighing boy in "The Gyres." Even while writing lyrics that expound tragic joy in destruction, Yeats could nevertheless protest in a letter of 1936: "I am not callous, every nerve trembles with horror at what is happening in Europe, 'the ceremony of innocence is drowned'" (*L,* 851). Mocking his "philosophy" in "Nineteen Hundred and Nineteen," a poem written at the time of the Black and Tan atrocities, Yeats intimates that he developed his system in part as a defense against the "terror" of war (207); indeed, it was during the First World War that he drew up the system's blueprint, *Per Amica Silentia Lunae.* Because the mass death in modern warfare threatens to disrupt or even petrify mechanisms of representation,[11] Yeats clutches all the more vehemently to exemplary heroes who belong "to a dead art"; he suppresses the dehumanization of death by keeping before his mind heroes who claim deaths uniquely and irreplaceably their own—heroes whose last moments "will, it may be, haunt me on my death-bed" (*Ex,* 416). This last phrase suggests that, for Yeats, the literary reconstitution of a disappearing heroism provided above all an *ars moriendi,* a way of training himself aesthetically for his own death. Although he tried to use the death-centered lyric to preserve his place among other "unique irreplaceable individuals," Yeats worried that such individuals were being endangered not only by technological warfare but also by Ireland's new middle class, by scientific "externality," by the city's "pushing world," and by education's enforcement of a "growing cohesiveness, . . . everybody thinking like everybody else" (*E&I*, 41, 189, 224; *Ex*, 423).

Just as the death rite and the heroic code became parts of Yeats's aesthetic while they were disappearing around him, so too more recent poets, such as Geoffrey Hill, James Merrill, Seamus Heaney, and Louise Glück, seem intent on sustaining in the lyric a meditative discourse about death—a discourse that much of contemporary Western society, say sociologists and historians, regards as taboo.[12] A similar compensatory effort may also be seen in the discussions of death in recent literary criticism. With an array of approaches to death in literature—deconstructive, psychoanalytic, generic, old and new historicist—literary critics are now groping for ways of talking about what the culture at large relegates to silence and pornography (AIDS notwithstanding).[13] Even critics embarrassed over a language that might become homiletic or existential often smuggle death into discussions of a more technical kind, where it becomes a term for the gaps in signification, rhetorical opacities or rifts, defeat by one's precursors, and so forth. Regarded as displacements, these sometimes illuminating concepts also inform the more overt "thanatology" of this work. When critics and poets write about death—an absence beyond empirical and linguistic determination—they must inevitably rename its absence as something else; Kenneth Burke calls such necessary translations the "deflections" of death.[14]

Because death is neither "an immediate experience" (Burke) nor "an event of life" (Wittgenstein), a poet's representation of it must draw heavily on cultural traditions, and no modern poet was more steeped in literary tradition than was Yeats.[15] Although the historical contexts I have been invoking (war, religion, and so on) shape the contours of Yeats's dialogue with death, that dialogue inherits its specific, literary discourses from the more transhistorical codes known as "genres." Many poetic responses to death have been encoded immemorially within literary genres, so Yeats's poetry of death should not be bound exclusively to a diachronic axis. Exemplifying the danger of such an overemphasis, Philippe Ariès claims that during the nineteenth century death ceased to be the "death of the self" and became the "death of the other"; yet, the elegiac and self-elegiac genres, codified since antiquity, make available to Yeats both dramatic relationships with death.[16] Further, death from the perspective of the Romantic lyric has a peculiar kind of historical status, because the death at issue is often the poet's own, from Keats's "When I have Fears that I may cease to be" and Dickinson's "Because I could not stop for Death" to Yeats's "Under Ben Bulben." Neither an "event" nor an "experience," one's own death is utterly ahistorical—a nothingness always in excess of its historical representations—and yet utterly historical—nothing more than its time-bound representations because nothing itself.

My primary interest lies in interpreting the psychological, ontological, and rhetorical dimensions of Yeats's poetry of death and its informing genres. The generic framework of this study thus draws on several theories of death. These include Freud's psychoanalysis of human attempts to master death in dreams, tragedy, obsessional neuroses, and religion—attempts to master death by representing it as its opposite: a wish-fulfillment.[17] This perspective contradicts Freud's more limited views on death, from which I depart: that the fear of death is always secondary, that there is no correlative for death in the unconscious, and that death anxiety is ultimately the fear of castration.[18] Because psychoanalysis describes death in terms of object-loss and cannot explain the specificity of one's own death, I turn to Heidegger for his ontological theory of death as one's "ownmost" or "authentic" (*eigenst, eigentlich*) possibility. But I also modify this analysis to show how access to one's "own" death is always culturally and psychologically mediated.[19] Neither the ontological nor the psychological perspective accounts for the intimate relationship between death and writing. So this inquiry also draws on a rhetorical tradition that goes back to Plato's *Phaedrus* (where "written discourse" is "dead discourse") and that extends to Jacques Derrida ("All graphemes are of a testamentary essence") and Paul de Man ("Death is a displaced name for a linguistic predicament").[20] But the reduction of death to a purely "linguistic predicament" is an essentialist stance contrary to my hermeneutic interest in the various displacements of death. Death is, as Richard Wollheim observes, an "impure" and "hybrid" concept; literary thanatology therefore needs, in my view, to sustain a measured pluralism.[21]

Yeats's poetry is unusually various in its articulations of death, partly because it rejoins and revises a remarkable diversity of genres and modes. Cutting across individual poems, volumes, even the entire corpus, many genres can help us interpret Yeats's polymorphous responses to death—his elegiac pathos, for example, as against his apocalyptic joy in destruction.[22] Yeats remakes the genres he appropriates, while also revealing their hidden logic. In calling the dead person a "nobody" or a "drunken, vainglorious lout," for example, he brings a new candor to the elegy and discloses the ambivalence that has long been latent in the genre (156, 181). Although Yeats reinvigorates the elegy, he also writes many poems that are anti-elegiac. Rejoicing in death and ruin, the poems of tragic joy and the sublime uncover the gaiety buried in such traditions as prophecy and tragedy, carpe diem and the curse. And the self-elegies both expose and intensify the self-mourning implicit within the autobiographical lyric, the invocation, and the ekphrasis. Not only can these genres help us to read Yeats's lyrics; the lyrics can, because they often describe their own genesis, help us to read the genres they draw upon. As hermeneutic filters, these genres direct our attention to the traditions that Yeats enters and modifies in his dialogue with the "rocky voice." They sometimes overlap—an elegy like "The Municipal Gallery Re-visited" is also self-elegiac—and they sometimes dialectically invert one another—many of the anti-elegies are covertly elegiac, and many of the elegies resound with an anti-elegiac joy. "The purpose of criticism by genres," as Northrop Frye states, "is not so much to classify as to clarify such traditions and affinities, thereby bringing out a large number of literary relationships that would not be noticed as long as there were no context established for them."[23] Balancing genre criticism with close reading, this book traces the interrelations between Yeats's lyrics and the traditions that inspired them. Despite some fine interpretive studies, Allen Tate predicted in 1942 the general emphasis of Yeats scholarship—"the more difficult problem of the poetry itself will probably be delayed."[24] Although the significance of "the poetry itself" can be interpreted only in relation to other horizons, such as genre and theory, it is to the difficulties of the poetry itself that the rest of this work is devoted.

1

"BREATHLESS FACES"

The Elegy

*This special human dimension is the in-built capacity
of man to think beyond his own life in the world, to
think about death. This is why the burial of the dead
is perhaps the fundamental phenomenon of becoming
human. . . . [B]y a remarkable expenditure of human labor and sacrifice there is sought an abiding
with the dead, indeed a holding fast of the dead
among the living. . . . [W]e are dealing here with a
conduct of life that has spiraled out of the order of nature.*
—Hans-Georg Gadamer
    Reason in the Age of Science

*The only thing grief has taught me, is to know how
shallow it is. . . . In the death of my son, now more
than two years ago, I seem to have lost a beautiful
estate,—no more.*
—Ralph Waldo Emerson
    "Experience"

Although the young Yeats writes few formal elegies,
his early work is suffused with elegiac pathos, an affective inclina-
tion he shares with many late Romantic contemporaries. His
early love poems, for example, repeatedly bemoan the loss or
death of the beloved. Like the melancholy lovers ever "full of
tears," the Sad Shepherd tells a *"piteous story,"* and Oisin mourns
his lost companions with "drooping head"—one of Yeats's nu-
merous echoes of "Lycidas" (20, 9, 358). The elegiac, in this
broad, modal sense of the term, undergirds Yeats's early concept

14

of the poetic, as we shall see from the elegiac love lyrics.[1] In his well-known essay "The Symbolism of Poetry" (1900), elegiac tone more than "symbolism" links the exemplary passages, such as Burns's "melancholy cry" ("And Time is setting with me, O!"), Nashe's lament over mutability ("Dust hath closed Helen's eye"), and Timon's final anticipation of his own death ("Timon hath made his everlasting mansion") (*E&I*, 156). Even though Yeats becomes disenchanted with the "overcharged colour" of his early laments, elegy would remain an important model for his understanding of the imagination (*Au*, 48). During the twenties and thirties he sometimes depicts the imagination's basic work in a language that very nearly describes the elegy. By creating substitutes for what death has taken away, the elegist attempts to compensate for loss, and Yeats formulates in just these terms the creative victory of what he calls *subjective* men—their "daily re-creation of all that exterior fate snatches away" (*Au*, 128). This is also the principal activity of the "imagination" in his own phase, a phase in which the "Body of Fate" is termed "loss": the imagination "must substitute some new image" for the "object" seized by fate (*AV*, 142).

In spite of these strong affinities with elegy, the mature Yeats resists some of its governing conventions when he writes poems directly in the genre. Whereas most English elegists lament with high pathos the death of an individual, Yeats subdues pathos to an unusual extent, and he typically commemorates the death not of one person but of a small group. These departures from the defining subject matter and psychic action of the elegy have received little analysis, except for some suggestive observations by Helen Vendler.[2] Further, Yeats's elegies are strikingly frank about their aggression toward the dead—a frankness made possible in part by the flexibility of the group form. Never before had an elegist used such terms for the dead: "A nobody in a great throng," "half a lunatic, half knave," "much falling," "sluggish," "ignorant," "A drunken, vainglorious lout," "bitter," "Blind," "withered old and skeleton-gaunt," "loose-lipped demagogue."

How can we explain these remarkable departures from elegiac

tradition? First, I should make it clear that I am not making an ad hominem argument about Yeats's moral character; his kindness as a human being is not in question. I am interested in how the poetry works, how it says it works, and how it says the genre of elegy works. Yeats's elegies bring close to the surface the dramatic and affective tension inscribed within the form throughout its development. Although Ben Jonson disclaims an elegy that would "think to ruin, where it seemed to raise," he manages to raze quietly the daunting edifice of his "Beloved" Shakespeare: he remarks his "small" learning, his less art (it "must enjoy a part"), and ends with an apotheosis that might also be a damnation— "for thy volume's light." Yeats's criticism of the dead is harsher than ever before in the elegy, as we shall see from the elegies for the Easter rebels, the Pollexfens, several companions (including Robert Gregory), fellow enthusiasts of the occult, and the Gore-Booth sisters. Yeats heightens the competition usually concealed within the form, manifestly battering the dead while he woos them.[3] Even though some of the elegies affectionately commune with the dying or dead and castigate the living (those for Mabel Beardsley, Romantic Ireland, Parnell, Augusta Gregory, and the beautiful lofty things), I focus initially on the reverse stance because of its unprecedented prominence. Critics usually write of elegy as a means for identifying and "abiding with" the dead, but Yeats's elegies also reveal the genre's other impulse: to divide the dead from the living.[4] Apparently writing in a genre of acquiescence but refusing to yield to the potentially tyrannical power of the dead, Yeats illustrates his Nietzschean dictum: "all noble things are the result of warfare" (*E&I*, 321). Even so, in contentiously distinguishing himself from the dead, Yeats also opens himself to them with a frankness usually reserved for intimate relationships with the living.

By candidly stating his ambivalence toward the dead, Yeats helps to remake the elegy for the modern period. When Auden inherits the form from Yeats and Hardy (who risks describing his dead wife as "indifferent"), he can admit that Freud was often "wrong and at times absurd" and that Yeats himself was "silly like us." These modern poets prepare the way for the still more aggressive elegies by Americans like Lowell, Plath, and Berryman, poets who say of their dead fathers: "'Anchors aweigh,' Daddy boomed in his bathtub," "Daddy, daddy, you bastard, I'm through," and "I spit upon this dreadful banker's grave."[5] Yeats plays an important role in renewing the genre and in making it central to the history of twentieth-century lyric.

We can best interpret his elegies by dividing them into two smaller groups: the private elegies, or lyrics that mourn the deaths of friends and family, and the public elegies, or lyrics that mourn the deaths of political figures. But first, before turning to the elegies proper and Yeats's signal contributions to the form, we should consider his earlier poems of mourning, laments in a different genre: the elegiac love poems.

THE ELEGIAC LOVE POEMS:
A WOMAN DEAD AND GON(N)E

Although Yeats later resists it, pathos clearly predominates over other moods in his early work, particularly in the elegiac love lyrics. Since no one is really dying or dead, these poems are elegiac in mode without being formal elegies. Descending primarily from erotic verse, the early love poems make up a recognizable group, as a 1985 collection reminds us—*A Poet to His Beloved: The Early Love Poems of W. B. Yeats*. Even so, many poems in the collection are generically hybrid, lyrics in which erotic song has been crossed with epitaph, love poem with elegy. Indeed, such love poems as "A Dream of Death" (1891) and "He wishes his Beloved were Dead" (1898) could also be called death poems. This ambiguity may help to explain the uneasy introduction to the volume, which praises the lyrics as "warm" and "ideal types of romantic poetry" but also calls them "too soft, dreamy, languorous, indolent."[6] To generate their "love," some of the love poems conjure a death. They imagine that the beloved "had died in a strange place" and that she is "lying cold and dead" in the ground (42, 72). Surrendering the beloved in effigy, they enact a symbolic rite of presence and absence that resembles not only the fertility rituals Yeats knew from Frazer and other comparative anthropologists but also Freud's famous *fort/da* game. Like the anthropologist's rituals and the psychoanalyst's game, the elegiac love poems both lament the beloved's death and yet require it as their condition of possibility. Although they are written neither in the group form nor in the querulous tone of many later elegies, the early love lyrics call attention to their aggressive absenting of the beloved, thereby raising one of the questions that haunts elegies like "In Memory of Major Robert Gregory" and "Parnell's Funeral"—namely, whether the elegist in some sense wills the death he mourns. In the early love poems as in the later elegies, Yeats guiltily acknowledges his reliance on thoughts of death to produce poetic mourning.

Lamenting the death that he imaginatively projects, Yeats increases the traditional inaccessibility and absence of the beloved. In this regard he is hardly alone: the dead woman is an aesthetic obsession during the period of his early poetic development. Partly in response to the nascent socioeconomic empowerment of women, Decadent poets and Pre-Raphaelite painters of "the tragic generation" dwell lugubriously on such literary types as the dead Ophelia, Elaine, and Lady of Shalott. Yeats writes of "pearl-pale" ladies and the "White woman that passion has worn" during the epoch of what has been called the "consumptive sublime" (355, 361, 369, 378; 63).[7] Earlier in the century, Poe had concluded that "the death, then, of a beautiful woman is, unquestionably, the most poetical topic in the world." Much androcentric love poetry since Petrarch and Dante presupposes this eerie view. Thus, late nineteenth-century laments for dead women belong to and intensify tendencies within older male traditions that define "woman" as the silent, absent referent.[8] Articulating the implicit link between the Petrarchan idealization of the beloved and her mummification, Yeats asks, when a man loves, does he not choose "that beauty which seems unearthly because the individual woman is lost amid the labyrinth of its lines as though life were trembling into stillness and silence, or at last folding itself away?" (*E&I*, 243–44). In the Petrarchan and courtly traditions, the idolized woman is a woman "lost," her being designated as "labyrinth," her life consigned to "stillness and silence."

But if pervasive social and cultural traditions help to define woman as the mute, dead "other"—the absent center around which male love poets elaborate their symbolic rites of mourning—how does Yeats stand apart? To an extraordinary extent, he thematizes his dependence on the beloved's death and absence for the life of his poetry. In the midst of "The Tower," a later sequence that uses the figure of the poet's blindness to reaffirm that the beloved must exist only in the mind's eye, Yeats echoes his earlier question about the woman lost; but this time the question is almost a self-accusation:

> Does the imagination dwell the most
> Upon a woman won or woman lost?[9]   [197]

He considers only one possible answer. Sometimes boldly, sometimes subtly, often unknowingly, Yeats's early love lyrics ruminate over their own implicit logic and that of their engendering tradition, even while perpetuating that same logic. The self-analysis in Yeats's love poetry does not "save" it from androcentric culture, but it can help us to probe the connections between that culture's erotic and elegiac poetry.

Because the titles of Yeats's elegiac love lyrics signal their thematic, generic, and psychic structures, these titles themselves deserve consideration for what they suggest about the interrelation between love and mourning in the early Yeats. Proposing a theme for elaboration, titles like "The Pity of Love" and "The Sorrow of Love" thematically commingle desire and melancholy. Other titles guide us into the poems by establishing their genre or subgenre, such as "Two Love Poems" and, strikingly, "An Epitaph" (*VP*, 154, 170, 123). A third kind of title combines these Victorian conventions of designating the theme and genre of the poem, while offering a brief description of its psychic action.

Again love and lament interfuse—for example, "The Lover
mourns for the Loss of Love" and, in a title that traces the
conversion of elegy into apocalyptic yearning, "He mourns for
the Change that has come upon Him and his Beloved, and longs
for the End of the World." The verbs in these descriptive titles—
mourns, remembers, longs, wishes, but also *bids, tells, speaks*—suggest that for the early Yeats mournful love is the wellspring of
poetic utterance. In his formal elegies Yeats tries to strip himself
of this protracted despondency, a change reflected in the new
directness ("In Memory of Alfred Pollexfen") and brevity ("Easter, 1916") of the later titles.[10]

Long before asking the famous question of "The Tower,"
Yeats begins to suggest that the (male) imagination dwells the
most upon a woman lost. The early dream-poem "A Dream of
Death" raises the disturbing possibility that many a love lyric may
ultimately be, as he had originally entitled the poem, "An Epitaph":

> I dreamed that one had died in a strange place
> Near no accustomed hand;
> And they had nailed the boards above her face,
> The peasants of that land,
> Wondering to lay her in that solitude,
> And raised above her mound
> A cross they had made out of two bits of wood,
> And planted cypress round;
> And left her to the indifferent stars above
> Until I carved these words:
> *She was more beautiful than thy first love,*
> *But now lies under boards.*   [42]

The beloved is at first merely an anonymous "one," lost in the
solitary landscape, where even the peasants' memorial mound,
cross, and cypress cannot save her from the indifference of the
stars. Dead, she can be humanized only by the poet: he carves
words on the cross that celebrate her beauty (in the earlier version

he "wrote" upon the cross). But to idealize her, the poet has had to imagine her dead—inhumed and requiring his rehumanizing "hand." The astonishing image of nailing "boards above her face" is initially displaced onto the agency of the peasants; yet, the poet's own inscription repeats the word *boards*, relating the defacement to his act of writing. The lyric enacts and exaggerates the contradictory movements of courtly love poetry, idealizing but defacing the beloved. In a later autobiographical celebration of Maud Gonne, to whom Yeats sent this poem, he rhapsodically invokes a brief moment when "her face, like the face of some Greek statue, showed little thought" and "might outface even Artemisia's sepulchral image," but alas, her face soon resumes its place among the merely living (*Au,* 242). Embedded within the larger epitaph of the whole lyric, the beloved's two-line epitaph is not really hers at all, particularly if we accept the traditional association of "thy first love" with Yeats's cousin, Laura Johnston, and the second with Maud Gonne. On that reading, the epitaph is not merely a formulaic boast to the passerby; self-reflexive, it is an apostrophe to the poet himself, writing the second love into a comparison between his relationships. The epitaph that the beloved's imagined death has allowed the poet to create is a miniature of the epitaphic process of much love poetry.

Although Frank Kermode calls "the dead face and the dancer . . . the central icon of Yeats and of the whole tradition," we have heard a lot about the dancer, while this dead face has been largely ignored.[11] Perhaps the poem's unsettling representation of the way it and other love lyrics work, burying and idealizing the beloved, is incongruous with our sentimental notions of the early Yeats; but the poem meditates on its own genesis as rigorously, if not as spectacularly, as "Byzantium" does. In its reflection on writing and the dead woman, "A Dream of Death" rivals its predecessors in a troubling line of Romantic love elegies, from Wordsworth's Lucy poems to Dante Gabriel Rossetti's paradoxically entitled *The House of Life* and Wilde's stilted "Requiescat," a line subsequently resumed by Hardy's *Poems of 1912–13.*[12] Because the poem is about itself and precisely not about women, because it is indeed about the erasure of women in love poetry, it is *about* Maud Gonne or Laura Johnston only in the root sense of *about*—outside. Gonne recalls in her autobiography that, recovering from a serious illness, she received the poem in France: "I was getting steadily better and was greatly amused when Willie Yeats sent me a poem, my epitaph he had written with much feeling."[13] Only imagined to be dead can she inspire such an impassioned love epitaph.

"A Dream of Death" is a poetic representation of a dream-representation of the beloved's death; but if we are hesitant about concluding that it therefore expresses a wish-fulfillment, the title of a companion dream-poem is more direct: "He wishes his Beloved were Dead." In their self-analysis, "A Dream of Death" and "He wishes his Beloved were Dead" share much with Freud's commentary on "Dreams of the Death of Beloved Persons" *(Die Traüme von Tod Teurer Personen)*, a commentary included in another work of the nineties—*The Interpretation of Dreams*. Indeed, Freud's opus and Yeats's *Wind Among the Reeds* appeared in the same year (1899). Freud attributes the wish for the loved one's death to a repressed childhood desire that the parent be "gone" *(fort)*, the child, like the adult unconscious, not distinguishing between death and other kinds of absence.[14] Yeats's lyrics reveal less the personal pathology of a necrophiliac than an awareness of unconscious desires—their materia poetica. Suggesting that their desire-charged language depends on the imagined absence or death of the loved one, these poems exemplify and highlight the psychological basis of much erotic poetry—perhaps even of Eros itself, at least according to the Lacanian theory of desire. As Lacan remarks in his *Discours de Rome*, "The symbol manifests itself first of all as the murder of the thing [*le meurtre de la chose*], and this death constitutes in the subject the eternalization of his desire."[15]

Aedh, the original speaker of "He wishes his Beloved were Dead," is appropriately enough both a poet and a "God of death" (*VP, 794*):

Were you but lying cold and dead,
And lights were paling out of the West,
You would come hither, and bend your head,
And I would lay my head on your breast;
And you would murmur tender words,
Forgiving me, because you were dead:
Nor would you rise and hasten away,
Though you have the will of the wild birds,
But know your hair was bound and wound
About the stars and moon and sun:
O would, beloved, that you lay
Under the dock-leaves in the ground,
While lights were paling one by one.   [72–73]

The disjunction between the two levels of the poem's rhetoric is
even more jarring than in "A Dream of Death." The beloved is a
dead woman, "lying cold and dead," and she is a divine principle
of the cosmos, dispersed in interstellar space. To borrow de
Man's terms, she is both a natural image and an emblem.[16] Critics
tend to suppress the natural imagery in such poems and perceive
only the apotheosis of the dead woman as Sophia, Wisdom, or
the holy Shekinah. But the poem shows us that it must "kill" the
beloved as natural image in order to transfigure her into a divine
principle of the imagination.[17] Though the beloved in Yeats does
differ from the corpses in Poe and Baudelaire, this woman is both
a disembodied essence and a cold, dead body, lying in the
ground. Yeats even specifies the coarse weeds—dock-leaves—
that cover her grave. In the dream-logic of this wish-poem, the
poet "wishes his Beloved were Dead" because dead, she would
generate language, not her own language but the words he wants
to hear: "you would murmur tender words, / Forgiving me,
because you were dead." These words forgive *d'outre-tombe* his
transgressions, possibly even his having wished her dead. Dead,
she would submit to his control, unable to articulate her own
desires or to "rise and hasten away." This lover is indeed both
poet and "God of death."

Together, the two early dream-poems partially anticipate a view shared by later theorists: that the sign is a carrier not of presence but of death and absence (in spite of Yeats's avowedly mystical theory of the symbol).[18] Thus, Raftery's words seemed to kill Mary Hynes, a young man explains to Yeats in *The Celtic Twilight:* "It is said that no one that has a song made about them will ever live long" (*Myth,* 27). For Yeats, a living woman and the nothingness in a man's song sometimes seem incompatible.[19]

Not all of Yeats's elegiac love poems represent the beloved as dead. If not dead, she may be dying or fallen, thus leaving a space between her present and past selves for the elegiac imagination to fill. Even when she is not dead, it is only the absent self that the poet records, as Yeats reminds us as late as "Fallen Majesty" (1912):

Although crowds gathered once if she but showed her
    face,
And even old men's eyes grew dim, this hand alone,
Like some last courtier at a gypsy camping-place
Babbling of fallen majesty, records what's gone.

The lineaments, a heart that laughter has made sweet,
These, these remain, but I record what's gone. A crowd
Will gather, and not know it walks the very street
Whereon a thing once walked that seemed a burning
    cloud.   [123–24]

Although he confesses that something remains of her physical beauty, the Blakean and Paterian word he chooses for it, *lineaments,* is itself a figure for absence, suggestive of an out*line* that de*line*ates a void. What remains is almost irrelevant to the poet: "I record what's gone," he proudly declaims. As in "A Dream of Death," the beloved has lost her former "face," and the "hand" of the poet refigures her. The hand is now the agency of love and language, a last courtier, and the elaborate simile of the gypsy camping-place situates it in the belated and homeless realm of words.

The poem's effacement of the beloved is visible in the buried pun on her name, emphasized by its repetition. Unlike the Innominata in most love poetry, the nameless beloved is named in the lines that proclaim her absence: the hand "records what's gone"; "I record what's gone." The trace of the name remains in the word that excludes it. If a "last courtier," Yeats certainly is not the first to pun on his beloved's name, as we know from Petrarch, who celebrates his poetry *(l'aura, lauro)* in puns on Laura's name. Following Petrarch's example, Yeats's pun makes a proper name improper by detaching it from its referent and making of it a sign of the poetic process.[20] Yeats's pun may be even more revealing than Petrarch's, because the word that displaces the name of the beloved signifies her absence—gone—an absence apparently necessary for the poem's own presence. Striking out one letter from her name, the poet renames the beloved as absence. "Her Praise" opens with the pun, and goes on to describe the poet wishing he might find someone with whom he could "Manage the talk until her name come round" (150). Similarly, in "Fallen Majesty," the poet excludes the beloved's name, but through the pun makes us supply it, so that we become complicitous in reading the poem with a desire structured around a lack.

The famous early love poem "When You are Old" (1892) also elegizes the youth of the beloved, but this poem represents her loss of youth as the poet's fancy. Yeats revises Ronsard's sonnet by putting his own book instead of distaff in the hand of the beloved; and what she reads there is not simply her youth but her youth recast as the prelude to old age:

> When you are old and grey and full of sleep,
> And nodding by the fire, take down this book,
> And slowly read, and dream of the soft look
> Your eyes had once, and of their shadows deep. . . .   [41]

Yeats imagines her to be old, alienated from herself, with the book alone preserving what's gone. He wills away her present self so that he may create a love elegy for her youth. He opens a gap for his poetry between her actual and imaginary selves, and thus, in her hypothetical reading of this poem, she reaches her present self by the detour of reading his book in her old age. She now depends upon the mediation of the poet's language, a mediation that cancels her externality and independence.[21] Once again a "love poem" turns out to be epitaphic, based on the forceful negation of the beloved. Tracing how his poems generate their constitutive desire, Yeats helps us to see more clearly an assumption shared by many poems of courtly love—poems that eclipse the beloved to produce their work of mourning. Even in his full-fledged elegies, where the death is not only imagined, Yeats still worries that he has contributed to the death he laments.

PRIVATE ELEGY

But Maud Gonne's amused response to her supposed "Epitaph" reminds us that the early love poems are not true elegies, that her oft-imagined death did not coincide with extra-poetic fact. In addition to such love epitaphs, Yeats was indeed writing formal elegies during the nineties, elegies that include the public lament for Parnell, "Mourn—And Then Onward!" (1891), and the private lament for Maud Gonne's first child, "On a Child's Death" (1893).[22] But these stiffly conventional works neither approximate the self-understanding of his early love poems nor foreshadow the power of his best elegies, written in the middle and late periods, from "Upon a Dying Lady" (1912–14) to "The Municipal Gallery Re-visited" (1937).

Much as Yeats heightens the self-consciousness of the love poem, so too he brings an intense self-scrutiny to the elegy. Gradually turning the elegy away from its memorial duties, the mature Yeats makes a space for meditative freedom not, as some pastoral elegists had, by discarding the dead behind a eulogistic cloud, but by writing elegies that are unabashedly about the poet and the poet's ambivalent responses to the dead. Every elegist, in Shelley's phrase, "in another's fate now wept his own," or as Spenser puts it in the pastoral eclogue Yeats avowedly imitated,

"Mourning in others, our owne miseries" (*L*, 646); this self-absorption becomes ever more evident in such Victorian elegies as Tennyson's *In Memoriam*, Elizabeth Barrett Browning's "Mother and Poet," and Swinburne's "Ave Atque Vale."[23] Nevertheless, the increased ambivalence of Yeats's elegies makes them seem still more inwardly focused. They dramatize the poet's effort to create a new self out of the conflicted process of mourning. Yeats's recurrent creation of a simplified mask is shaped dialectically by the opposite impulse: mournful self-negation. The danger posed by the elegist's contact with the dead is what Yeats calls in *A Vision* "Dispersal"—the false mask of self-surrender that tempts particularly those of his own phase. The challenge for the elegist is to meet the demand of "renunciation" while achieving his true mask: "Simplification through intensity" (*AV*, 140–42). Yeats's elegiac combativeness is therefore partly defensive, spurred by the fear of a contrary impulse toward the loss of self in mourning. Various paradigms may help us interpret the complex dialectic in the elegies between "Dispersal" and "Simplification." Ontologically, the elegist is drawn toward the ultimate dispersal of himself in death, and yet also toward simplifying himself as a totality, defined against the horizon of death. In psychoanalytic terms, he reencounters the dispersal of self threatened during the "mirror stage" and the oedipal crisis, but he also recapitulates the aggressive simplification and assertion of self that characterize these episodes.[24] Sometimes, as we shall see, an understanding of this vacillation requires rhetorical, psychosocial, and other modes of analysis.

Joyful Mourning: "Upon a Dying Lady"

Countering the danger of what he calls "the submission in pure sorrow," Yeats restrains the pathos of his pre-mortem elegies for Mabel Beardsley, both by containing it within a defensive joy and by encompassing her within a representation of his own craft (*E&I*, 252). Aside from this unusual joy (relegated by Milton and others to the end of their elegies), the seven poems in

the sequence are much more traditional than the later elegies.
Not yet manifesting two of Yeats's major departures from elegiac
norms, the sequence neither criticizes the dying friend nor
mourns more than one person. Instead, it rearticulates such major conventions of the genre as the apotropaic offering (the
"toys" and Christmas tree), the establishment of continuity by
lineage ("Her Race"), self-reflection ("no speech but symbol"),
and apotheosis by association ("Achilles, Timor, Babar, Barhaim,
all") (157–60). Formally, the variations in size recall the dimen-
sional oscillations of such elegies as "Lycidas" and *In Memoriam,*
and maybe even the to-and-fro movement of long and short lines
in elegiac couplets. From one poem to the next, line length
expands and then narrows, with the exception of the fifth and
sixth poems; and, leaving aside the first lyric, the number of lines
in each poem alternately exceeds or falls short of its predecessor.
The visual template of the poems is a figure for the vacillations of
mourning, the mind tossed between denial and resignation.

Already in the first poem, "Her Courtesy," the elegist begins
to check the genre's potential for submissive sorrow—an affective countermovement that will reach its extreme form in the
poems of tragic joy. He imagines the dying lady as a joyful hero,
and his emphasis on her linguistic competition with him indicates that he has turned her into a particular kind of joyful hero.
Poet and surrogate poet playfully vie in their responses to death,
her resolute acceptance challenging the poet to triumph over
grief. But here and throughout the sequence, traditional elegiac
identification regulates the mild competition with the deceased:

> With the old kindness, the old distinguished grace,
> She lies, her lovely piteous head amid dull red hair
> Propped upon pillows, rouge on the pallor of her face.
> She would not have us sad because she is lying there,
> And when she meets our gaze her eyes are laughter-lit,
> Her speech a wicked tale that we may vie with her,
> Matching our broken-hearted wit against her wit,
> Thinking of saints and of Petronius Arbiter.   [157]

Like the poet and his lyric, she seems to impose form on death. Her head is framed by hair and pillows, her rouge inscribed on the blankness of her face. And her exuberant speech defeats the pure silence that approaches. Like other elegists, Yeats is drawn toward death, but, in Blanchot's Heideggerian terms, he attempts to cancel its uncertainty, constructing through the woman a relationship of freedom with it.[25] By its end, the brief elegy has even switched the dying woman's gender that she may more closely resemble the male poet. It has refashioned her into an emblem of the "old" aristocratic courtesy and form; she too evokes a loveliness "long faded from the world" ("He remembers forgotten Beauty," 62).

Although it risks some sorrow, this and other of Yeats's elegies leave behind the heavy pathos not only of his early love poems but also of elegies by Milton, Gray, Shelley, and Tennyson, attempting instead to create a heroic mask for the poet. Elsewhere, Yeats supplies a philosophical context for this affective turn from pathos to ethos. In *A Vision* he defines the divine Christ's "pity" as a "primary" affect, as opposed to the "antithetical" anxiety he knew as a man in the Garden of Gethsemane (*AV*, 275). Christ's pathos diffuses the self; his anxiety gives it individuality. In the play *Calvary*, Yeats dramatizes the distinction in a conflict between an antithetical Lazarus and a primary Christ. Lazarus accuses Christ of robbing him of his death, not understanding that he wants to die: "You took my death, give me your death instead" (*VPl*, 782). For Yeats as for Heidegger, death may afford "an unshakable joy" if seized as one's own.[26] Death confers such joy in part because it permits one to unify one's life.

But that unity eludes the poet and his female counterpart. In one of the most ascetic elegies in the sequence, "The End of Day," Yeats explores through the metaphor of play the tension between the desire to totalize the life and its inevitable openness:

> She is playing like a child
> And penance is the play,
> Fantastical and wild

Because the end of day
Shows her that some one soon
Will come from the house, and say—
Though play is but half done—
'Come in and leave the play.'   [158]

Through the overdetermined metaphor of play, the poet finds a reflection of his own mournful play in Beardsley's childlike play of penance; then "play" widens out even more in the last line to become "the play of life" of the *theatrum mundi* topos. The elegy consoles by diminishing death's authority to that of a parent. But it also warns that the final call arbitrarily interrupts the half-completed work of self-mourning. By rejoining the friend to her origins, the next poem tries to compensate for this harsh admission that closure is inaccessible. Her life has a wholeness because she accepts both her personal past—"Happier days"—and her familial past—"Her Race" (158–59). In *A Vision* Yeats makes the Pythagorean claim "that men die because they cannot join their beginning and their end" (*AV*, 68–69). Trying to find the dying woman's end in her beginning, Yeats would immortalize her as an aesthetic whole. This attempt leads him into unfortunate bravado about lineage or "race"—a word transplanted from the Renaissance elegy.[27] Heroic integrity and self-possession distinguish the woman not only from death but also from the middle class, which Yeats bitterly labels "a common / Unreckonable race."

The tensions in the sequence between pathos and joy, dispersal and totality, persist in Yeats's later elegies. They reflect the poet's alternating confidence and uncertainty about the effectiveness of art's war on death. Superficially, art would seem to be the loser. The "wit" of the poet is at first "broken-hearted"—an image duplicated by the broken outline of the sequence; and he has "naught for death but toys," mere dolls or drawings that ineffectively substitute for the lost life ("Certain Artists bring her Dolls and Drawings," 158).[28] But by representing in the story the very substitution of art for life that he is poetically enacting,

Yeats calls attention to the performative power of his own work. He concedes the limited sway of his verse over death: "(I have no speech but symbol, the pagan speech I made / Amid the dreams of youth)" ("Her Courage," 159). But he also vaunts the woman's immortality and foregrounds his enlistment of her in a chorus of literary heroes, the initial disavowal permitting him to swell the bluster. This momentary regression to "youth" also joins his end with his beginning, thus establishing his own continuity in memory as against the discontinuity threatened by death. Critics have remarked that this poem ignores the plight of the real, dying woman.[29] In a dynamic familiar from the elegiac love poems, Yeats even supplants her with heroic emblems of his own joyful language, and he unites not so much her as himself to a literary tradition of such heroes as Achilles and Timor—heroes who have "laughed into the face of Death."[30]

After the mixture of swagger and restraint in the penultimate poem, the sequence ends in the quieter mode of prayer. The focus remains the power of art to stay death:

Pardon, great enemy,
Without an angry thought
We've carried in our tree,
And here and there have bought
Till all the boughs are gay,
And she may look from the bed
On pretty things that may
Please a fantastic head.
Give her a little grace,
What if a laughing eye
Have looked into your face?
It is about to die.
                    ["Her Friends bring her a Christmas Tree," 159–60]

Again the narrative recapitulates what the poem is itself doing. The friends bring in a Christmas tree that, like the drawings, dolls, and pagan dreams, is a figurative substitute for the dying lady, as archetypally for the dying god. Joyful, much as the elegiac sequence as a whole is joyful, the tree would displace sorrow and death. Because the elegy's laughter is defiant, the poet apologizes if the "laughing eye" of woman and lyric has seemed to challenge the ultimate authority of death. Having remade himself as the heroic plaintiff for Beardsley, he asks on her behalf for "a little grace"—a phrase that also recalls the "little ease" that he, like Milton, has himself interposed.[31] But humbled before the great enemy and great father, he finally acknowledges the reality principle: "It is about to die."

Group Elegy

In spite of such exceptions as the Beardsley sequence, most of Yeats's private and civic elegies are for more than one person. And yet their collective focus—a significant contribution to the genre—remains largely uninterpreted. With few precedents, Yeats reserves the majority of his elegies neither for individuals (the elegiac mainstream) nor for an anonymous mass (a sparse form instanced by Milton's sonnet "Avenge O Lord . . ." and Gray's "Elegy Written in a Country Churchyard"), but for small groups. According to the elegy's standard fiction, a collectivity mourns for an individual; Yeats inverts this dramatic configuration. There are, of course, some precedents for Yeats's group elegies. Shelley incorporates into *Adonais,* his lament for Keats, the images of other dead poets. And Hardy, adapting Gray, communes with the dead of Mellstock churchyard in "Friends Beyond" and other poems. The epic tradition offers many catalogs of the dead, catalogs that purge the dead of accidental qualities and select one characteristic or deed as a synecdoche for the life. In his own prose Yeats proceeds serially past a range of personalities—witness sections of his *Autobiography,* such as "The Tragic Generation" and *Dramatis Personae,* and the section of *A Vision* entitled "The Twenty-Eight Incarnations." But these and other relatives of the group elegy, such as the *de casibus* tradition and the "character," are too distant and uncertain to help us get at the significance of the collective form; for this, we must closely read Yeats's group memorials.

Neither "The Secret Rose" nor "Introductory Rhymes" presents itself as an elegy, but both poems prefigure in their catalogs of the dead the group form of the major elegies. Because these poems predate "Easter, 1916," they counter the possible impression that the Easter Rising alone made Yeats develop the group form. In "The Circus Animals' Desertion" Yeats states succinctly the principle of these linked miniature portraits:

> Character isolated by a deed
> To engross the present and dominate memory.   [347]

In the apparent paradox shared by Joyce's "epiphanies," the deeds that isolate character are impulsive and unpremeditated. They include giving up everything for a kiss, driving the gods out of their habitation, flinging the crown away, and selling house and goods for a lock of golden hair ("The Secret Rose," 69–70). The most spontaneous of the *"old fathers"* in the later poem is the

> *Old merchant skipper that leaped overboard*
> *After a ragged hat in Biscay Bay. . . .*
> ["Introductory Rhymes," 101]

In each case the unforeseen deed both reveals the character's potential for reckless courage and violates social, religious, or moral norms. It mirrors the poet's capacity for heedless or even amoral self-surrender and for the defiance of death; the skipper, for example, risks his life for a hat and, therefore, seems momentarily to have triumphed over death. By purifying the dead of everything except the poetic moment of their lives, the speaker proves a continuity between them and himself. In the apostrophe to the old fathers, the speaker exemplifies the line he addresses, his barren passion the latest in a sequence of *"wasteful virtues."*[32]

But, as in many of Yeats's elegies, the identification with the dead is combined with another impulse: the antithetical impulse of separation. Though the speaker seems to apologize to the dead and submissively request their acceptance, he also refutes their imagined accusation of impotence. From the point of view of the poem, the lineage and permanence of the two families depend on the poet's creative act, and their mere moments of poetic being signify his constant being as a poet. The lines

> *I have no child, I have nothing but a book,*
> *Nothing but that to prove your blood and mine*

allude to another introductory poem in which an author similarly announced his "booke" with disingenuous humility and called it his "child": Spenser's "Goe little booke . . . / As child whose parent is unkent"—a dedication that in turn echoed Chaucer's "Go litel book."[33] Yeats's allusion to an allusion implicitly sets up a poetic lineage that "overgoes" the merely familial one. Having refashioned everyone in the family into a trope for his poetry's triumph over mortality, the speaker by the end stands out as the only poet in the group. He calls attention to the *"book"* and this introductory poem of the book, a progeny that subtly distinguishes him from the literary impotence of his fathers.

Although it may not be self-evident that this oedipal impulse lurks beneath the pious surface of this address to the fathers, the group elegy for (or perhaps against) the dead males of the poet's maternal family is more explicit about its resistance. The title, "In Memory of Alfred Pollexfen," is misleading, since the elegist crowds other dead people around the ostensible subject of the elegy, anticipating the strategy of "In Memory of Major Robert Gregory." We reach Alfred's recent death only by picking our way through the paratactic string of earlier deaths, ranged sequentially and dated as if they were tombstones. Despite the appearance of mere sequentiality, the latent organization of these mini-epitaphs clarifies the function of the group form.

The portraits make up collectively a story of degeneration, with Alfred Pollexfen as the nadir. The poem begins with a memorial for the most daunting figure in the group, the *"silent and fierce old man"* of "Introductory Rhymes" (101). Two active verbs suggest that his power even extends to his relationship with death: instead of being buried, "old William Pollexfen / Laid his strong bones down in death"; and not in a tomb that merely was made but "In the grey stone tomb he made" (156). Personifying the Law and the Father, William alone achieves an active self-burial. For in the next line we read that "they laid / In that tomb" George, and John has had so little control over his death that the verb switches to the passive mode: "But where is laid the sailor John . . . ?" At least George "ended where his breath began," his circular life somewhat countering the placelessness of death, whereas John, like Lycidas and Tennyson's Ulysses, "never found his rest ashore, / Moping for one voyage more" (156). The manner of the sailor's death is itself emblematic of death's home-lessness. His defeat by death contrasts with the elegy's attempt—an attempt even more characteristic of epitaphs—to fix death in a specific place and time, thereby gaining some control over its absolute indeterminacy.[34]

The movement of decline terminates in the anticlimax of the poem's titular hero:

> And yesterday the youngest son,
> A humorous, unambitious man,
> Was buried near the astrologer,
> Yesterday in the tenth year
> Since he who had been contented long,
> A nobody in a great throng,
> Decided he would journey home,
> Now that his fiftieth year had come. . . .

Before Yeats, no elegist had dared to call the deceased "A no-body." The precipitous drop from William's steadfast individu-ality to John's placeless corpse leads to a man inseparable from the crowd. Alfred's only apparent virtues, all undistinctive, are his humor, his lack of ambition, and his long contentment. His death repeats the anonymity of his life; lost in the throng, he redisperses at death into the speech and memory of merely "common men" (157).

But the elegy does not end with this mourning procession of

commoners. Against the undifferentiated crowd and the increasingly undistinguished dead, an individual suddenly appears:

> At all these death-beds women heard
> A visionary white sea-bird
> Lamenting that a man should die;
> And with that cry I have raised my cry.

Although the visionary seabird would represent the apotheosis of the dead person in a traditional elegy, here the mourner—the visionary poet—achieves transcendence. The function of the group and its decline should now be clear. Joining in song an image of itself, the lyric "I" constitutes its solitary voice over against the dead throng, just as the seabird is distinguished from the passive auditors by its cry. As a coda, the ending reframes the poem, converting a testimony to the dead into an occasion for self-construction. The climactic cry reverses the gyrelike movement of the elegy toward passivity, placelessness, and commonality. Warding off the contagion of dispersal that attends the act of mourning, the poet draws a line of discontinuity between himself and the dead multitude.

In "All Souls' Night" (1920), epilogue to *A Vision* and collective elegy for occultist friends, Yeats seems more willing to blur the line between himself and the dead. Mourner turned magus, the speaker tells us that "the living mock" the truths he has to tell, so he winds himself and the reader into the imperturbable "mummy-cloth" of death (230). Yeats sometimes intimates that poets are subject to a kind of aesthetic death; when Fergus, for example, leaves his kingship for poetic "dreams," he abstracts himself from life: "now I have grown nothing, knowing all" ("Fergus and the Druid," 33). The genre of elegy threatens to draw a poet still deeper into that nothingness. Some great poets, Yeats says, "look at life deliberately and as if from beyond life," and indeed, by the end of this group elegy, the speaker pictures himself "bound" and "[w]ound" like a dead man (*E&I*, 278; *P*, 230). But it is exactly because the elegist opens himself to the dead that he wants to assert his distinctness from them, and so he magisterially summons his friends and comments skeptically upon them.

The organizing principles of the three portraits might help to establish further the value of the group form for Yeats. As in the Pollexfen elegy, the overarching pattern is one of decline. From the first two people, the confused Horton and the withered Emery, to the third, the crazed MacGregor, the lives grow worse. Although in each portrait the speaker isolates character in a first stanza and then hints at an apotheosis in the second, the somewhat saving movement toward transcendence is never really made by the deceased: it is Horton's wife who, because Horton has confused her with God, seems transfigured into a heavenly but silly "gold-fish"; an Indian tells Emery about the "delight" of the afterlife; and the poet alone forgives MacGregor (227–30). The first stanza of each portrait initially makes a criticism and then very tentatively repairs the damage: Horton's "pride" modulates into "love"; Emery's "wrinkles" appear on a "beautiful" face; MacGregor is "half a lunatic, half knave," leaving no part available for praise, but the speaker magnanimously allows that "friendship never ends." Vacillation between responses toward the dead is characteristic of elegy, but rarely had an elegist's blame so nearly undone the praise. Yeats gives us both his "CELEBRA-TIONS" and his "DETRACTIONS," as he called his divided thoughts on Synge after his death (*Au*, 346). Although Yeats groups his dead friends and identifies with them on the basis of a common interest in the occult, each portrait draws more attention to the botched life than to any knowledge of a life beyond that life. Yeats tells us elsewhere that MacGregor had introduced him to the hermetic practices that seemed to grant access to the afterlife (*Au*, 124). Here, however, the poet will not peer beyond this life, and the friend's postmortem existence dwindles into an unflattering hypothesis: MacGregor "may have grown more arrogant being a ghost." In the last stanzas of the elegy, the speaker casts out the elegiac project of conferring at least some individuality on the dead ("What matter who it be") and draws our attention to his mastery in "meditation" of all the mere "parts," himself the only whole and the only survivor.[35]

For all their candid bullying of the dead, these elegies often leave us feeling, oddly enough, that the poet has created a stronger fellowship with the dead than he could have done through mere eulogistic praise. As Georg Simmel and others have suggested, aggression can be a way of strengthening social bonds; even while the poet defines himself over against the group, his self-definition ultimately depends upon the community of the dead. And Freud associates the melancholic ambivalence of mourners with the ambivalence in love-relationships.[36] This sampling of Yeats's group elegies is too small to draw comprehensive inferences, but we can at least see that the group form gives Yeats the freedom to play out ambivalences in his relations with the dead and to break the constraints of one-to-one identification— an hypothesis we can test and elaborate in such group elegies as "In Memory of Major Robert Gregory" and "The Municipal Gallery Re-visited."

The Gregory Elegies

The four poems on Robert Gregory's death are a microcosm of the polymorphous poetics with which Yeats could respond to death.[37] The generic code of each work shapes its representation of death. In the dramatic monologue "An Irish Airman foresees his Death," the subjectively anticipated death challenges the speaker to assert his heroic resolve; by contrast, the satiric apostrophe "Reprisals" presents Gregory's death as a pointless waste, linking him to "the other cheated dead" (562). More closely related to the elegiac mainstream are the pastoral elegy in dialogue form, "Shepherd and Goatherd," and the monody on Gregory and other friends, "In Memory of Major Robert Gregory." Like many traditional elegies, these poems brood over themselves, but their concern that they may somehow have willed or caused death disturbs the conventional hope that elegy may conquer death. Extending our analysis of the group form, we may also consider more directly Yeats's elegiac meditation on the relation between death and writing.

In the pastoral dialogue, the Shepherd briefly reflects on this relation:

> I am looking for strayed sheep;
> Something has troubled me and in my trouble
> I let them stray. I thought of rhyme alone,
> For rhyme can beat a measure out of trouble
> And make the daylight sweet once more; but when
> I had driven every rhyme into its place
> The sheep had gone from theirs.   [142]

The neoclassical conceit may be artificial, but artifice is its subject. Poetry alone can triumph over sorrow because its aesthetic wholeness—every rhyme driven "into its place"—repairs the dispersal of the troubled mind, although unmastered thoughts, like the straying sheep, may still roam abroad. Drawn toward fragmentation, elegy simplifies through intensity. The dialectic describes not only the psychology of elegists but also the course taken by the image of the dead person in elegies. At the moment of death, the life is cut off abruptly and distributed to many minds. Then the elegist tries to replace the discontinued life and fragmented corpse with a harmonious image, reviewing the life synoptically and putting every phase and every limb—like every rhyme—"into its place." Peter Sacks complains, understandably, that the final myth in the Goatherd's song "has little connection to the generic context," but it could be seen as Yeats's version of elegy's consoling image of totality. The myth that Gregory lives backward his life through war, courtship, playtime, and infancy is a novel way of fulfilling our expectation of elegy—that the life should pass before our eyes, reconfigured.[38]

Nevertheless, the poem represents elegy and artifice not only in terms of wholeness. Seen from the opposite end of the same psychic and rhetorical movement, this impetus toward reconstruction presupposes a prior disintegration, as we saw in the disfiguration and refiguration of the elegiac love poems. Even in life the dead man seems to have been disjoined from himself, for the tunes—his only remains—are lonely and elegiac, as if he had mourned himself while living. They signify a self-separation only accentuated by death:

> And now that he is gone
> There's nothing of him left but half a score
> Of sorrowful, austere, sweet, lofty pipe tunes.   [143]

Gregory is himself an elegist, and Yeats imitates him in his lament, much as he rehearses Mabel Beardsley's "play," or as Spenser recapitulates Sidney's prior unhappiness.[39] Predicated upon rupture, elegy consoles by reintegrating the dead person with himself or herself; this poem projects rupture backward onto the life, grief onto the earlier landscape. When Gregory "played his pipes," the "loneliness" of the hills "cried / Under his fingers"—in a fine turn on the pathetic fallacy (142). The poem's pastoral characters inhabit the austere and lonely landscapes of Gregory's artifacts; it is *because* of Gregory's absence that they can inhabit this space and the mourning mind revisit it.

Embedded in this pastoral elegy, the recognition that the poet's art requires death and gains by it comes closer to the surface of "In Memory of Major Robert Gregory." This poem has attracted some of the best close reading and generic study in Yeats criticism, but its articulation of the economic problem of poetic mourning remains unexplicated.[40] Tennyson writes of trying to "find in loss a gain to match," and Yeats's poem makes visible this elegiac trade-off between aesthetic gain and mortal loss. We can discern it in the elegy's contrasts between the dead and the living, and between painful and familiar loss. Whereas a living wife or friends produce mere "talk" or "quarrels," the dead yield lyric meditation. And whereas the accustomed dead generate only detached portraits, Gregory's fresh loss impassions the poetic imagination. This economic logic further suggests that the elegy as a form is self-consuming: an elegy undermines its own basis by healing the psychic wounds that generate it, by paying off the debt that sustains it. We shall also trace this elegy's use of the group form to develop the poet's self-image, from a self absorbed by the social world to a self unified and irradiated by the confrontation with death.

The first two stanzas of the elegy are casual and conversational, but both hint in their last lines that the dead are best at setting the poetic process in motion. Although Yeats says of himself and his new wife, "we're almost settled in our house," he turns instead to "name the friends that cannot sup with us. . . . / All, all are in my thoughts to-night being dead" (132). Dead friends defeat the living wife in competition for the poet's attention, or as Yeats states elsewhere, "the dead at whiles outface a living rival" (647). In the phrase "being dead," there is an ambiguity over whether "being" has not merely temporal force ('they are now dead') but perhaps causal force as well ('all are in my thoughts because dead').[41] It is because they are absent, this latent construal implies, that the friends can dominate memory and engender the poem, unlike the nearby woman. The second stanza resumes the contrast between, on the one hand, the mere conversations or "quarrels" the poet might have with the living and, on the other, the poetic discourse fashioned out of contact with the dead, who cannot "set us quarrelling." In accordance with Yeats's distinction between oratorical "rhetoric," made of the "quarrel with others," and "poetry," of the "quarrel with ourselves," the dead can be taken up more easily into the internal, poetry-making dialogue of self and shadow (*Myth,* 331). While the living come in at eye or ear, the dead come into the mind alone; "all that come into my mind are dead." In these initial contrasts between the living and the dead, Yeats obliquely suggests that the imagination may live most vigorously in the absence or death of its object.

But even though the elegist implies in these stanzas that death may provide the best fuel for poetic life, he goes on to suggest, conversely, that each death may supply only a finite ration of fuel. The deaths of Lionel Johnson, John Synge, and George Pollexfen no longer call for the expenditure of libido in mourning; so in the great pivotal stanza of the elegy, Yeats laments less having lost them than having lost his sense of loss:

They were my close companions many a year,
A portion of my mind and life, as it were,
And now their breathless faces seem to look
Out of some old picture-book;
I am accustomed to their lack of breath. . . .   [133]

We have just seen the dispassionate "old picture-book" in the
preceding stanzas about these friends. Having fixed the friends in
lifeless pictures, Yeats has made himself ever more "accustomed"
to their once painful deaths. Each man had been a "portion of my
mind and life," and by healing the wound left when each portion
of the ego was torn away, the poet has sealed himself off from the
feelings that once denoted their loss. The very success of mourning has meant its termination. Previous writers had also worried
about this economic problem of elegy. Shelley grieves that "grief
itself be mortal!" and Tennyson regrets that "regret can die!"
Emerson confesses in "Experience" that he feels the loss of his son
only as if it were the loss of an estate.[42] Although the expenditure
of feeling pays off the debt of loss, it may finally induce imaginative sterility. In the detached perspective of the elegy's first half,
Yeats almost seems endangered by the same "lack of breath" (or
spiritus) he perceives in his friends' "breathless faces," until the
thought of Gregory suddenly lifts the poem into a different
rhetorical register. The fresh loss supplies a new space for the
imagination to fill. Using elegiac repetition, allusion, and hyperbole to describe Gregory, the poem prepares us for its influx of
grief: "my dear friend's dear son, / Our Sidney and our perfect
man." Thanks to the "discourtesy of death," the poet can demonstrate his literary courtesy.

The next stanza's turn shows how Gregory's death reinvigorates the imagination, drawing the poet away from dry calcula-
tions about his friends to a visionary encounter with the landscape:

For all things the delighted eye now sees
Were loved by him; the old storm-broken trees
That cast their shadows upon road and bridge;

The tower set on the stream's edge;
The ford where drinking cattle make a stir
Nightly, and startled by that sound
The water-hen must change her ground;
He might have been your heartiest welcomer.   [133–34]

"Delight" is one of Yeats's key terms for imaginative excitement, and here it is Gregory's absence that permits the poet's "delighted eye" to see freshly the broken trees, the tower, and the ford. Death, like trope, turns the poet from his customary access to the scene, providing a mental space through which he can re-encounter his own estate, defamiliarized. The verbs describing the cattle and water hen—*stir, startled, change*—suggest the new imaginative life Gregory's death has given to the scene. A stark bed, stair, and fire had earlier characterized the setting, but it now grows animate with shadows and sounds, animals and trees. In death Gregory can become our and the poet's "heartiest welcomer"— the superlative playing on the elegiac synecdoche of the heart developed two stanzas later. The "gazing heart doubles her might" by taking upon itself the "discipline," or mental framework, now vacated by Gregory. So the poet's heart, consuming Gregory's, is exactly doubled (134).[43]

Over the course of the Gregory elegy, the poet gathers strength by dramatizing his triumphant relationship with the dead. At the beginning of the lyric, he inscribes himself in a comic matrix, a man chatting with equals about friendship and quarrels; but as he begins to unfold the catalog of dead friends, his implied transcendence, signified by irony and evaluation, becomes palpable. By extracting the less flattering moments from the sometimes eulogistic rhetoric, we can clarify the poet's tactic of self-definition by contrast. Johnson, Synge, and Pollexfen are dead not just now; in life they also seemed to be suffering a kind of death-in-life. Johnson, "much falling," lived entombed in his "Greek and Latin learning," ever trapped in the deferral of his dreams (132). In the next portrait Synge is also "dying," his life a search and preparation for death; unprepared, he "never could have rested in the tomb" (133).[44] Even the "old" uncle, despite his muscular horsemanship, is at the end "sluggish and contemplative" (133). Each life prefigures death. Then the process of mourning and the passage of time further deaden the dead, distancing the recollection of their lives, as if sealing their breathless faces in an old picture book. The day before Synge's death, Yeats writes that anticipatory mourning for a living man rendered him dead to the poet's mind: "He seemed already dead" (*Au*, 343). Mourning paradoxically increases the poet's distance from the dead, reconsigning them to the grave.

Yeats may not seem to distinguish himself from Gregory as from the other dead. But as Marjorie Perloff argues, he differentiates his own successful achievement of Unity of Being from Gregory's merely potential accomplishments.[45] Although he praises Gregory more than the three companions and uses Gregory's diverse aspirations to construct a theoretical totality, he also indicates that Gregory failed to achieve that imago. Gregory "had the intensity / To have published all to be a world's delight," but since Gregory did not publish as Yeats did, Yeats both distances himself from the unfulfilled life and identifies with the dead man's mask. The broader context of this dramatic relation is worth considering. In *A Vision* Yeats writes: "All unity is from the *Mask*, and the *antithetical Mask* is described in the automatic script as a 'form created by passion to unite us to ourselves', the self so sought is that Unity of Being compared by Dante in the *Convito* to that of 'a perfectly proportioned human body'" (*AV*, 82). An image of coherence, Gregory's mask unites Yeats to himself; a Dantean perfect body, it also replaces Gregory's fragmentary corpse. Unity of Being reclaims a victory over its implied dialectical counterpart, the Dispersal of Being. We can see this clearly in an example that Yeats borrowed from his father—the story of a "Frenchman who frequented the dissecting rooms to overcome his dread in the interest of that Unity" (*Au*, 235). Like Yeats's other elegies, "In Memory of Major Robert Gregory" renews the crisis between Unity and Dispersal because it draws the poet closer to death and to the self-surrender of mourning that can resemble death.[46]

By the last stanza, the poet has sloughed off comic indefi-
nition, having internalized some aspects of the dead while ex-
orcizing others. The reintegration is nearly complete: he consoli-
dates his "manhood," "childhood," and "boyish intellect" in a
synchronic whole. This totality recalls the life passed backward
before our eyes toward the end of "Shepherd and Goatherd,"
even though it is stated here as a forsaken possibility:

> I had thought, seeing how bitter is that wind
> That shakes the shutter, to have brought to mind
> All those that manhood tried, or childhood loved
> Or boyish intellect approved,
> With some appropriate commentary on each;
> Until imagination brought
> A fitter welcome; but a thought
> Of that late death took all my heart for speech.   [135]

Often said to be a significant motif in the poem, the totalizing
word *all* now applies neither to "all" the dead that come into the
poet's thoughts nor to "all life's epitome" that was Gregory's
potential, but to "all my heart"—the poet alone. As in the elegy
written almost two years earlier, "In Memory of Alfred Pollexfen," the many deaths recede by the end, having thrown the
poet's own solitary figure into sharp outline; and he hints a last
time that he has had to expend his "heart" to purchase poetic
"speech."

The Later Group Elegies

With "Beautiful Lofty Things" and "The Municipal
Gallery Re-visited," Yeats brings the form of the group elegy to
its highest articulation. Although the poet's battle with his own
death is central to both of these late elegies (probably written in
1937), the Gallery elegy displaces it onto the lesser battle with the
paintings. In "Beautiful Lofty Things," by contrast with many of
the other elegies, Yeats shows little hostility toward the dead; he
openly identifies with their august masks to construct his own

mask—a unifying self-image that guards against the final in-coherence. In one of his last publications, "I Became an Author," Yeats describes his weaknesses as a schoolboy, adding: "Even today I struggle against a lack of confidence, when among aver-age men, come from that daily humiliation, and because I do not know what they know." He was at the bottom of the class but found his friends at the top, just as he always had an "interest in proud, confident people" (*UP2*, 507). Anxious about his ulti-mate powerlessness in facing death, Yeats identifies with the "proud, confident people" whom he enumerates in "Beautiful Lofty Things" and "The Municipal Gallery Re-visited." "I have sometimes wondered," he admits in the same essay, "if I did not write poetry to find a cure for my own ailment, as constipated cats do when they eat valerian." Poverty, in Stevens's sense of the word, initiates poetic making: out of such deficiency, Yeats calls forth masks of serene, totemic force.

At first glance, "Beautiful Lofty Things" seems to be a list both haphazard and detached. But each person plays a part in this collective image of victory over death:

> Beautiful lofty things; O'Leary's noble head;
> My father upon the Abbey stage, before him a raging
>   crowd.
> 'This Land of Saints,' and then as the applause died out,
> 'Of plaster Saints;' his beautiful mischievous head thrown
>   back.
> Standish O'Grady supporting himself between the tables
> Speaking to a drunken audience high nonsensical words;
> Augusta Gregory seated at her great ormolu table
> Her eightieth winter approaching; 'Yesterday he
>   threatened my life,
> I told him that nightly from six to seven I sat at this table
> The blinds drawn up;' Maud Gonne at Howth station
>   waiting a train,
> Pallas Athena in that straight back and arrogant head:
> All the Olympians; a thing never known again.   [303]

In spite of its apparent randomness, the poem is built upon a "spatial" design—itself a unifying talisman against death. The outermost frame of the elegy consists of synoptic comments on the pantheon—"Beautiful lofty things"; "a thing never known again." Toward the beginning and end of the poem, the miniature portraits are purely visual: the silent heads of O'Leary and Maud Gonne enclose the speaking portraits in the poem's middle. The placement of the two quotations around O'Grady's unquoted utterance continues the concentric pattern. To this formal framing, Yeats adds the framing of the heroes by a lowly environment; characteristically—and snobbishly—he conflates the reckless disdain for death with the aristocratic disdain for commoners. Multiplying an elegiac synecdoche, he sets each head off against the backdrop of a crowd, a drunken audience, a possible attacker, or a train station. He also elevates the heroes above their surroundings by what almost seem to be their brief stage-performances.

In all of their utterances, the lofty speakers defy danger or death. With a taunting remark, Yeats's father risks enraging the hostile crowd. O'Grady speaks high words though he is about to fall. And Lady Gregory defies her potential assailant by telling him where she can be found. These utterances aspire to the condition of lyric; elsewhere, recalling "the night of the '*Playboy* debate,'" Yeats implicitly relates his father's danger-defying utterances to lyric, or what he and Mill call speech overheard: "No man of all literary Dublin dared show his face but my own father, who spoke to, or rather in the presence of, that howling mob with sweetness and simplicity" (*Au*, 327). As early as "The Secret Rose" and "Introductory Rhymes," the defining deed has been one of reckless courage in the face of death; but now Yeats pares away even more of the narrative content from each defiant act, giving the lyric moment a greater intensity. Because the characters are linked neither by family nor by narrative, their very disparateness puts in relief the poet's act of synthesis. The "lofty things" are memories that resemble Wordsworth's "spots of time," and they invisibly repair the imaginative power because they sustain the "depressed" mind amid banal surroundings and intimations of mortality.[47] But the "spots" in *The Prelude* are developed stories, whereas Yeats offers his minimalist spots without the supporting coordinates. Each spot is a synecdoche for the whole life, expressing its essence as if a proleptic epitaph. It has been cut loose from a narrative by death, and the elegist amasses the lapidary memories as a fragile bulwark against dissolution.

Each fragment of time has been laid beside the others, forming a nearly static mosaic. In some of Yeats's elegies this static quality counterweighs the poet's rapidly shifting and ambivalent responses to the dead, but in this elegy there is little evidence of such turmoil. Yeats hazards a first line that is immobile, pinioned at both its medial caesura and its end: "Beautiful lofty things; O'Leary's noble head;" (303). "Upon a Dying Lady" also opens with a still, pictorial image—a head framed by hair and propped on pillows. But now, despite the active syntax of the late period, the elegy has almost no finite verbs; they appear only in Lady Gregory's quotation, where the fact of quotation insulates them from the rest of the poem. Verbals—past and present participles—suspend the "spots" in the vacuum of an indefinite time. The fragments merge not only in the elaborate "spatial" structure of the poem but also in the global "all" and "thing" of the final line: "All the Olympians; a thing never known again." In the course of the poem, a single "thing" has amalgamated the earlier "things." Elegiac pathos, driven underground throughout the poem, suddenly flashes backward over its entire surface. Restrained in its claims up to this point, the elegy now raises the traditional lament for the fleeing of the gods. Although all the Olympians except for Maud Gonne have died, their moments of proud disdain for death join them to the immortals. In a rueful ending that recalls "Upon a Dying Lady," "In Memory of Alfred Pollexfen," and "In Memory of Robert Gregory," the poet seems strengthened and thus more willing to risk "the submission in pure sorrow." Against his own death he holds out the pantheon of momentary triumphs over oblivion.

Fragmentary images of the past besiege the poet at the beginning of "The Municipal Gallery Re-visited," where Yeats again
uses the techniques of suspended syntax and serial enumeration
to suggest the simultaneity of the dead, buried in the human
mind:

> Around me the images of thirty years;
> An ambush; pilgrims at the water-side. . . .   [319]

As usual in Yeats, the dead ambush the mind in groups. These
images are pictures in a museum, not mere phantoms recollected
in tranquillity. Even so, Yeats turns out to have been the invisible
artist:

> 'This is not' I say
> 'The dead Ireland of my youth, but an Ireland
> The poets have imagined, terrible and gay.'   [320]

Reading the paintings, Yeats finds the "terrible beauty" and
"tragic gaiety" he has himself given to Ireland. He refuses to
allow the paintings to usurp the meditative prerogatives of the
elegist, implying that in looking at the gallery, he gazes on the
contents of his own mind. He has created the images encircling
his consciousness, as also suggested by a latent meaning of the
possessive adjective *my*:

> Wherever I had looked I had looked upon
> My permanent or impermanent images. . . .

Yeats recasts his usual contest with the dead as a contest with
the visual images of the dead. Each portrait threatens to supplant
the space of poetic meditation, but he responds with a subtle
counterattack:

> Mancini's portrait of Augusta Gregory,
> 'Greatest since Rembrandt,' according to John Synge;
> A great ebullient portrait certainly;
> But where is the brush that could show anything
> Of all that pride and that humility[?]

The poet corrects Synge's lavish praise for this inadequate portrait; what's more, he rhetorically suggests that no painter could show "anything" of the two qualities that he, as poet, begins to show in the very act of asking his question.[48] Here, as we shall see in some of his other ekphrastic poems, Yeats wars against the limitation of the visual image—perhaps a metonymy for death's ultimate limitation; he refuses the eye's dominion over the imagination. By the end of the elegy, he has triumphed over the inadequacies of "the brush": he has made the external gallery seem to depend on the gallery of his own mind. He happens upon Synge's portrait ("And here's John Synge himself") only after he has already begun to paint Synge's lyric portrait within his own thoughts (321).

In defeating the primacy of the paintings and the dead, nothing less than the poet's imaginative life is at stake. The anxiety about death contaminates the poem's language in subtle ways. For example, Yeats chooses Antaeus to signify the immortality of the dead; but this mortal giant also brings a trope of physical decay into the poem—"contact with the soil." Such metaphors as "that rooted man" and the "grave deep face" also give voice to this thought (321). And yet, Yeats joins himself to the dead less defensively than in most of his elegies, perhaps reassured by the persistence of his own Ireland and by his superiority to the painters.

This openness at the end of the Gallery elegy recalls the mood of the fine pre-mortem elegy for Lady Gregory, "Coole Park, 1929"—a similar elegy that may also help us to understand Yeats's elegiac use of place. In the elegiac coda of "The Municipal Gallery Re-visited," Yeats positions himself among the dead and speaks to us as if from beyond the grave:

> You that would judge me do not judge alone
> This book or that, come to this hallowed place
> Where my friends' portraits hang and look thereon;
> Ireland's history in their lineaments trace;
> Think where man's glory most begins and ends
> And say my glory was I had such friends.   [321]

As we have seen, the Yeatsian Gallery has gradually superseded the Municipal Gallery, so that the deictic phrase "this hallowed place" must signify at least in part the poem itself. Although Yeats acknowledges that the Gallery is an extra-poetic place, he does so only after he has proven the primacy of his immaterial cenotaph. "Coole Park, 1929" resembles the Gallery elegy in seeming to defer to a commemorated structure; but it also substitutes its own poetic "rooms and passages" for the house (243). Double in meaning, the deictic *here* again points to both the poem and the physical dwelling, while alerting us to their differences. One place established by the poem's epitaphic *sta viator* ("Here, traveller, scholar, poet, take your stand") is an oddly homeless and place-less place, inhabitable like other lyrics by "poets after us." In contrast, "those rooms and passages" of the real home will soon be a "shapeless mound," inhabited only by weeds and ill-fated saplings:

> Here, traveller, scholar, poet, take your stand
> When all those rooms and passages are gone,
> When nettles wave upon a shapeless mound
> And saplings root among the broken stone. . . .

Against the coming shapelessness, Yeats sets his poem's ex-quisitely sculpted stanzas in *ottava rima*. Earlier in the poem, he puts his self-portrait among the portraits of his friends—"one that ruffled in a manly pose / For all his timid heart"—just as in "The Municipal Gallery Re-visited" he seems to resign himself to being a mere portrait among other portraits of the dead.[49] But there again he is subtly different in his postmortem exis-tence. The friends' images are fixed in the real portraits that hang in the gallery, whereas his self-portrait is unmoored, placeless, linguistic, and therefore capable of encompassing theirs. The poet magnanimously identifies himself with his dead friends, but in doing so, he also bids us to see their portraits as signifiers of himself, as we have done in reading this poem partly as a self-elegy.

PUBLIC ELEGY

By the term *public elegy,* I mean an elegy whose subject is the death of a political figure, such as Parnell or the leaders
of the Easter Rising. Yeats's "private" elegies are also, of course,
public and political, whether in setting the aristocratic speaker
above the crowd, heightening the genre's predilection for male
rivalry, or resuming its often contentious relations with female
figures (as in Milton's berating of the female muses or Shelley's
dismissal of Urania). But many obstacles would lie in the way of
assigning to the elegiac genre a unitary "politics." Although the
form may seem inherently pacifist, we have already seen that
Yeats's elegies sometimes war on the dead. And although many of
the public elegies by Yeats's Anglo-Irish predecessors, such as
Thomas Davis's "Lament for the Death of Eoghan Ruadh,"
would convert sorrow into political anger and activism, Yeats's
public elegies rarely pursue this program. Nineteenth-century
elegists had often used the genre's cult of the dead to inflame
patriotic sentiment. Recalling the manner typical of Young Ireland, the "Lament for Thomas Davis" by Sir Samuel Ferguson
proposes not that one imitate the stillness of the dead but that
one strive to make "Erin a nation yet, / Self-respecting, self-
relying, self-advancing"; Yeats turns this verse on its head when
he echoes it in "A Prayer for my Daughter," now as a description
of the innocence gained in part by throwing out chauvinist
hatred.[50] Repeating Arnold's characterization of the Celtic imagination as "melancholy," Yeats implies that elegy has a special
national base in Ireland; his best public elegies, however, resist
the patriotic huzza of much Anglo-Irish elegy (*E&I*, 184).

Even though we cannot identify a single "politics" with the
form of the elegy, we can enumerate the disturbing political
attitudes expressed in Yeats's public elegies: antifeminism, anti-
egalitarianism, anti-Catholicism, and so forth. I have no interest
in absolving Yeats or his elegies of their sometimes provincial,
haughty, and hieratic views; indeed, the political views of those
whom he attacks are, at least for me, much more appealing than

his own. But these elegies are political not only in the views they expound but also in the language by which they expound—a language of lyric interiority and equivocation. Complex and elusive, this political dimension of Yeats's elegies deserves but has not received much analysis.

The language proper to the lyric was at the center of Yeats's quarrel with Young Ireland.[51] The poets of this movement had, in Yeats's view, corrupted the lyric with the language of the political press. Their writing was "but excellent journalism for the most part," and it had, in turn, infected the rhetoric of the new Irish middle class (*UP2*, 34). Of the typical bourgeois, Yeats writes bitterly: "Every thought made in some manufactory and with the mark upon it of its wholesale origin—thoughts never really thought out in their current form in any individual mind, but the creation of impersonal mechanism—of schools, of textbooks, of newspapers, these above all. He had that confidence which the first thinker of anything never has, for all thinkers are alike in that they approach the truth full of hesitation and doubt. . . . The newspaper is the roar of the machine" (*Au*, 311–13; see also *UP2*, 395–96).

In public elegies like "Easter, 1916," Yeats sets the rhetoric of "hesitation and doubt" against the anonymous phrases of the machine. Like Blake and Shelley on the left, he grapples, from the right, with the "mind-forg'd manacles" that have threatened to bind and commodify language since the Industrial Revolution.[52] Yeats writes: "One must not forget that the death of language, the substitution of phrases as nearly impersonal as algebra for words and rhythms varying from man to man, is but a part of the tyranny of impersonal things" (*E&I*, 301). Theodor Adorno puts it this way in "Lyric Poetry and Society": "The idiosyncrasy of poetic thought, opposing the overpowering force of material things, is a form of reaction against the reification of the world, against the rule of the wares of commerce over people."[53] But Yeats does not imagine that he can retreat from the reified space of the market to an autonomous and natural space called the "self." The poet's alternative to capitalist anomie is a fabricated

self, a Wildean, artificial construct: "Style, personality—deliberately adopted and therefore a mask—is the only escape from the
hot-faced bargainers and the money-changers" (*Au,* 311).
Shaped by the world it rejects, this individual mask carries dialectically the imprint of its social counterpart: Through satire Yeats
defines his solitary mask over against the many-faced multitude;
through "hesitation and doubt" he defines his ambivalent language over against journalistic univocity.

Satire and Lamentation

Satire is one of the devices by which Yeats tries to
cleanse his elegies of newspaper rhetoric. He directs the satire not
only against a "language" but also, of course, against the class
that uses the language. He attacks the middle class rather than the
elegy's usual muses, nymphs, animals, or deities—those much-
berated personifications of social groups and psychic forces. Even
though Jonson, Donne, and Milton incorporate satire into their
elegies, we expect the form to be relatively quiescent, so that the
rhetorical onslaughts in "September 1913" and "To a Shade" can
be startling. Writing out of the sharp temper of his middle phase,
Yeats mythologizes the Catholic bourgeoisie as foe to poetry's
spontaneity and recklessness: "It likes to see the railway tracks of
thought. . . . It loves rhetoric because rhetoric is impersonal and
predetermined, and it hates poetry whose suggestions cannot be
foreseen" (*UP2,* 396). Denouncing the mirror-image of his own
class origins, Yeats pretends to an aristocratic persona and seeks
in poetry the freedom he associates with his desired social class.[54]
He imagines the members of the middle class to threaten poetry
itself, so they assume ominous proportions. Commenting on
Shelley, Yeats may aptly describe himself: "His political enemies
are monstrous, meaningless images. . . . [H]e can never see
anything that opposes him as it really is" (*AV,* 143). Even so,
Yeats occasionally recognizes that this enemy without is partly a
shadow cast by the enemy within. In *A Vision* he explains that
such Romantic poets as Wordsworth, Shelley, and implicitly

himself "are almost always partisans, propagandists and gregarious" (*AV*, 143). They must either struggle to defeat the temptation of "Dispersal" by adopting a mask of individuality, or drag out their years like Wordsworth, "shuddering at his solitude" and filling his art "with common opinion, common sentiment" (*AV*, 134). This is a psychosocial version of the Yeatsian dialectic between the impulses toward "Dispersal" and "Simplification through intensity." When aggression reappears in the satirical elegies, its target is not the elegized dead but the anonymous "they" of the middle class—perhaps a projection of the "they-self" within, though Yeats forgets this possibility when ire holds sway. His angry accusations sometimes suggest an eagerness to deflect self-accusation, though later, in "Parnell's Funeral," the elegist turns the full force of his melancholic anger against himself.[55]

Long before the satirical elegies of midcareer, Yeats's first public elegy lacks satire, doubt, equivocation, or anything else that distinguishes his later efforts in the genre. Published four days after Parnell's death and excluded from Yeats's collections of his poetry, "Mourn—And Then Onward!" might have been written by a member of Young Ireland, since it dutifully obeys the conventions of nineteenth-century public elegy. An apostrophe to the mourning nation, the lyric celebrates Parnell not only as a Shelleyan hero—he was "derided, hated, / And made the tyrant bow"—but also as a modern Christ—he showed the "way" to a nation by "the waves" (531). The biblical allusions culminate in Parnell's metamorphosis as "a tall pillar, burning / Before us in the gloom!" Here the elegist's rhetoric is that of a public orator—a Mark Antony addressing his countrymen, no hint of satire separating his mind from theirs.[56]

How different Yeats's rhetoric in a later, informal elegy for Parnell, "To a Shade" (1913), distinguishing the poet at every turn from the "they," from the "old foul mouth," from the "pack." This poem is also an apostrophe, but instead of addressing a nation of fellow mourners, it can stand to address only the deceased:

If you have revisited the town, thin Shade,
Whether to look upon your monument
(I wonder if the builder has been paid)
Or happier-thoughted when the day is spent
To drink of that salt breath out of the sea
When grey gulls flit about instead of men,
And the gaunt houses put on majesty:
Let these content you and be gone again;
For they are at their old tricks yet.   [110]

Banished are the earlier elegy's harmonious pastoral setting of "broad high mountains" and "grass-green plains," replaced by the alienating world of commerce. No longer does Parnell metamorphose into a burning pillar; his apotheosis is as a city monument built on credit. Instead of a mourning procession of "men," only the gray gulls and gaunt houses accompany the lament.

Hostile and playful in tone, the speaker not only separates himself from the "they"—the Catholic middle class whose religious leaders "betrayed" Parnell—but also unites himself with a line of martyrs. Analyzed by Simmel and Freud, this psychosocial tactic is prevalent in Yeats's satirical elegies: they arouse antagonism toward an external power to intensify the unity of a group—here, the victimized Parnell, Lane, and Yeats.[57] Hugh Lane is a man of Parnell's "kind," both because he tries to serve the people (by offering his collection of French paintings for the Dublin gallery) and because the people turn on him, drive him away, and dismember him like Orpheus or Goethe's Irish Actaeon (they refused to house the paintings properly).[58] By the images he uses to describe Parnell and Lane, Yeats makes himself the third in the line of aristocratic victims. He too has brought in his "full hands" a poetry that could have given the nation "loftier thought," but he has received little reward for his "open-handedness." What Saint Peter had called "Blind mouths!" in the satiric outburst of "Lycidas," Yeats calls "an old foul mouth." William Martin Murphy's mouth is the enemy of lyric not only because it represents figuratively his two newspapers but because it had attacked the lyric "To a Wealthy Man . . ." (as well as Parnell and Lane). By making himself and the lyric the covert victims in the elegy, Yeats animates two public events, recasting Parnell's death and the Lane controversy in highly personal terms. He echoes Hamlet ("dust stops") and advises Parnell's ghost, like the ghost of Hamlet's father, to rest while the time is out of joint, thus implicitly dubbing himself Parnell's filial inheritor.[59] After deploring the present, he must half-humorously invert elegy's conventional transcendence and bid the dead man go bury himself again. Continued death in the tomb is preferable to rebirth among the depraved. "Reprisals," the satiric elegy for Robert Gregory, repeats this gesture of re-interment, though that poem's bitter tone so predominates that it spares not even the dead man: his apparently heroic death was a waste, a meaningless sacrifice for the brutal murderers of Irish mothers.

Yeats's elegiac satire is not always so fierce as in "Reprisals" nor so temperate as in "To a Shade." "September 1913" is somewhere between the two poles, and Yeats marks off its satiric sections to allow eulogy also a part, especially in the refrains. By juxtaposing satiric and eulogistic discourses or "voices" (in a useful though imperfect metaphor), Yeats recalls the *genera mixta* of Renaissance poems for the dead. Amplifying the part of satire in the elegy, he, together with Hardy, Stevens, Owen, Pound, and Eliot, saves a genre of pathos for the Age of Irony.[60] In the social psychology of "September 1913," the configuration of voices helps distance Yeats from one community and identify him with another. Each stanza shifts discursive registers, opening with a satiric reproach to the blindly religious and materialistic member of the middle class, and closing with a ceremonious lament for a lost Ireland. The satire is at its sharpest in the first stanza:

> What need you, being come to sense,
> But fumble in a greasy till
> And add the halfpence to the pence
> And prayer to shivering prayer, until
> You have dried the marrow from the bone;

For men were born to pray and save:
Romantic Ireland's dead and gone,
It's with O'Leary in the grave.   [108]

The first voice is itself bivocalic, partly narrating in the free
indirect mode the imagined thoughts of a Dublin Catholic: "men
were born to pray and save." The poet's voice frames and wars
against his enemy's imagined voice. The colon allows us to read
the refrain as the Dubliner's explanation for surrendering to the
marketplace—"after all, Romantic Ireland's dead"; but because it
resonates proleptically with the other refrains, we may also read it
as the speaker's eulogistic comment. According to the second
reading, the earlier irony opens a psychological divide between
the speaker and the pious materialist, and then the refrain's pathos identifies the speaker with the disappearing Anglo-Irish
legacy of O'Leary and Romantic Ireland. As in "To a Shade," we
recognize the interdependence between the poet's affectionate
communing with the dead and his aggressive separation from the
crowd. The pathos inverts the irony: it brings the distant dead
near as the irony moves the nearby living apart.

But in successive stanzas the relation between the two voices
changes, as the poem gradually shifts its emphasis from satire to
panegyric. The bitterness slackens with each rhetorical question—each focused less on the ignorant addressee and more on
the martyrs with whom the poet identifies. The first question
buzzes with the antagonist's supposed thoughts, then the second
is less tense, less bivocalic, asserting for the most part the heroism
of the dead, until the third seems almost entirely caught up with
the apotheosis—"All that delirium of the brave" (108).[61] In each
stanza the speaker comes closer to accomplishing an identification with the dead, so that the angry questions subside and, in the
last stanza, disappear. This dialectical interpretation of the satiric
and eulogistic voices may help put into perspective the disagreement between two critics, one of whom sees the poem as a
"satiric taunt," while the other's emphasis falls on the poem's
"compassionate celebration" and "tenderness."[62] The poem has

both voices, and the one depends upon the other. Having dis-
tanced himself from the person groping for money in a drawer,
the speaker can affectionately embrace the mercenaries, patriots,
and finally himself—the lover-poet whose delirium or *enthou-
siasmos* implicitly unites him with the heroic madness of the
martyrs.[63]

"Easter, 1916" and the Balladic Elegies

In "To a Shade," "September 1913," "Easter, 1916,"
and "Parnell's Funeral," Yeats confronts his own imagined death
through the historic occasion of loss, foreshadowing the public
elegies of Robert Lowell and Geoffrey Hill. By bringing language to the horizon of death, his lyrics seek to wrest words from
their entanglement with the market; they would prevent journalistic "idle talk" from concealing death as something that always happens to others and therefore to no one.[64] By means of
this Romantic strategy—surely imbued with Romantic ideology—Yeats avoids in "Easter, 1916" the eulogistic cant that
often clogs the public elegy. At the beginning of "Easter, 1916,"
much as in "September 1913," satire predominates; but now
Yeats directs the satire at his own "polite meaningless words"
(180). Robert Bly echoes Yeats's claim that we make out of "the
quarrel with ourselves, poetry" (*Myth,* 331): "A true political
poem is a quarrel with ourselves. . . . The true political poem does
not order us either to take any specific acts: like the personal
poem, it moves to deepen awareness."[65] Though not relevant to
all such poetry, Bly's statement can alert us to one political aim of
"Easter, 1916": to fasten words to the human experience of death
and history rather than capitulate to formulas about the death of
statesmen and the anonymous other. The discourse of the poem
shifts from the first stanza's evocation of the monologic prattle
that conceals death to the last's many-tongued confrontation
with death in the language of mourning. The pressure of death
discloses the collectivity within the poet's language and historical
consciousness, so the nation is transformed from "a subject of

knowledge" into "a dumb struggling thought seeking a mouth to utter it" (*E&I,* 317). As Adorno writes of history and the lyric: "through the individual and his spontaneity, objective historical forces rouse themselves within the poem, forces which are propelling a restricted and restricting social condition beyond itself to a more humane one. . . . [V]arious levels of society's inner contradictory relationships manifest themselves in the poet's speaking."[66] "Easter, 1916" articulates the social and historical forces of revolution as an internal, polyvocalic debate about death.

To disclose the "quarrel with ourselves," Yeats must expunge the "idle talk" that Heidegger ascribes to "the everyday"—a talk so rigidly controlled by convention ("polite") and so mindlessly passed from one atomistic subject to another ("meaningless") that it can bespeak neither death nor historical transformation:

> I have passed with a nod of the head
> Or polite meaningless words,
> Or have lingered awhile and said
> Polite meaningless words . . .
>
> . . . .
> Being certain that they and I
> But lived where motley is worn:
> All changed, changed utterly:
> A terrible beauty is born.   [180–82]

The stanza announces the historical shift by enacting it within its own language, leaping up several levels of discourse—from mechanical repetition to a sublime bewilderment before rupture. Because no *but* or other conjunction marks the transition, we seem to witness in the rhetorical break the birth of the terrible beauty.[67] Taking up an elegiac counterconvention that extends from Tennyson's "bald street" to Auden's "hundred cities," the poem opens with an urban setting—its "grey" houses as anonymous and interchangeable as the "faces" and "words."[68] Rising out of this public world's undifferentiated drabness, the nativity ode that is also a death song seems strange and inexplicable. To accentuate further the logical chasm between the new world, new consciousness, new language and the old, Yeats brilliantly formulates the crossing in the passive voice—"All changed" and "is born"—a formulation best explicated in the context of the next stanza.

An epistemological rift generates the poem: a rift between the knowledge that a change has occurred and the absence of an "efficient cause" to explain the change. The relation of the event to what precedes it is inorganic or "allegorical."[69] Thus, in the second stanza Yeats enumerates the personal characteristics of the rebels only to show that these qualities cannot have brought about the historical transformation. Although his skepticism may be partly rooted in disagreement and animosity (against Maud Gonne's husband, for example), it develops into a powerful subversion of hero-historiography. Whereas an elegist like Davis would have marshaled personal attributes to explain heroic action, Yeats shows them to be almost irrelevant. As if the leaders were immediately before him and the verse merely pointing them out one by one, each portrait begins with a demonstrative adjective—"That," "This," "This," "This." The poet summons four rebels immediately before us to prove that, much as his own heightened awareness could not have been deduced from his earlier distraction, so too the heroic event could not have been predicted from the antiheroic participants. One had a sweet voice that grew shrill; another was a school-keeper who wrote poetry; his friend was sensitive and promising; the last seemed a "drunken, vainglorious lout." They hardly forebode terrible beauty, singly or together. Although Yeats allows them some responsibility for the change—the lout "has resigned" his former part—dropping out cannot explain the creation of new beauty. Yeats glories in the rhetorical disjunction: he implies that the lout and his compatriots had some role in creating the terrible beauty *and* that the beauty gave birth to itself:

> Yet I number him in the song;
> He, too, has resigned his part

In the casual comedy;
He, too, has been changed in his turn,
Transformed utterly:
A terrible beauty is born.

As the comedian leaves his former role, something larger than
him transforms him. The agency of change remains unstated,
because the verbs—"has been changed" and "Transformed"—
are in the passive voice. Yeats is remembering and secularizing
that earlier reflection on mutability included in his edition of
Spenser: the "Mutability Cantos." In her final judgment Nature
concedes that things "changed be," but when she repeats this
verb with still more emphasis on the passive voice—"all shall
changed bee"—she indicates the enormity of the final, apocalyptic change, a leap from time into eternity.[70] In Yeats's refrains, the
passive mood suggests likewise that the change is definitive and
inexplicable, but this poem's terms of reference are aesthetic
rather than theological. Like Yeats, the patriots have left behind
the "casual comedy" of the everyday. Their entry into a historical
process larger than themselves engenders an unforeseeable event,
just as the poet's surrender to a genre, a tradition, or a discourse
occasions the birth of a work that transcends personality and
intention (E&I, 509). For Yeats, the dislocations in history and
writing are analogous.

The analogy may be more than an analogy and more than a
mere aestheticizing of history, according to Blanchot: "The
writer sees himself in the Revolution. It attracts him because it
is the time during which literature becomes history. It is his
truth."[71] The strength of the elegy for the rebels is that Yeats sees
himself in their revolutionary act, not only because they are
analogues for his writing but because they concretize his writing
in their historical actions. As Maud Gonne states: "Without Yeats
there would have been no Literary Revival in Ireland. Without
the inspiration of that Revival and the glorification of beauty and
heroic virtue, I doubt if there would have been an Easter
Week."[72] Over the years, Yeats worries about the historical enact-

ment of his scripts, especially of an apparent script for martyrdom like *Cathleen ni Houlihan,* asking himself in "Man and the Echo":

> Did that play of mind send out
> Certain men the English shot?   [345]

From this perspective the concession "Yet I number him in the song" has a darker meaning: the poet has numbered the "lout" and the other rebels not only in the song we read but also in the text of revolutionary action. The martyrs and history are not the only authors of the change; because of the poet too, all is transformed utterly.

In spite of the elegy's overall movement toward identification with the rebels, the next stanza distinguishes their work from the poet's. With their "one purpose alone," the rebels have become "a stone," the opposite of the running stream, the tumbling clouds, horse, rider, birds, moorhens, moorcocks—every "living" thing that "Changes" in the pastoral landscape. The stone cannot be an image of this poem's "lyric stasis," since there is nothing static about the lyric, except for the momentary pauses in the refrains, and even these are about metamorphosis.[73] Unlike such stilled elegies as "Her Courtesy" and "Beautiful Lofty Things," this restless lyric tries to *be* the transformation it describes.

If we need more evidence for this view of the poem, the final stanza is a dizzying spiral of changing responses to the dead—Yeats's derailing of the newspaper narrative of history from its "railway tracks of thought":

> Too long a sacrifice
> Can make a stone of the heart.
> O when may it suffice?
> That is Heaven's part, our part
> To murmur name upon name,
> As a mother names her child
> When sleep at last has come
> On limbs that had run wild.

What is it but nightfall?
No, no, not night but death;
Was it needless death after all?
For England may keep faith
For all that is done and said.
We know their dream; enough
To know they dreamed and are dead;
And what if excess of love
Bewildered them till they died?

Assertion leads to question, question back to assertion, anger to
acceptance, acceptance back to anger and then acceptance again;
the rhetoric eddies back and forth; the mourning mind gropes
between consolation and demystification. The poet's inner quarrel becomes a nation's quarrel: one voice says sacrifice hardens the
heart, another that only heaven should judge, a third dallies with
the false surmise that death is sleep, a fourth counters that death is
death, a fifth adds that the sacrifice may have been unnecessary,
and so on. The multiplicity of voices even brings about a momentary shift in gender, when the poet leaves behind the stern and
judgmental voice of the paternal Minos for the loving murmur of
the elegiac mother. Corrective distance alternates with identification, and the final embrace of the rebels assimilates their vision to
the poet's "dream" and "love," as in "September 1913." Scorning
his own "polite meaningless words," Yeats accuses himself in the
first stanza of having nearly suffered what he calls elsewhere "the
death of language"; but the renewed proximity to extra-linguistic
death awakens his language to the "quarrel with ourselves" and
within language itself—the quarrel that may be the Romantic
lyric's authentic grasp of history. The poet, in Adorno's words,
"comes to full accord with the language itself," until "the voice of
language itself is heard."[74] The deeply personal meditation before death oddly allows a nation's language, with its many con-
flicting voices, to be heard.

How can we explain the prominent role of proper names in
effecting the elegy's linguistic shift? A review of naming in Yeats's

other elegies might help us with this question. Elegists from Jonson to Yeats use names as if they were verbal switchboards, allowing or barring access to the dead. In some of the elegies, such as "On a Child's Death," "Mourn—And Then Onward!" "Upon a Dying Lady," and "Shepherd and Goatherd," Yeats obeys the elegiac convention of not naming the dead; similarly, he withholds names in the brief portraits of this poem's second stanza. Apparently to protect Parnell from the jaws of the pack, "To a Shade" leaves him nameless, thinking him "safer in the tomb." In other elegies, such as "All Souls' Night," "Beautiful Lofty Things," and "The Municipal Gallery Re-visited," the poet names the dead with much pomp, as if this performative act would call them among us. Having summoned the dead in "All Souls' Night," he dismisses them with the disavowal, "But names are nothing" (229). In still other elegies, he skillfully uses names to organize the work; for example, he names Johnson, Synge, and Pollexfen in vignettes but sets Gregory apart by naming him only in the title, "In Memory of Major Robert Gregory." "September 1913" is closest to "Easter, 1916" in its pacing of names, withholding its roll call until the climactic moment when the martyrs are interfused with the poet's "delirium." Yeats claims that his use of names in "Easter, 1916" arose partly from the shame of hearing an old Irish member of Parliament recite a ballad, "repeating over his sacred names, Wolfe Tone, Emmet, and Owen Roe, and mourning that new poets and new movements should have taken something of their sacredness away"; in this elegy and in "September 1913," Yeats adopts this Irish tradition of repeating over the names of the dead (*Au*, 199). Frazer and Freud discuss the taboo on the names of the dead, names whose utterance might bring the dead into one's presence; but for Yeats, such "contagious magic" or "omnipotence of thoughts" facilitates the desired contact.[75] In "Easter, 1916" he figures this communion as a mother's murmuring her child's name; the echoic verb *murmur,* unlike *say* or *speak,* helps to blur further the distinctions between signifier and signified, subject and object. But lest we think Yeats has given himself over to the dead, he reasserts the power of the namer, grasping in the name all that remains, conferring existence on the nonexistent dead:

> I write it out in a verse—
> MacDonagh and MacBride
> And Connolly and Pearse
> Now and in time to be,
> Wherever green is worn,
> Are changed, changed utterly:
> A terrible beauty is born.

Dramatizing his act of writing the names into a verse, the poet again suggests that it is he who has changed them utterly. By the synecdoche of a name, he inscribes each rebel into this lyric, "Now and in time to be." He reenacts a historical change as a perpetual linguistic event.

In two later balladic elegies on the Rising, Yeats invokes ritualistically the names of the patriots—one of several techniques for distancing his own language from idle "talk," from "words" that "are lightly spoken," from the withering "breath of politic words" (182–83). As if having released ambivalent feelings in the earlier elegy, he now more uniformly identifies with the rebels. In "Sixteen Dead Men," the elegist also uses another kind of synecdoche to distinguish his rhetoric from the inauthentic rhetoric of the enemy: body parts. No mere "logic" could "outweigh / MacDonagh's bony thumb," no mere conversation of the living penetrate his "ear." Yeats spreads before us the thingliness of the dead bodies, setting his own language of brute fact against speculative talk about "What should be and what not." Parts of the body had played a significant role in elegy before, but when Surrey, for example, invokes Wyatt's head, face, hand, tongue, and eye, he shrouds each part in its corresponding heavenly virtue until we almost forget the physical thing.[76] Not so with Yeats. Because the patriots "converse bone to bone," their language seems irrefutable. Yeats even presents his rhetorical questions as gestures of indication, seeming to point transparently to inalienable facts:

You say that we should still the land
Till Germany's overcome;
But who is there to argue that
Now Pearse is deaf and dumb?
And is their logic to outweigh
MacDonagh's bony thumb?

The addressee can "say" what he likes, but the poet's questions seem to "say" nothing, invisible except as indices aimed at the inevitably real—the opposite strategy from the self-indication we have seen in a number of Yeats's poems.

If some critics were right to decry "Easter, 1916" for its ambivalence toward the rebels, then the zealous identification in these ballads might make them the better poems—though for me they certainly are not. Indeed, such identification makes the poems more ideological in their verbal strategies, for these elegies efface themselves as written constructs and present their interpretations as natural, inarguable fact. "The Rose Tree" is cast as a dialogue, its dramatic form aligning it with real speech. This "naturalizing" effect is heightened by the apparent inevitability built into the ballad's structure: the rose tree is withered and needs to be watered; there is no water; ergo, "plain as plain can be," we must water it with our blood. The steamroller momentum of the ballad, like the names, body parts, and questions of the preceding ballad, helps suggest that the poet's language is a window onto history—a history immediately present and readable. But for all their technical interest, these balladic elegies are not Yeats at his best, and so, by way of synopsis, I glance back at Yeats's more significant public elegies before passing on to the Gore-Booth poems.

The Gore-Booth Elegies

Yeats's elegies for public figures overturn some of the guiding principles and structures of the genre. The participants in the Easter Rising are mundane antiheroes, incommensurable with the epic event. The satire of "To a Shade" and "Reprisals" chokes off the elegiac movement toward transcendence and consolation. More generally, we often find in place of the expected, univocal discourse of public eulogy a discourse fragmented into competing voices, and in place of the expected rallying cry over the corpse, a cry of despair, wonder, or disgust.

Yeats's two poems for the Gore-Booth sisters, "On a Political Prisoner" (1919) and "In Memory of Eva Gore-Booth and Con Markievicz" (1927), more deliberately invert the priorities of public elegy. The sisters did not realize their potential greatness through political action; rather, it was politics that robbed them of their greatness. "Easter, 1916" had already taken a step in this direction, showing the rebels to have achieved greatness in a political event almost in spite of themselves. But now politics—at least in the sense of a particular political allegiance and involvement—suffocates the practitioner. These two lyrics are antipolitical public elegies, or, from another perspective, private elegies for friends who have died into politics. Both lyrics have, of course, their own sexist and anti-"humanitarian" politics—Yeats's original adjective deriding Eva Gore-Booth's "dream." And we may well sympathize more with the allegiances of the sisters: Eva Gore-Booth worked with the suffragists and the trade unionists; Con Markievicz also worked with the trade unionists, assisted the Dublin slum-dwellers, and took part in the 1916 Rising as deputy leader (for which she was initially sentenced to execution).[77] Yeats portrays these political activities as a kind of death for the sisters, a death from which he tries to restore them in what seems a prepolitical harmony with himself.

Like the sequence "Upon a Dying Lady," "On a Political Prisoner" is not technically an elegy, since Yeats writes it for Con Markievicz during her imprisonment. He mourns her premature spiritual death much as Shelley mourns Wordsworth's (though for the opposite political reasons) in the pre-mortem elegy that ends: "thou leavest me to grieve, / Thus having been, that thou shouldst cease to be."[78] Yeats attempts to recreate the life that, like Shelley's Wordsworth, Markievicz has lost. This recuperative

effort is common to Romantic poems of the compensatory imagination, and yet earlier Romantics usually try to repair the loss
suffered by their own imaginations, not by others'. An exception,
Shelley's lyric is comparatively gentle with Wordsworth, whereas
Yeats characteristically refuses to temper his hostility for the sake
of elegiac decorum. Imagining Markievicz feeding a gull in her
jail cell, Yeats launches an assault, though it is couched not in
anger but in sorrow and celebration:

> Did she in touching that lone wing
> Recall the years before her mind
> Became a bitter, an abstract thing,
> Her thought some popular enmity:
> Blind and leader of the blind
> Drinking the foul ditch where they lie?   [183–84]

As in his portrait of her in "Easter, 1916," Yeats first confronts
her present image—ignorant and shrill—before moving backward in time to her youthful beauty. Her mind has lost its
integrity, penetrated by readymade thought, political cliché,
other people's hatreds, while the poem distinguishes its own
enmity as supposedly nonpolitical disappointment. Yeats's usual
bifurcations of woman inform the attack. In much of his poetry, a
woman is either an aesthetic totality incarnating "uncomposite
blessedness," or broken fragments disturbed by "unresting
thought"; only if she "gives up all her mind" can she attain the
wholeness of the beautiful (176, 49, 146).

But in terms of the internal dynamic of the elegy, what is the
purpose of this aggressive gesture? To adapt Wordsworth's line,
does Yeats "murder" to resurrect? After the detraction of the
poem's first half, the second moves in the opposite direction. The
person drinking from a ditch now rides on horseback by a mountain. The mind diffused in other people's thoughts regains
"youth's lonely wildness." The change from passive to active,
downward to upward, and anonymity to individuation calls our
attention not only to the distance Markievicz has fallen but also
to the distance the poet travels in imaginatively restoring her.

Similarly, traditional elegists often establish the deadness of the body early in the poem, and so their power to transfigure it seems all the more astonishing.

If the earlier stanzas destroy so that the later stanzas may rebuild, the poem's figure for this imaginative process is the remarkable pair of bird images. In the first stanza, the bird is merely a "grey gull" like any other real gray gull that happens to be hungry. It is a natural image. But the second bird is a creature of a different rhetorical order. The poem introduces it with the preposition *like* to indicate its status as an emblematic image, akin to Swinburne's passionate bird in "To a Seamew." Markievicz

> seemed to have grown clean and sweet
> Like any rock-bred, sea-borne bird:

> Sea-borne, or balanced on the air
> When first it sprang out of the nest
> Upon some lofty rock to stare
> Upon the cloudy canopy,
> While under its storm-beaten breast
> Cried out the hollows of the sea.

The transformation of the gray gull into the seaborne bird rhetorically parallels the metamorphosis of Markievicz, from her seemingly literal death in spirit, to her figurative rebirth in the poem. Assurance of her death permits the poet to replace the natural image with an emblem, and it is in the emblem that poet and deceased can converge; for the seabird represents not only the absent woman but also the poet, recalling the "visionary white sea-bird" at the end of "In Memory of Alfred Pollexfen." Indeed, the seabird represents the poet in the very act of mourning that the lyric carries out—facing danger and death, and resonant with a swelling cry. The vertical movement above rocks, clouds, and sea completes the ascent from the foul ditch. The compensatory regression to origins leads the martyrs of "Easter, 1916" back to childhood under Yeats's maternal protection, Gregory back to the cradle-side in "Shepherd and Goatherd," and here Markievicz back to the nest. Placing Markievicz between the two horizons that apparently would neutralize her political programs, Yeats sees her as a seabird newly sprung from its nest and sublimely facing down the risk of death.

"In Memory of Eva Gore-Booth and Con Markievicz" renews the fight to rescue Markievicz and her sister from the death of politics. The lyric reverses the teleology of public elegy—transcendence in heroic political service—by countering it with the Romantic paradigm of loss. Here, "politics" lures both sisters into time and death, severing them from the "light" of their youthful innocence, or what Wordsworth calls "the fountain light." The poet's task, as so often in the English elegy and the Romantic lyric, is to override darkness with a consoling image of light: Yeats substitutes an apocalyptic "conflagration" for the lost natural "light" of the first stanza.[79]

Because his elegies can shift turbulently from one response, voice, or discourse to another, Yeats sometimes frames these vacillations with the kind of static picture we find at the first stanza's beginning and end—steadying the poem like the refrains in "September 1913" and "Easter, 1916." The first picture gives an impression of stillness because it excludes all verbs:

The light of evening, Lissadell,
Great windows open to the south,
Two girls in silk kimonos, both
Beautiful, one a gazelle.   [233–34]

The phrases seem to be laid side by side, freed from any syntactical momentum. A visual movement inward establishes the former intimacy between Yeats and his friends. The sequence of images guides the mind's eye from the outermost, panoramic vision of the light, to the narrower focus of the house, then at still closer range to the windows, to the two girls within and their appearance, and finally to the particular girl. But the final image, though the most "close-up," also reverses the visual movement; the metaphor of the gazelle suddenly widens out the frame of reference. Postponing the announcement of grief and death that usually opens an elegy, Yeats takes up instead the traditional scene of peace and fellowship—Milton's "we were nursed upon the selfsame hill."[80]

This crystalline image shatters with the announcement of death. The aural movement of the poem is a trope for the sisters' fall from the timeless harmony of their world and from the good graces of the poet. Languorous dactylic rhythms—*Lissadell, Beautiful*—and liquid sounds—*light, Lissadell, Beautiful, gazelle*—had stilled the iambic lines. But the next two verses are rhythmically broken by their initial headless feet, sonically disturbed by insistent *r*-sounds, and, together with the ensuing lines, syntactically overloaded with verbs:

> But a raving autumn shears
> Blossom from the summer's wreath;
> The older is condemned to death,
> Pardoned, drags out lonely years
> Conspiring among the ignorant.
> I know not what the younger dreams—
> Some vague Utopia—and she seems,
> When withered old and skeleton-gaunt,
> An image of such politics.

Instead of the usual recognition of the corpse that we expect in elegy, the women here are corpses before they are fully dead. Con Markievicz's condemnation to death seems not to have been reversed by the briefly mentioned pardon, for she "drags out" a moribund life. Her sister Eva betokens death in her self-separation, drying up into an allegorical "image" of the politics she espouses. Skeletons had appeared in elegies before, but this elegist risks comparing the deceased to a skeleton prior to death; he does so in the disturbing line that withholds respite from its severe string of adjectives—"withered old and skeleton-gaunt." Forcefully separating himself from the two women, the poet adds the statement "I know not" as yet another indicator of his distance from them.

But in the latter part of this stanza and in the next, the poet reunites with the women. As in many of Yeats's elegies, the psychological process of marking off the dead from the living seems to be the necessary precondition for the process of re-identification. After what he has just said about the women, his ruminative hope of speaking with them seems at face value absurd; his own poetic speech is a token of its impossibility, since their absence enables him to "mix / Pictures of the mind." As if to anchor these swings in affect and rhetoric, the first stanza returns to the image of an intimate interior. Dropping the present-tense suggestion that the women still live, the second stanza acknowledges their death; and drawing them into the plural pronoun "We," it assimilates them as "shadows" to the identity of the poet:

> Dear shadows, now you know it all,
> All the folly of a fight
> With a common wrong or right.
> The innocent and the beautiful
> Have no enemy but time;
> Arise and bid me strike a match
> And strike another till time catch;
> Should the conflagration climb,
> Run till all the sages know.
> We the great gazebo built,
> They convicted us of guilt;
> Bid me strike a match and blow.

The women have learned about their folly through posthumous wisdom, partly because the elegist has incorporated them as "shadows" into his mourning mind.

We have become familiar with Yeats's variations on the elegiac coda—the final reflection of the elegist on his persona and "doric lay." At the end of "September 1913" and "Easter, 1916," Yeats likens himself to the dead because of their commonality of desire; in the later poem he then recapitulates what he has been doing all along: "I write it out in a verse." Although more pained at the end of "In Memory of Major Robert Gregory" ("a thought / Of that late death took all my heart for speech"), the backward glance allows Yeats to focus the image of himself, with childhood, boyhood, and manhood coming together. At the end of "The Municipal Gallery Re-visited," Yeats asks us to recognize his "glory" in the friends he has just mourned. This larger context suggests that we may plausibly read the coda of "In Memory of Eva Gore-Booth and Con Markievicz" as a reflection on the poet and his task of mourning. Foregrounding himself at the end of the elegy, the poet asks the dead and internalized sisters to bid him rise and destroy time, in effect asking them to ratify the work of his poem. By bracketing their fall into time within two static tableaux and by seeking to demolish their temporal lives, the poet has burned up time in a microcosm; this purgation of their political lives has allowed him to absorb them within his own private meditation. The "conflagration" he would create is in part the elegy he has just created, replacing as it does the merely natural "light" at the beginning of the poem with this poetic light at the end. After the poet's contradictory responses to the dead, the coda reassembles a coherent persona and voice. Reconstructed, the poet is now ready to embrace his own fundamental "guilt." By intimating this willingness to accept guilt for a share in the temporal and political world, Yeats mutes the harshness of the poem's earlier attack on the sisters, and he anticipates the self-accusation in "Parnell's Funeral."

"Parnell's Funeral"

Unlike the elegies for the Gore-Booth sisters, a handful of Yeats's last elegies display a passion for political events. They depart from some guiding principles of the earlier public elegies. Yeats had avoided a public poetry that would merely "hiss the villain" or "preach a doctrine" in favor of a practice more sensitive to the "quarrel with ourselves" (*Au*, 138; *E&I*, 257). To turn within, as we have seen in an elegy like "Easter, 1916," does not necessarily mean to turn from the political to the merely personal; it may also permit the articulation in lyric of the complex forces and voices of history. In Robert Bly's typically Romantic assertion, "the political poem comes out of the deepest privacy."[81] Yeats's political consciousness narrows in such elegies as "The O'Rahilly" and "Come Gather Round Me, Parnellites." The internalized collective drama of "hesitation and doubt" disappears behind the journalistic hiss of the balladic elegy "Roger Casement" and the more amusing mock-elegy for John Bull, "The Ghost of Roger Casement." Together with "Three Songs to the Same Tune" and the later "Three Marching Songs," these elegies suffer both because of their political agenda—leaning toward fascism in the "Songs"—and because of their psychological project of mechanically arousing pathos to convert it into anger at external foes, a project that can allow much less attunement to the multiple voices within ourselves and our language.

This is not to say that the earlier public elegies disdained hatred altogether. Yeats often established his own community and inheritance through satiric dissociation. "Parnell's Funeral" (1932–3), the richest of the late public elegies, questions the role satire played in the earlier elegies. In "Easter, 1916" the poet began to turn the weapon of satire on himself, and at the end of "In Memory of Eva Gore-Booth and Con Markievicz," he even convicted himself of the same guilt for which he had just attacked the sisters. But the self-condemnation is much more persuasive in "Parnell's Funeral." Yeats satirized the materialists in "September 1913" and thereby intensified his bond with the delirium of Emmet, Fitzgerald, and Tone; but when these names reappear in "Parnell's Funeral," they no longer set the poet apart from the rest of the nation. Yeats adopts a conscience so collective that even Parnell's downfall has become partly his own doing. Whereas "To a Shade" derides the "pack" for dragging down Parnell and his like, Yeats now numbers himself in the pack:

> But popular rage,
> *Hysterica passio* dragged this quarry down.
> None shared our guilt; nor did we play a part
> Upon a painted stage when we devoured his heart.
>
> Come, fix upon me that accusing eye.
> I thirst for accusation. All that was sung,

All that was said in Ireland is a lie
Bred out of the contagion of the throng,
Saving the rhyme rats hear before they die.   [279–80]

The language echoes and inverts the locus classicus of elegiac satire, Saint Peter's angry denunciation of the clergy in "Lyci-das"—specifically the verbal constellation *devoured-contagion-nothing*. Unfed, the sheep rot and

> foul contagion spread:
> Besides what the grim wolf with privy paw
> Daily devours apace, and nothing said.[82]

Milton's Peter dissociates himself from the devouring wolves and the contagion, but Yeats accuses himself and all Irishmen of having devoured the totemic Parnell. Even Yeats's own lyrics ("All that was sung") were bred out of the national sickness. Satire is directed more completely inward than in earlier elegies like "Easter, 1916," the accuser now accusing and convicting himself. The former revulsion for the outside world has given way to what Freud calls the "self-reproaches and self-revilings" of melancholia, "self-reproaches to the effect that the mourner him-self is to blame for the loss of the loved object, i.e. that he has willed it."[83] Paradoxically, Yeats sees his own Parnellite rage against fellow Irishmen—the satiric intensity displayed in his public elegies—as sharing in the Irish hatred that brought down Parnell. Whitaker usefully compares the speaker of this poem to a tragic scapegoat who recognizes his own participation in the evil that has made him a victim.[84] This recognition has antecedents not only in tragedy and religious ritual but also in elegy. Yeats often quotes and echoes Shelley's *Adonais*. In one of its climactic moments the poet, having called down the curse of Cain on the murderers of Adonais, exposes what may be that brand on his own brow.[85] Like the poet of "Parnell's Funeral," Shelley's mourner knows his own guilt belatedly. As Heidegger remarks, "*Being*-guilty is more primordial than any knowledge about it."[86] But Yeats goes still further. By literalizing the identification in elegy as the devouring of the dead person's heart, he suggests that elegy—this elegy too—shares in the murder. The first part of the poem was originally entitled "A Parnellite at Parnell's Funeral." To bear the identity and transmit the tragic legacy of Parnell, the elegist must share in dismembering him—like the ancient mourner of a vegetation god. Alluding to the ancient sacrifice by arrow of a child that represented the tree spirit, Yeats asks: "Can someone there / Recall the Cretan barb that pierced a star?" In the following stanza, the answer is that the artist carries and preserves the knowledge of ritual sacrifice: "Some master of design / Stamped boy and tree upon Sicilian coin." By encoding this knowledge in his own elegiac craft, the artist perpetuates ritual sacrifice. The coin is an internal emblem for the work of this poem—reenacting the destruction and incorporation of Parnell to identify with him.[87]

Many of Yeats's elegies reveal an awareness that the loving sympathy of the genre also includes a component of aggression, and this elegy is even more explicit in laying bare that aggression and the attendant guilt: "Come, fix upon me that accusing eye. / I thirst for accusation." Yeats takes the genre back to its supposed origins in the ritual sacrifice of the dying god—Orpheus, Dionysus, Adonis, Attis, Charles Stewart Parnell. But according to the poem's second half, this rite fails to be perpetuated in history. Neither de Valera, nor Cosgrave, nor O'Higgins, nor the fascist O'Duffy ate Parnell's heart, as the elegist does, to become a true "Parnellite"; that is, none of them had the fortitude to take up the cannibalistic act of mourning that is fundamental to identification. Having associated himself with his countrymen in the first half of the poem, he now asserts his distance, interrupting the elegiac rite of naming:

> Had even O'Duffy—but I name no more—
> Their school a crowd, his master solitude;
> Through Jonathan Swift's dark grove he passed, and
>   there
> Plucked bitter wisdom that enriched his blood.

The poet constitutes his own literary line of descent against the historical failure to obviate the "loose-lipped demagogue" and to satisfy "Imagination." Parnell has eaten Swift's heart in a sacred "grove," and now Yeats symbolically eats Parnell's—solitary heroes apart from the crowd. But Yeats's language includes another precursor in the lineage, whose words have been disjoined again and incorporated into the last verse of the elegy. The mourner announces at the beginning of "Lycidas" that he must "pluck" from the plants that represent imagination because of "Bitter constraint." What, then, is the *bitter* wisdom Parnell *plucks*? Like Yeats in Milton's grove, Parnell plucks the bitter wisdom of the artist from Swift's grove—the elegiac knowledge of death. Here, death's constraint is bitter, however much it may profit the poet. But in the poems of tragic joy, Yeats asserts that there is joy in being compelled to pluck laurels, myrtles, and ivy, even for one's own laureate hearse.

2

"LAUGHING TO THE TOMB"

Tragic Joy and the Sublime

*Not only laughter and gay wisdom but the tragic, too,
with all its sublime unreason, belongs among the
means and necessities of the preservation of the species.*
—*Friedrich Nietzsche*
    The Gay Science

*It is a violence from within that protects us from a
violence without. It is the imagination pressing back
against the pressure of reality. It seems, in the last
analysis, to have something to do with our self-
preservation; and that, no doubt, is why the expres-
sion of it, the sound of its words, helps us to live
our lives.*
—*Wallace Stevens*
    "The Noble Rider and the Sound of Words"

Yeats's poems of tragic joy are his most familiar and
controversial achievement. Since they defy appropriation by any
single generic category, we must interpret these poems not,
strictly speaking, in terms of genre but in the cognate vocabulary
of mode.[1] As modes, the tragic, the sublime, the curse, the
prophetic, and the apocalyptic have significant family resemblances, since all potentially encode affirmative responses to
death and destruction. They can help in approaching the family
resemblances that connect an array of lyrics: such late poems as
"The Gyres" and "Lapis Lazuli," such middle poems as "The
Fascination of What's Difficult" and "The Second Coming," and
even an early poem, "The Valley of the Black Pig." Not any one of
the modes is relevant to every poem, but together they reveal

various emphases in this recognizable group of lyrics. The group
has traditionally been discussed in terms of tragedy, a view that I
build on in the first half of the chapter; their relation to the
sublime has not been discussed, and it becomes the subject of the
ensuing argument. Because critics have not sufficiently mapped
out the generic affiliations of these poems, I attempt to do so by
reading the lyrics synchronically rather than one by one.

The poems of tragic joy tend to divide critics into modernists
like Ellmann, who applaud their apparent rejection of Romantic
pathos for a harsher tone, and romanticists like Bloom, who
dislike their relinquishment of elegy and quest-romance for tragic
realism.[2] The critical division obscures the genealogy of these
poems. Even though Nietzsche's tragic joy is their most visible
debt, the antithetical exultation in violence is a powerful undersong through much Romantic writing, from Blake's apocalypses
and Shelley's Necessity to the later tragic affirmations of Freud,
Heidegger, and Stevens. In the Romantic dialectic of joyous
innocence and painful experience, Yeats's tragic joy represents the
final and synthetic moment. The generic affiliations of these
poems extend, still more broadly, to tragic catharsis and sublime
ecstasis, and to such lyric modes as carpe diem and the ruins
tradition, and even to the elegy.

TRAGIC JOY

"We that look on but laugh in tragic joy," proclaims
the gleefully antithetical speaker of "The Gyres" (293). The
disturbing gaiety of this tone and stance seems to have no generic
locus. Instead, the poem signals negatively its generic orientation
as anti-elegy. The poems of tragic joy may be seen as a countergenre to elegy—a countergenre that rages, in Yeatsian fashion,
against its shadow. With its rhetoric of abnegation and sorrow,
elegy seems to be everything these poems reject. The dialectic is a
complex one, however, since many of Yeats's formal elegies are
openly joyous and triumphant. For the present discussion I sim-

plify drastically the "elegiac," defining it in terms of the pathos of traditional elegy, of the early Yeats, and of his Romantic precursors. This definition simplifies partly because, as we have seen, his own elegies and those of his predecessors often share the heroic ethos of the poems of tragic joy. And despite the pervasive sorrow in Yeats's early poems, even they sometimes anticipate the anti-elegiac impulse of the later poems. "The Gyres" is hardly his first lyric to turn against elegiac pathos with its recommendation, "Heave no sigh, let no tear drop." The opening lyric of *The Collected Poems*— although mourning the death of Romantic pastoralism, resuming the *ubi sunt* tradition ("Where are now the warring kings?"), and paired with a "Sad" companion poem— pictures the last Arcadian on the way to a grave where he will sing not a dirge but "mirthful songs" ("The Song of the Happy Shepherd," 7–8). In another early lyric, "Ephemera," a lover upbraids the beloved for throwing dead leaves on herself in mourning their lost love: "Ah, do not mourn" (15). And at the end of *The Wanderings of Oisin,* the hero breaks off his dialogue with Saint Patrick, disgusted by the saint's advocacy of sorrow and repentance—laughter and combat are Oisin's calling. Even so, the elegiac tone is dominant in the early Yeats and tends to override such moments; it links an apostrophe like Fergus's "And no more turn aside and brood" not to a countergenre but to the renunciation of mourning within elegy itself—an interpretation Joyce suggests in *Ulysses* by following this quotation soon afterward with the parent-line in Milton's "Lycidas": "Weep no more, woful shepherds, weep no more" ("Who goes with Fergus?" 43). As it is cast by the poems of tragic joy, the shadow of the literary past—Romanticism—is even more distorted than that of Yeats's own early poetry; it requires lengthier examination.[3]

Internalized Tragedy: The Poet as Hero and Chorus

In Yeats's own essays and in subsequent criticism, tragedy has been the primary generic paradigm for discussing his anti-elegiac poems.[4] Because this view has often been formulated ahistorically, we might recall the generic transformations that allow Yeats to modulate a dramatic genre into lyric. Surveying his aesthetic writings, we see that Yeats builds on the Romantic appropriation of tragedy: he casts the lyric poet as both the hero and chorus of tragic drama.

First, the poet as hero. Yeats takes for granted the Romantic reading of tragedy, and especially of Shakespeare, which effects the transition from dramatic to lyric (or "closet") tragedy. Writers as diverse as Goethe, Coleridge, Wordsworth, Byron, and Tennyson assimilate the tragic hero to the lyric poet. When Yeats writes of the energy of "the hero of a play or the maker of poems," the casual *or* reflects these generic assumptions (*E&I*, 266). He uses the term "personality" for both the writer and the tragic hero, as contrasted with the clearly delineated "character" of comic persons (*Ex*, 154; *E&I*, 240). The distinction between personality and character is largely a distinction between lyric and dramatic conceptions of self, the one defined by the confrontation with death—a confrontation that seems to deepen and essentialize consciousness—the other by social relations with a community. Historically, this lyric overhaul of tragedy is part of what Gadamer calls "the subjectivization of aesthetics," writers reproducing in their transformation of genre their increasing isolation in bourgeois societies.[5]

Historians of lyric have perhaps made too much recently of the Romantic and post-Romantic internalization of romance, not enough of the concurrent internalization of tragedy—a generic tendency that culminates in the modern period.[6] Wyndham Lewis represents Timon of Athens as a precursor; the young Yeats thinks of Hamlet "as but myself," and the older Yeats imagines himself as Oedipus, Timon, and Lear (*Au*, 30). In "An Acre of Grass," Yeats turns Timon and Lear into heroic poets analogous with Blake:

Grant me an old man's frenzy.
Myself must I remake
Till I am Timon and Lear

> Or that William Blake
> Who beat upon the wall
> Till Truth obeyed his call. . . .   [301–2]

Yeats annuls the distinction between the rhetorical imitation of previous masters (as in Quintilian) and the ethical imitation of heroic types (as in Aristotle). In his dramatic practice, he absorbs tragedy into lyric, believing, contrary to Aristotle's *Poetics,* that "the motives of tragedy are not related to action but to changes of state" in the "soul" (*Au,* 319). Despite his interest in drama, Yeats attributes to the daimonic men of his own phase "an intensity which is never dramatic but always lyrical" (*AV,* 141). He applies his favorite terms for lyric consciousness to tragic drama—"passion," "personality," "reverie," "trance," "energy"—and commends above all those moments when "all is lyricism" (*E&I,* 240). Already in *The Prelude* the poet tells us that he is incapable of responding to tragedy unless it enables him to recognize his own solitary thoughts and feelings. Yeats also says of successful tragedy that "it is always ourselves that we see upon the stage" (*E&I,* 241; *Ex,* 154). There is, however, this difference between the poets: although Wordsworth thinks that "Poetry is passion," he fears that tragic passion dangerously wanders toward "pain," whereas Yeats celebrates the tumultuous "wandering of passion" in tragedy—"Tragedy is passion alone" (*Au,* 318).[7]

Adopting but modifying the pervasive Romantic conflation of hero and poet, Yeats identifies the poet specifically with the hero who is about to die. Arnold and Wilde had already privileged last lines spoken by Shakespeare's dying heroes. Yeats quotes repeatedly Arnold's tragic "touchstone" (from the dying Hamlet), "Absent thee from felicity awhile," and he echoes Wilde on the joy of Shakespeare's heroes at their last.[8] But it is Yeats who time and again celebrates these final utterances as models for the lyric. Discussing the impersonality of the lyric self, he takes these dying characters as his paradigm: "The heroes of Shakespeare convey to us through their looks, or through the metaphorical patterns of their speech, the sudden enlargement of their vision, their ecstasy at the approach of death: 'She should have died hereafter,' 'Of many thousand kisses, the poor last,' 'Absent thee from felicity awhile'" (*E&I*, 522–23).[9] The context of this much-quoted sentence from "A General Introduction for my Work" suggests its relevance to Yeats's poetry: the lyric, often projecting death as its horizon, aspires to the condition of tragic utterance. Sometimes Yeats even refers to his own poems as "soliloquies" (*Au*, 359; *E&I*, 521). Although tragic soliloquy is one of Yeats's recurring models for the lyric, we need not see the speakers of his "tragic" poems as defined characters. Even when they adopt specific personae, death essentializes their utterances, situating their discourse somewhere between dramatic monologue and nondramatic lyricism. If dramatic tragedy leads characters to an encounter with the external forces that destroy them, lyric tragedy internalizes this process by leading the poetic mind to a heroic reflection on death. Empirically, there can be no such thing as internalized tragedy, since the poet does not "die" but only encounters an obstacle troped as death and then quests onward. But in their phenomenological structure, the poems of tragic joy are staged as imaginative encounters with death, meditations at the brink of catastrophe.

Many poems instance Yeats's association of lyric consciousness with the dying hero, and such lyrics as "Vacillation" and "Parnell's Funeral" even present the poet as scapegoat. "An Irish Airman foresees his Death" is the clearest example in the Yeats canon of a lyric in the form of a tragic soliloquy. Its single stanza does indeed lead to "death," its final word:

> Nor law, nor duty bade me fight,
> Nor public men, nor cheering crowds,
> A lonely impulse of delight
> Drove to this tumult in the clouds;
> I balanced all, brought all to mind,
> The years to come seemed waste of breath,
> A waste of breath the years behind
> In balance with this life, this death.   [135]

A modern and unmystified Othello, the tragic speaker of the poem reviews his life from the privileged vantage point of its final moments. Heidegger's "being-towards-death" so closely approximates Yeats's understanding of the tragic here that we might say the speaker encounters his death with anticipatory resoluteness *(Entschlossenheit)* as the everyday withdraws from view, its morality and purposes reduced to anonymous crowds. The airman affirms this intense life of death as his chosen fate and freedom.[10] By making the encounter with death an entirely subjective trial, Yeats would elevate the speaker above the politics of the First World War.

The airman is perhaps too successful in his effort to grasp his life as a whole, an aim that Yeats and Heidegger elsewhere show to be impossible, though alluring. The poem lacks the "lyric heat" of Yeats's other meditations on death because it so closely approximates the model of tragic soliloquy, leaving the reader to peer over its thick wall of character—to modify Pater's phrase (*E&I*, 240). Yeats is no Browning, however dramatic some of his poems aspire to be, and the mechanical symmetries of the poem's beginning and end, while demonstrating self-possession, do not help to convince us that the speaker meditates at the edge of darkness. In such poems as "The Second Coming," "Nineteen Hundred and Nineteen," and "The Gyres," the outlines of character fade, although the resolute poet-hero still reveals his generic genealogy in fighting a social world that threatens to engulf him.

Yeats assimilates the poet not only to the tragic hero but also to the tragic spectator. The most important mediator of tragic tradition in this regard is Nietzsche. His Zarathustra, for example, combines the Apollonian hero's impulse to overcome himself with the satyr chorus's Dionysian joy in destruction.[11] But there is also an important precedent in English Romantic poetry for Yeats's recasting of the poet as both hero and tragic chorus. Shelley's *Prometheus Unbound,* for Yeats "a sacred book," plays a large part in his reception of tragedy, as "The Second Coming" indicates (*E&I*, 65). In noting the first stanza's echo of *Prometheus Unbound,* commentators have not wondered that it is the

chorus of Furies whose discourse Yeats rewrites.[12] Their choral
joy in wreck and ruin marks the ecstatic tone of the speaker, as he
works up to his "revelation." Yeats uses their phrase "lidless eyes"
in an earlier poem, "Upon a House shaken by the Land Agitation": there, the phrase describes his emblematic eagle, a spectator similarly unperturbed by destruction; and it is an eagle (or
vulture), of course, that torments the mythic Prometheus (95).[13]
But *lidless eyes* evokes both hero and chorus, because in Shelley,
the Furies use the phrase to describe Prometheus, the hero who
tries to conquer his pain and woe with courageous "endurance."[14] The tag may lie behind Yeats's avowal about his youthful
ambition: "I wished to become self-possessed, to be able to play
with hostile minds as Hamlet played, to look in the lion's face, as
it were, with unquivering eyelash" (*Au*, 62).[15] Perhaps to look
into the lion's face with unquivering eyelash, one must become
part lion, and the seer who imagines the "shape with lion body"
in "The Second Coming" partly shares its "pitiless" gaze. So too
the lines that evoke it move rhythmically with the slowness of "its
slow thighs"—an effect heightened as the poem "Slouches" to its
close:

>   . . . somewhere in sands of the desert
> A shape with lion body and the head of a man,
> A gaze blank and pitiless as the sun,
> Is moving its slow thighs, while all about it
> Reel shadows of the indignant desert birds.
> The darkness drops again; but now I know
> That twenty centuries of stony sleep
> Were vexed to nightmare by a rocking cradle,
> And what rough beast, its hour come round at last,
> Slouches towards Bethlehem to be born?   [187]

† The poem effects what I later describe as a *sublime* transfer of
energy from the violent scene to its own aesthetic work, as we see
here from the rhythmic mimesis of the beast's movement. In this
and other poems of tragic joy, Yeats internalizes further the
already internalized drama of Shelley, compounding hero with

chorus, the resolute Hamlet or Prometheus with the dauntless eagle, fury, or lion. *Spiritus Mundi* rends the veil to show the Promethean visionary a terrifying image that tests his courage, except that Prometheus is now more overtly his own tormentor.

The oxymoron "tragic joy" makes sense generically only if we see that it amalgamates hero and spectator, Apollo and Dionysus—a claim we can now begin to test in some exemplary lyrics. Yeats objects to drama that lacks the Dionysian, or what he calls "the emotion of multitude," and he demands "that tragedy must always be a drowning and breaking of the dykes that separate man from man" (*E&I*, 215, 241). This imperative of aesthetic collectivism may be viewed in part as compensating for the unavailability of such collectivism in the real, atomistic social world—a world that shunts to its margins the modern poet. Aesthetically, Yeats tries to break down "the dykes that separate man from man," and he tries to do so even in some poems that defend Apollonian form, such as "A Prayer for my Daughter" and "Meditations in Time of Civil War": in one poem, the speaker imagines "in excited reverie" the maenadic years dancing out of the Dionysian sea, and in the other, he "all but cried / For vengeance" along with the senseless multitude (188, 206). The words "all but" preserve the speaker's Apollonian integrity, in a typically Yeatsian hesitation at the brink of choral dissolution.

"Lapis Lazuli" fuses tragic hero and spectator more brilliantly than any other of Yeats's poems. Describing how the actors ought to respond to their roles if "worthy" of them, the second stanza conceives of the *actors* as *spectators* of the *heroes* whose roles they play:

> All perform their tragic play,
> There struts Hamlet, there is Lear,
> That's Ophelia, that Cordelia;
> Yet they, should the last scene be there,
> The great stage curtain about to drop,
> If worthy their prominent part in the play,
> Do not break up their lines to weep.

> They know that Hamlet and Lear are gay;
> Gaiety transfiguring all that dread.
> All men have aimed at, found and lost;
> Black out; Heaven blazing into the head:
> Tragedy wrought to its uttermost.
> Though Hamlet rambles and Lear rages,
> And all the drop scenes drop at once
> Upon a hundred thousand stages,
> It cannot grow by an inch or an ounce.   [294]

The subtly ambiguous proper names play out the tension between merging the hero with the actor-spectator and keeping them distinct. The proper names slide between two referents: the characters and the actors. This blurred semantic space, opened by the actor's reflective imitation and observation of a role, for Yeats resembles the ambiguous psychic space between a spectator and a hero. At first, the names Hamlet, Lear, Ophelia, and Cordelia refer principally to actors who "perform" Shakespeare's plays, deictis summoning them before us, like the rebels in "Easter, 1916." They prove themselves more or less "worthy" of their noble roles by how they act the "last scene." But the line "They know that Hamlet and Lear are gay" transfers the referent of the names from the actors to the heroic characters. With the antecedent of "They" spelled out, the line would read, "Hamlet and Lear [the actors] know that Hamlet and Lear [the characters] are gay." The proper names belong improperly to both actor-witness and hero, so that as actors, Hamlet and Lear may wrongly weep, but as characters, Hamlet and Lear exult. Just as hero and spectator coexist in these names, they also coexist, Yeats suggests, in each person's encounter with death. For this stanza represents one's own death as ineluctably dual: on the one hand, it is private and single, experienced as a "Black out; Heaven blazing into the head"; on the other, it is collective and recurrent, observed inevitably at a spectatorial distance, as if on "a hundred thousand stages."

Psychologically and aesthetically astute, Yeats's fusion of hero and spectator is also a response to various painful realities of his historical moment. His amalgamation of lyric poet with heroic character with reflective actor with cathartic spectator may help to compensate in part for the modern poet's sense of estrangement from an audience. Further, Yeats wrote most of his poems of tragic joy, including "Lapis Lazuli" and "The Gyres," in wartime—the First World War, the Troubles, the Civil War, and the conflicts preceding the Second World War. When he composed "Lapis Lazuli" in late July 1936 and "The Gyres" in this same general period, he was indeed a "spectator" of war and death. That March, Hitler had sent ten thousand troops into the Rhineland; in May, Mussolini had quelled the Ethiopian resistance by aircraft and poison gas; and in mid-July, Spanish generals had ferried Foreign Legionnaires to Andalusia from Morocco, beginning the Spanish Civil War. Nietzsche also conceived his theory of tragic spectatorship in wartime—a theory of tragic affirmation that deeply informs Yeats's poem; the later preface to *The Birth of Tragedy* historicizes the book in terms of the Franco-Prussian War.[16] Partly in response to the outward pressure of such violence, Yeats modulates into lyric not only tragedy but also an ancient warrior ethos, just as Nietzsche absorbs it into his philosophical writings. During the Great War, Yeats briefly encapsulates this ethos: "In an Anglo-Saxon poem a certain man is called, as though to call him something that summed up all heroism, 'Doom eager'" (*Per Amica Silentia Lunae, Myth,* 336). But in casting heroes as spectators rather than agents, Yeats and Nietzsche diminish the scope of heroism; both writers, perceiving themselves shackled to choral roles as witnesses of warfare, restrict their heroes largely to affective reactions to their finitude and to global cataclysm.

The abrupt transition from the first to the second stanza of "Lapis Lazuli" silently articulates the relation between spectators of war and spectators of dramatic tragedy. To refute the demand of the "hysterical women" that something drastic be done to stop the war, the second stanza demonstrates that, regardless of the circumstances, "All" must in the end die their own death—so

they might as well embrace this necessity. But this rebuttal relies
on an underlying conflation of death's inevitability with the
apparent inevitability of war, a mystifying conflation distinct
from the poem's finer ambiguities. Although each person's death
is unavoidable, each war is not; death comes to all, but war death
need not do so. Yeats refigures political violence as theater, thus
following Nietzsche in the further conflation of death's necessity
with aesthetic necessity. Modernizing the *theatrum mundi* topos,
he translates the political and social catastrophe of war into the
aesthetic encounter of each character with a scripted death.
Nietzsche describes the tragic spectator's delight in the face of
destruction: "a metaphysical solace momentarily lifts us above
the whirl of shifting phenomena."[17] Yeats the prophetic spectator
rises above his historical moment until King William of Orange
merges with Kaiser Wilhelm II, Elizabethan England with Attic
Greece, the Orient with the Occident. As in Nietzsche's *Artisten-
Metaphysik,* this distance solaces the spectator, for the political
contingencies of war take on the appearance of necessity. Yeats's
Hamlet and Lear share much with Nietzsche's Dionysian spectator and Hamlet: "both have looked deeply into the true nature of
things, they have *understood* and are now loath to act. They realize
that no action of theirs can work any change in the eternal
condition of things, and they regard the imputation as ludicrous
or debasing that they should set right the time [Welt] which is
out of joint."[18] We may grant Nietzsche's and Yeats's tragic
spectators that death is part of the "eternal condition of things,"
but it is harder to grant that each war is as well; the possibility of
nuclear annihilation—all the drop scenes dropping at once, never
to rise again—has made it even harder.

Lyric Modes and the Question of Elegy

Yeats develops his poems of tragic joy not only by
internalizing tragic drama but by reworking an array of traditional lyric modes and subgenres closely related to tragedy. Critics are sometimes led astray in the interpretation of these lyrics

because of a failure to recognize their literary templates: *carpe diem, carpe florem, contemptus mundi,* the happy death, the ruins tradition, the Romantic lyric, and the elegy. From Fitzgerald's *Rubaiyat* to Stevens's "Sunday Morning," late Romantic poets have taken up the carpe diem song, "Death is the mother of beauty." Yeats frequently quotes Ernest Dowson's version of the carpe diem chant, and borrows its phrase, "bitter and gay," to characterize his own poems of tragic gaiety (*E&I*, 492; *L*, 836; *Ox*, x). Such is the mood of his own blessing of transience in "Lapis Lazuli":

> All things fall and are built again
> And those that build them again are gay.   [295]

Much earlier, he had written a mock-elegy for Father Rosicross, "The Mountain Tomb," which draws in its opening from the familiar repertoire of the carpe diem song:

> Pour wine and dance if manhood still have pride,
> Bring roses if the rose be yet in bloom. . . .   [121]

Given the importance of the rose in Rosicrucian rituals, Father Rosicross would no doubt have been pleased with this use, along with many others in the early Yeats, of the carpe florem tradition. In one of his most Paterian sentences, Yeats writes that the poet must take his pleasure in the temporary beauty of women, flowers, and heroic passion—"in whatever is most fleeting" (*E&I*, 287). Not that the acceptance of death as the condition of all value comes easily to Yeats. *A Vision* attempts to absorb time into logical oppositions. And when he echoes the language of Pater's "Conclusion" to *The Renaissance,* his thoughts turn from "moments as they pass" to death itself.[19] Indeed, Yeats's principal modification of Pater's aesthetic moment is that he makes it the final moment, intensifying Pater's sense of each perceptual moment as *eschaton.* Yeats's heroes and speakers have their enlargement of vision at their death, uttering as his Faust does a "last cry to the passing moment" (*Au*, 348).

The lyrics of tragic joy also resume the tradition of the "happy

death"—a tradition that flourished with such Renaissance ex-
empla as Sir Thomas More and Sir Walter Raleigh, and that has a
separate classical and Christian heritage.[20] Defying the possible
threat of mass death to this heroic ideal, Yeats has his Irish airman
and other warriors respond whimsically to their own deaths.
Furthermore, some of these poems draw on the ruins tradition,
familiar in its Renaissance adaptations by Joachim du Bellay,
Spenser, and Shakespeare, and especially evident in Yeats's ekphrastic modulation, which we analyze in the context of the self-
elegy. The speaker of "Meru" reflects on the cycles of decay that
have destroyed Egypt, Greece, and Rome (this last the favorite
ruin in the tradition); and the hermits know that before dawn,
man's "glory and his monuments are gone" (289). Yeats himself
identifies a major historical reason for the mode's appeal: as a boy
he rebelled against the pervasive "myth" of "progress," and therefore "took satisfaction in certain public disasters, felt a sort of
ecstasy at the contemplation of ruin" (*Ex,* 392). One could trace
this generic strand backward from "Meru" to "Nineteen Hundred and Nineteen," *The Wanderings of Oisin,* and then back to
Shelley's *Hellas* and Byron's *Childe Harold.* Yeats unbinds the
eerie glee that much of the tradition keeps just beneath the
surface. Sometimes his use of the mode also absorbs the contemptus mundi attitude—for example, the refrain of "Vacillation," "Let all things pass away" (251–52), or the call of "Nineteen Hundred and Nineteen" to "mock at the great" who toiled

To leave some monument behind,
Nor thought of the levelling wind.   [209]

The happy death, the ruins tradition, and contemptus mundi
mark an extreme of detachment in this array of subgenres, unlike
the carpe diem exhortation to affirm beauty and life because of
death. The poems of tragic joy tend sometimes in one direction
and sometimes in the other: when they move toward Schopen-
hauerian or Buddhistic dismissiveness, the tragic element is at
risk, as in "Meru" and the other *Supernatural Songs;* when they
cling to passing beauty or people, the joyful element is at risk.

This latter end of the spectrum leads into the elegiac, the mode whose relation to the poems of tragic joy is most difficult to assess.

Let us consider two possible arguments about elegy and tragic joy: that the poems of tragic joy are a countergenre to elegy and, at the opposite extreme, that they are a covert form of elegy— elegy as conventionally defined in terms of pathos and mourning. "The Gyres," a controversial lyric in this group, will be our primary point of reference, along with Yeats's writings on aesthetics. Yeats lends support to the countergenre argument by setting "pity" or "pathos," which he associates with self-consciousness and Ophelia, against "tragedy" and "passion," related in his work to self-forgetting and Shakespeare's heroic characters (*Ex*, 428; *Au*, 353, 355). Yeats's resistance to pathos is evident in the very name he chooses for his bards—*gleemen*—a term richly suggestive of the bond between joy and song. Among his lyrics, "The Mountain Tomb" and "Tom O'Roughly" are clearly presented as anti-elegies. The former recommends wine, dance, music, and kissing instead of the solemn behavior one would expect at a tomb, the latter provoking us with the fool's declaration that

'. . . little need the grave distress.'

.   .   .   .

'And if my dearest friend were dead
I'd dance a measure on his grave.'   [141]

The poem has been attacked for being anti-elegiac, but its generic task is to flout the norms of elegy. Similarly, the heroic posturings in "Under Ben Bulben," amid the gravediggers, limestone, and self-epitaph, should be seen as efforts to dispel elegiac sorrow and submission, and gain self-mastery: "for only when we are gay over a thing, and can play with it, do we show ourselves its master, and have minds clear enough for strength" (*E&I*, 252).

Many of Yeats's poems of tragic joy contrast the heroic and the elegiac along gender lines, as we might expect from the association of pathos with Ophelia. In this regard, Yeats participates in the period's patriarchal tendency to feminize grief and mourning.

"Lapis Lazuli" belittles "hysterical women" for their elegiac response to war; in an earlier draft the gender division so predominates that, despite their heroic status, even Cordelia and Ophelia
weep.[21] In "The Gyres" the poet represents his youthful, elegiac
self as feminine, sighing for "boxes of make-up" (293). In part
this gender division suggests that the anti-elegiac strain is the
"masculine" side of Yeats's psyche in revolt against its own "femininity." Joyce Carol Oates puts the general conflict this way: "A
man's quarrel with Woman is his quarrel with himself—with
those 'despised' and muted elements in his personality which he
cannot freely acknowledge because they challenge his sense of
masculine supremacy and control."[22] Such poems of tragic joy as
"The Gyres" and "Lapis Lazuli" suppress the woman within—
troped as the sighing boy and the "hysterical women"—and
assert a masculine joy in victory. In "Upon a Dying Lady," Yeats
virtually transforms Beardsley into a male hero by identifying her
first with Petronius and then with a cast of warriors that includes
not only Grania but also

> Achilles, Timor, Babar, Barhaim, all
> Who have lived in joy and laughed into the face of Death.
>   [159]

Even though Yeats's resistance to the elegiac is partly a rejection of "femininity" and of the "feminine" pathos of Romanticism, it is itself a typically Romantic gesture and thus participates
in a larger male poetic tradition of suppressing the pathos sometimes linked with women and passivity. Shifting our focus from
gender and returning to the literary historical issue of Yeats and
Romanticism, let us consider some key examples of the anti-
elegiac strain in Romantic works that strongly influenced Yeats.
In *The Four Zoas* Blake represents elegy as a fallen mode of
discourse, Urizen moaning in sterility that his songs of "joy" have
"turned to cries of Lamentation," and reviving only when sorrow
leaves him—"he Exulted he arose in joy he exulted."[23] From
Wordsworth's "Intimations Ode" and Coleridge's "Dejection" to
Shelley's "Ode to the West Wind," the Romantic ode tries in its

final movement to break through elegiac pathos and into "joy!"
or "prophecy." Just so in the middle stanza of "The Gyres":

> What matter though numb nightmare ride on top
> And blood and mire the sensitive body stain?
> What matter? Heave no sigh, let no tear drop,
> A greater, a more gracious time has gone;
> For painted forms or boxes of make-up
> In ancient tombs I sighed, but not again;
> What matter? Out of Cavern comes a voice
> And all it knows is that one word 'Rejoice.'   [293]

Elegy, with its sighs, tears, and tombs, is parodied and silenced.
The poet renounces his own youthful and feminine indulgence of
Romantic pathos by substituting for his elegiac whimperings the
paternal voice of tragic affirmation. "What matter?" recalls Zara-
thustra's proverb, "What does it matter?" but it also resembles
Wordsworth's question in his ode,

> What though the radiance which was once so bright
> Be now for ever taken from my sight[?][24]

Nor should it surprise us that in the midst of destruction, the
Rocky Face declares—as does Coleridge in his effort to forego
mourning and Blake in response to a bloody apocalypse—"Rejoice."[25] Tragic joy is Yeats's own more assertive and aggressive
version of the final movement in high Romantic mythologies: it
is his equivalent for Blake's organized innocence after jubilant
innocence and despairing experience, Wordsworth's "joyous
song" despite the eye's "sober colouring," Coleridge's "luminous
cloud" of joy that issues from the dejected self, and Shelley's
exuberant though "autumnal tone."[26]

But another twist complicates this literary genealogy. In Romantic lyrics of loss, the literary parent of this imaginative drive
toward compensation is the final section of the paradigmatic
English elegy, "Lycidas." And Yeats himself incorporates tragic
joy into many of his formal elegies as a subordinate mode—the
heroic joy facing down death in "Upon a Dying Lady," the

terrible beauty born in "Easter, 1916." Is it possible, then, that
Yeats's apparently anti-elegiac works are fundamentally elegiac?

Unlike elegy, the poems of tragic joy seem to refuse mourning; that is, they seem to give up, as the Rocky Face does, all
attachment to lost objects. In its opening "Lapis Lazuli" ridicules
women who, instead of rejoicing like poets, bemoan the potential loss of their bomb-threatened towns. Yet the artists, heroes,
builders, and Chinamen differ from the women less than it may
appear if their gaiety is based on the faith that lost towns, lives,
civilizations, and works of art are never really lost—that they will
always be "built again." If so, then the psychological and linguistic task of the poems of tragic joy structurally resembles that of
elegy: they joyfully give up lost objects only to ensure that they
will return, much as Freud's grandson in *Beyond the Pleasure
Principle* throws his toys away *(fort)* to author their reappearance
(da). A paradigm more familiar to Yeats, and one that he works
directly into "The Valley of the Black Pig," "Her Vision in the
Wood," and "Vacillation," is the mourning rite as described in
The Golden Bough. Even as they wail and disfigure themselves,
Frazer's mourners conceal their gleeful knowledge that they are
assuring the deity's return. Their rites are a "Festival of Joy," not
sorrow.[27] Nor is even the Rocky Face indifferent, as we discover
in the last stanza of "The Gyres":

> Conduct and work grow coarse, and coarse the soul,
> What matter! Those that Rocky Face holds dear,
> Lovers of horses and of women, shall
> From marble of a broken sepulchre
> Or dark betwixt the polecat and the owl,
> Or any rich, dark nothing disinter
> The workman, noble and saint, and all things run
> On that unfashionable gyre again.

What the Rocky Face holds dear may be repugnant to us, but this
final section of the poem completes the disguised work of mourning. In a typically elegiac gesture, it prophesies the resurrection
from a Shelleyan "dark wintry bed" (a darkness multiplied with

Shelleyan abundance) of a very un-Shelleyan social order. However outrageously anti-elegiac in tone, "The Gyres" is at some
level an elegy for a lost feudal society and a former poetic self.
Yeats advises that the poet "find his pleasure in all that is for ever
passing away," not because pleasure in what passes away is, in
Paterian fashion, valuable for its own sake, but "that it may come
again" (E&I, 287).

The poems of tragic joy are thus neither anti-elegies nor elegies simple but anti-elegies with a strong elegiac undersong.
Without the elegiac undersong, these poems would be, in Yeats's
terms, primary, Asiatic renunciations; they retain, however, their
attachments and affections. And because their willful joy is pervasive rather than the last stage in a process of mourning, they
cannot be considered elegies simple.

An affective antinomy, "tragic joy" continues to shock in part
because it deliberately violates generic decorum. Dryden asks,
"are not mirth and compassion things incompatible?"[28] Not for
Yeats, whose Celtic Twilight opens with a teller of tales who
recommends "mirth" because he lives in depressing circumstances—a portrait of the artist with eyes that have "a melancholy
which was wellnigh a portion of their joy" (Myth, 5). Auden
captures in his elegy for Yeats this same joy that rises in the
moment of descent:

Follow, poet, follow right
To the bottom of the night,
With your unconstraining voice
Still persuade us to rejoice. . . .[29]

In his aesthetic writings, Yeats talks of "the mingling of contraries," a mingling that purifies the moods or passions and gives us
"the extremity of sorrow, the extremity of joy," one passion
"aroused into a perfect intensity by opposition with some other
passion" (E&I, 255; Ex, 155). His description of the moods,
particularly of the moods brought together when Shakespeare's
heroes approach death, can help us to perceive the affects con-
joined in the poems of tragic joy: "Shakespeare's persons, when

the last darkness has gathered about them, speak out of an ecstasy that is one-half the self-surrender of sorrow, and one-half the last playing and mockery of the victorious sword before the defeated world" (*E&I*, 254). We sometimes fail to detect the sorrow embedded in such poems as "The Gyres" and "Lapis Lazuli," so strong is their effort not to surrender but to wave the sword; yet we misunderstand them if we do not grasp their interplay of moods, for even a poem as mocking as "The Gyres" allows itself the rueful line, "A greater, a more gracious time has gone."

Toward the Impossible Mask

As a model for the poems of tragic joy, Yeats's theory of moods may by itself be too static since these poems are not inertly suspended between immutable affects. They dramatically enact a transition toward a mask—the "emotional antithesis" of the self (*Au*, 128). Borrowing the theory of the mask from Wilde and Nietzsche, Yeats links it to tragic joy: he associates the mask not only with the ideal and opposite self but also with remembered "moments of exaltation" (*AV*, 83). He crafts his joyful mask out of privileged moments and imposes it on the mournful self. Writing *Per Amica Silentia Lunae* during the First World War—a work that might have been called *Notes Toward a Supreme Vision*—Yeats anticipates Stevens by trying to equate the battles of poet and soldier: "The poet finds and makes his mask in disappointment, the hero in defeat" (*Myth*, 337). Like the heroic act, the joyous poem is a performative gesture, its occasion not victory but loss. Too often we assume that the exuberant mask has been won, whereas a poem like "Lapis Lazuli" or "The Gyres" must fail in its striving toward an unattainable mask: "To me the supreme aim is an act of faith and reason to make one rejoice in the midst of tragedy. An impossible aim" (*L*, 838). These poems rejoice in the midst of tragedy despite inevitable defeat, even as Shelley's trumpet of prophecy and Coleridge's luminous cloud of joy issue forth from a dejection that qualifies apparent victory. Emerson defines as power this process of self-transformation: "Power ceases in the instant of repose; it resides in the moment of transition from a past to a new state, in the shooting of the gulf, in the darting to an aim. This one fact the world hates, that the soul *becomes*."[30] Although we may be tempted to associate the perspective of "The Gyres" with the Rocky Face,[31] the poem is "knit by dramatic tension" between sorrowful face and antithetical mask, between elegiac youth and tragic maturity, between the "woman" within and the "male" warrior—in the knitting metaphor that Yeats uses both for his lyrics and for the relation of self and mask (*E&I*, 521; *Myth*, 335). The actor, Yeats writes in *A Vision* to explain his theory of the mask, "must discover or reveal a being which only exists with extreme effort, when his muscles are as it were all taut and all his energies active" (*AV*, 84). The taut, energetic body of this poem would replace the "sensitive body" it disdains; but its very tautness and assertiveness should alert us to the energy it must expend to occlude pathos and will its joyful mask into being.

The lyrics of tragic joy are efforts at self-overcoming, and Nietzsche's favorite metaphor for self-overcoming is birth, as Yeats knew: "I think that all happiness depends on the energy to assume the mask of some other self; that all joyous or creative life is a re-birth as something not oneself" (*Au*, 340, 321). Suppressing the "woman" within, the process of self-origination appropriates the female power to give birth to a new self. In its last stanza, "The Gyres" predicts the birth of a new order out of the "dark nothing," and in the middle stanza it symbolically enacts the birth of a new tragic voice out of the negated elegiac one—a substitution of tragic laughter for sighs and tears. In the first stanza, the poem thematizes this process of substitution in broad cultural terms:

> The gyres! the gyres! Old Rocky Face look forth;
> Things thought too long can be no longer thought
> For beauty dies of beauty, worth of worth,
> And ancient lineaments are blotted out.
> Irrational streams of blood are staining earth;

Empedocles has thrown all things about;
Hector is dead and there's a light in Troy;
We that look on but laugh in tragic joy.

Energetically trying to overcome its own belatedness by refigur-
ing elegiac sorrow as tragic joy, the poem also diagnoses the very
cultural condition ("beauty dies of beauty") of which it is a
symptom. The attempt to displace sadness is itself evidence of a
sadness over cultural loss—the loss from which the poem wills a
recovery. Even as it announces that cultural substitution is a
process of decline—distancing rather than recovering origins—
it returns to the "original" Western scene and violently re-origi-
nates it, substituting joy for the elegiac response to the Trojan fall
at the end of the *Iliad*. But the perspective it adopts on that
"original" scene is the already belated perspective of the *Aeneid*,
seeing in the *fire* that destroyed Troy the compensatory *light* of a
new civilization. Partly recognizing its own entanglement in the
decline it laments, the poem asserts its mask and fails heroically.

The process of self-overcoming carried out by the poems of
tragic joy often unfolds temporally as a recognizable structure.
Broken into its stanzaic components, "The Gyres" proceeds from
an initial shock at the present outward spectacle of streaming
blood and cultural self-destruction, to the retrospective movement inward of the middle stanza, and finally to the outward and
prophetic contemplation of a renewed social hierarchy. George
Bornstein has mapped onto some of Yeats's other poems M. H.
Abrams's description of the Greater Romantic Lyric as an out-in-
out movement.[32] This triadic formula works well with "The
Gyres." And it brings out the poem's major deviation: the middle
movement swerves from the Greater Romantic Lyric in refusing
to find consolation in its regressive, inward glance, and thus sets
itself against its more elegiac precursors.

And yet, in its psychic structure, the poem depends on elegy to
work up its joy. The middle stanza recalls the energy formerly
used in mourning and releases this energy from its objects, transforming it into joy. If mourning is the psychic correlative of

elegy, mania corresponds to tragic joy and the sublime; and mania, writes Freud, is the overcoming of mourning: "In mania, the ego must have got over the loss of the object (or its mourning over the loss, or perhaps the object itself), and thereupon the whole quota of anticathexis which the painful suffering of melancholia had drawn to itself from the ego and 'bound' will have become available."[33] The transition from elegiac mourning to tragic affirmation marks the middle movement of many poems of tragic joy. In the pivotal line of "Meru," gaiety supervenes when the poet releases lost civilizations from the grip of mourning: "Egypt and Greece good-bye, and good-bye, Rome!" (289). The mind again summons these fallen civilizations in the middle stanza of "Lapis Lazuli" but relinquishes them and recaptures gaiety. In "The Gyres," this structure is visible not only at the macroscopic level of the poem as a totality but also in each of the constituent stanzas. Each opens with an exclamatory and outward vision of present violence (gyres, nightmare, coarseness), followed by a retrospective meditation that raises and refuses the possibility of lament (Hector and Troy, sighs and tombs), and ends with a final and prospective affirmation. The last stanza modifies the pattern by eliminating the middle step and by collapsing past and future, elegy and joy, in its final moment of prayer.

Tragic Laughter

The energy released in the poems of tragic joy often takes the form of laughter, and laughing "into the face of Death" is one of Yeats's favorite symbolic gestures, though it remains largely uninterpreted (159). In "The Gyres" the choral witnesses of destruction "laugh in tragic joy" (293); in "Under Ben Bulben" the warrior-poet "Laughs aloud" at the moment before he completes his fate (326); in "Vacillation" the ultimate arbiters of poetic worth are "such men as come / Proud, open-eyed and laughing to the tomb" (250). At the end of "A Dialogue of Self and Soul," the poet frees himself from self-pity by affirming his fate:

When such as I cast out remorse
So great a sweetness flows into the breast
We must laugh and we must sing,
We are blest by everything,
Everything we look upon is blest.   [236]

The replacement of the self-mourning "I" by the laughing "We"
represents the unbinding of object-directed pathos and its sudden transformation into Dionysian catharsis—an unfocused libido that drowns the dikes in a moment of blessedness. Freud
usefully describes this redistribution of psychic energy: "If the
objects are destroyed or if they are lost to us, our capacity for love
(our libido) is once more liberated; and it can either take other
objects instead or can temporarily return to the ego."[34] Insofar as
the loosened quantity of libido returns to the mind, a narcissistic
joy floods the ego, giving rise to Yeats's power to bless—or at
least to bless himself. And insofar as the freed libido is turned
outward, everything the poet looks upon seems blessed—a moment analogous with the spectator's sense of affirmation and
reunion after the death of the tragic hero. But the communion
with others is based on a transient illusion, partly exhilarating to
Yeats because it seems to offer a momentary release from the
atomism of his social world. This and several other poems of
tragic joy draw modally on the blessing, yet we shall later see that
they incorporate even more frequently the curse.

In the psychic economy of the poems of tragic joy, laughter
represents the conversion not only of elegiac pathos but also of
the energy that holds defenses in place against death and destruction. By distancing, aestheticizing, and accepting the contemporary bloodshed in Europe, "The Gyres" frees defensive energy to
become laughter, much as Freud describes this process in his
study of jokes: "laughter arises if a quota of psychical energy
which has earlier been used for the cathexis of particular psychical
paths has become unusable, so that it can find free discharge."[35]
In Yeats the moment of laughter amid tragedy represents a temporary illusion of transcending the human, insofar as the human

is associated with the twin responses toward death of fear and pathos. His poetry persistently reverses the commonplace—derived from Aristotle—that of all living creatures human beings alone are endowed with laughter. In the early poetry, laughter often distinguishes inhuman stars, waves, gods, fairies, animals, madmen, and godlike heroes from human mourners.[36] The Immortals are called the "Laughing People" in *The Shadowy Waters* (416). In *The Wanderings of Oisin,* the Immortals laugh at the protagonist, who is covered with mortal "mire" like a babe returning to Spenser's Gardens of Adonis (360). Niamh's Danaan songs of laughter are an "unhuman sound" (358). But in the later poems of tragic joy, the laughter's forcefulness is a measure of the strength of the underlying fears and attachments that the poems wish to overcome.

This impulse toward transcendence has a social dimension. Yeatsian laughter sometimes represents the overcoming not only of the self but also of others. The squirrel in "An Appointment" makes a "low whinnying sound / That is like laughter" (and like poetry), a spontaneous sound that overrides the political sedimentation of "government" (126). In accord with Thomas Hobbes's theory of laughter, Yeats's surrogate selves laugh out of a "sudden glory" that springs from a sense of superiority to others, a superiority often disruptive to hierarchies of class and government.[37] Laughter in Yeats can be rebellious and anarchistic: Seanchan, the poet-hero of *The King's Threshold,* laughs in defiance of king, mayor, state, and his mournful disciples:

> And I would have all know that when all falls
> In ruin, poetry calls out in joy,
> Being the scattering hand, the bursting pod,
> The victim's joy among the holy flame,
> God's laughter at the shattering of the world.
> And now that joy laughs out, and weeps and burns
> On these bare steps.   [*VPl*, 266–67]

As Bakhtin argues of medieval laughter, Seanchan's laughter has no inhibitions or limitations; it signifies at least a temporary victory over fear, whether of political authority or of death—the final form of authority. But Seanchan's laughter is not communal, like Bakhtin's "festive folk laughter": it is the laughter of the isolated scapegoat in the sacrificial flame, the lonely apocalyptic laughter of God, or the affirmative sound of a lyric poem confronting alone the world's ruin.[38]

Rather than expound its radical potential, Yeats in the middle poems associates laughter with aristocratic disdain. In the topography of "Upon a House shaken by the Land Agitation," Castiglionian "high laughter" rises above the "Mean roof-trees" of the farmers (95). The breeding of the "Friend whose Work has come to Nothing" makes her capable of laughter, a self-present and self-authenticating form of speech that contrasts with the lies of the middle class (109). One of Yeats's dreamers would like to gaze

> At the old bitter world where they marry in churches,
> And laugh over the untroubled water
> At all who marry in churches,
> Through the white thin bone of a hare.
>
> ["The Collar-bone of a Hare," 137]

The derisive laughter signifies the speaker's identification with king and nobility (the opposite not only of Seanchan's but also of Bakhtin's laughter), an identification that allows him to miniaturize and distance the bourgeois world of the everyday. In such poems, the laughing mask is dangerously close to becoming a face.

The risk of seeking beyond the human, the elegiac, the everyday, of seeking the transcendence of the sublime, is enormous in Yeats. We have already seen that it presupposes the aestheticization of historical violence and the renunciation of what he thinks of as feminine and bourgeois; let us look further into its psychology. Laughter in Yeats as in Nietzsche is apotropaic. To defy death, the laughing hero must identify with that which threatens to destroy him, the poet turn into pitiless, rough beast. Recalling one of his beasts, Yeats wonders, "Had I begun *On Baile's Strand* or not when I began to imagine, as always at my left side just out of the range of the sight, a brazen winged beast that I associated with laughing, ecstatic destruction?" (*Ex*, 393). The muted excitement in "The Second Coming," as we have seen, betrays an implicit identification between poet and beast, Promethean hero and laughing Fury. In the discarded Nietzschean play *Where There is Nothing*, the protagonist responds jubilantly to his vision of what he calls "my wild beast, Laughter"—a beast with brass wings and claws, as well as hard, cold eyes (*VPl*, 1102). Laughter in the poems of tragic joy arises in part from the relinquishment of elegy—a relinquishment whose cost is an oedipal identification with the forces of destruction, represented variously as beast, war, gyres, and so forth. Laughter is an aggressive act for Nietzsche, a form of somewhat cruel delight in the suffering of others *(schadenfroh)*, and it is the best way to kill the burdens of the past and pathos.[39] Yeats occasionally joins the destructive chorus to share its Dionysian laughter. He associates laughter not only with forces of destruction but with death itself: the poet Seanchan exclaims at his last moment, "Dead faces laugh"—a remark that goes all the way back to Lucian's image of Menippus laughing in the kingdom of the dead (*VPl*, 310).[40] Laughter is for Seanchan the wordless speech of the dead. In the poems of tragic joy, it represents an attempt to become that which one fears most in order to defend against it. In brief, the sinister side of the lyrics of tragic joy is that the mask with which the poet identifies may ultimately be death itself.[41]

THE ANTITHETICAL SUBLIME

Like his modernist contemporaries Eliot and Hulme, Yeats rarely uses the word *sublime*. His critics have been all too willing to adopt his aversion to the term, even though his prophetic and apocalyptic lyrics of tragic joy descend from the Romantic sublime of Blake and Shelley, and even though many of his aesthetic categories—ecstasy, passion, terror, *sprezzatura*, joy—descend from the vocabulary of writers on the sublime from Longinus to Schopenhauer.[42] Yeats continually draws on this rhetoric—for example, when he defines the poet's "ecstasy" as arising "from the contemplation of things vaster than the individual and imperfectly seen," or when he recommends symbols in art as a means to "escape from the barrenness and shallowness of a too conscious arrangement," or perhaps less obviously when he theorizes about life and history as a turning between antithetical terms (*Au*, 319; *E&I*, 87). The poems of tragic joy recuperate the mood, imagery, structure, sound, and rhetoric of such works of the Romantic sublime as Blake's "Night the Ninth" in *The Four Zoas*. By reinterpreting the poems of tragic joy in the light of the poetics of the Romantic sublime, we can better understand the structure and genealogy of their affective movement from terror to joy (the psychological sublime) as well as their characteristically violent figures and fragmentary images (the rhetorical sublime). More generally, this approach can reveal the interrelations between the sublime and such related modes as prophecy and the curse. Although the sublime is not a unitary concept, I hope to show, with Yeats's help, that death is its ultimate occasion.[43]

The sublime is not a genre, and theorists of the sublime are happy to emphasize its fluid movement across generic boundaries. Nevertheless, the sublime has an affective structure and a rhetoric—among the qualities that define genre—and so it might be thought of as an extended mode, related in turn to other modes, such as the apocalyptic, the prophetic, and the curse. But how is the sublime related to tragedy, the generic category traditionally used in analyzing these poems? In most theoretical discussions, the sublime overlaps with epic, tragedy, lyric, and prophecy, but of these genres tragedy is the primary aesthetic example for Kant and Schiller, as well as a frequent touchstone for Longinus. Schiller cites "tragic art" as the aesthetic counterpart of the individual's sublime encounter with the spectacle of change in nature and history, "change which destroys everything and creates it anew, and destroys again." This view anticipates Iris

Murdoch's contention that the theory of the sublime apprehension of "formless strength" is close indeed to being a theory of tragedy.[44] It would be more nearly accurate to say that the theory of the sublime is close to being a theory of what Yeats calls "tragic joy," for the sublime transforms the painful spectacle of destruction and death into a joyful assertion of human freedom and transcendence. Yeats most memorably conjoins the tragic and the sublime in his description of Shakespearean heroes who encounter their deaths with an ecstatic enlargement of vision, "Heaven blazing into the head: / Tragedy wrought to its uttermost" ("Lapis Lazuli," 294).

Another tragic hero, Oedipus, is for Yeats a resonant emblem of tragic joy, as he is for Longinus an emblem of the sublime.[45] Recalling his own version of *Oedipus at Colonus,* Yeats writes in the introduction to *A Vision* that his book will "proclaim a new divinity":

> Amidst the sound of thunder earth opened, "riven by love", and he sank down soul and body into the earth. I would have him balance Christ who, crucified standing up, went into the abstract sky soul and body. . . . He raged against his sons, and this rage was noble. . . . He knew nothing but his mind, and yet because he spoke that mind fate possessed it and kingdoms changed according to his blessing and his cursing. Delphi, that rock at earth's navel, spoke through him, and though men shuddered and drove him away they spoke of ancient poetry, praising the boughs overhead, the grass under foot, Colonus and its horses. [*AV,* 27–28]

Oedipus is the new, antithetical divinity because he is the new Yeats, moving downward upon life rather than upward and beyond it (*L,* 469; *E&I,* 266–67). Thunder and riven earth objectify the sublimity of Oedipus's speech, a speech that summons up Yeats's favorite sublime modes: the tragic, the curse, and the prophetic. Like the earth that tears open to consume Oedipus, Oedipus's *curses* swallow and destroy Creon, his sons, and himself. And like Longinus's Pythian priestess at Delphi, Oedipus utters *prophecies* that originate from that sacred place with "the cleft in the ground."[46] As if with the language of the Yeatsian *Anima Mundi* or the Lacanian unconscious, Delphi "spoke through" Oedipus, leaving him cleft in an ecstatic rage that makes his hearers "shudder" and yet carries them beyond terror to bless joyfully Colonus and the language of ancient poetry. This transformation of terror into joy is the sublime's affective structure, and the spontaneous movement of language from one mind to another is the intersubjective course of the sublime. The powerful speech of Yeats's Oedipus makes overt the violence of the sublime—a violence that I trace through its modulations in Yeats's lyrics. But I first attempt to determine the affective basis for this violence of the Yeatsian sublime.

The Affective Sublime

"Tragic joy" expresses as well as any other formulation in the history of criticism the emotive ambivalence of the sublime, since the sublime involves the conversion of affects from defeat and terror to freedom and joy.[47] A consideration of the precedents for Yeats's evocative phrase reveals assumptions shared by various theorists of the sublime. In the first full discussion of the psychological sublime, Edmund Burke creates a comparable oxymoron: "delightful horror, which is the most genuine effect, and truest test of the sublime."[48] Schiller explicates the binary affect: "The feeling of the sublime is a mixed feeling. It is a composition of melancholy which at its utmost is manifested in a shudder, and of joyousness which can mount to rapture."[49] This remark so closely approximates Yeats's description of tragic ecstasy that, but for the word *sublime,* it could almost be the work of his pen. The sublime in Kant also seems, as Schiller phrases it, "two contradictory perceptions in a single feeling." But Kant tries to unpack the synchronic affect along a diachronic axis, separating it into moments of defeat and counterassertion. Threatening objects "raise the energies of the soul" and discover in us the "courage to measure ourselves against the apparent almightiness of nature."[50] Yeats's poems of tragic joy often aim at courage in the face of Blakean nature—a universe of death that would trap the mind.[51] Yeats remarks, much like Kant, that "only the greatest obstacle that can be contemplated without despair rouses the will to full intensity" (*Au*, 132). In his system, Yeats mythologizes this obstacle as the "Body of Fate," but in his lyrics the final form of the reality principle is death itself. In my view, death precipitates the emotional turning called the sublime, although theorists of the sublime often refer to death by other names, or by what Kenneth Burke terms "deflections": castration, physical destruction, semiotic collapse, defeat by a precursor, and annihilation of the ego.[52] Death is the recurrent obsession for these theorists, from Longinus to Heidegger and Bloom. Especially from the eighteenth century on, they increasingly pair the sublime with death, as death seems to become ever more solitary, final, and secular. But even Longinus makes it clear by his examples that death is of much importance to his understanding of the sublime—witness Sappho's broken-tongued gasp, "I seem near to dying," and Homer's terrified sailors, "carried away from under death, but only just."[53] The sublime strife between heroes and gods, aspirants and masters, is good for mortals, but only if the mortals survive the threatened annihilation.[54] For Edmund Burke to a greater extent, "ideas of pain, and above all of death," occasion the sublime. One of his most prominent examples is Death itself, in Milton's allegory.[55] Kant amends Burke's emphasis on terror by arguing that we must be secure while we picture to ourselves danger and destruction, but even then, the imaginary threat is so great that we know "all resistance would be altogether vain."[56] It is our apparent security that allows our fundamental insecurity to come into view. His notion of the first step in the sublime as a defeat of the imagination, a momentary checking, is a kind of momentary death, the equivalent of Yeats's "Black out" in "Lapis Lazuli" and Wordsworth's "when the light of sense / Goes out" in *The Prelude*.[57] This is comparable to the moment of anxiety over castration in Freud's oedipal struggle and to Heidegger's notion of the sudden call of conscience that discloses Dasein's guilt and nullity, a call that "comes *from* me and yet *from beyond me*."[58] For my interpretation of the sublime as a staged confrontation with death, I draw on the psychoanalytic accounts of Neil Hertz and Thomas Weiskel, supplementing them with a Heideggerian emphasis on the ecstatic encounter with death. But it is in Yeats that the sublime is explicitly a *staged* confrontation with death: his tragic heroes convey in their final utterances "the sudden enlargement of their vision, their ecstasy at the approach of death" (*E&I*, 522–23).

In the temporal structure of the sublime, the momentary death gives rise to a counterassertion of life. Having torn out his eyes in horror, Yeats's antithetical Oedipus reasserts himself with a rage that "seemed to contain all life" (*AV*, 28). In psychological terms, the hero and the poet surmount the threat of the destructive father through identification with him.[59] This oedipal dynamic is clear and pervasive in Yeats's personal history, even though *Reveries over Childhood and Youth* displaces the figure of aggression onto his grandfather Pollexfen, a man whom Yeats confused with God and Lear, prayed to for punishment, and emulated as a model of courage (*Au*, 3, 4, 22).

This psychoanalytic model of the sublime can help us interpret the overarching affective movement of Yeats's poems of tragic joy. To rejoin our earlier discussion, these poems introject the violent, paternal threat, thereby permitting the conversion of defensive and pathetic energy into joy, sometimes manifested as laughter. Having faced his own death, Yeats writes in a letter: "How strange is the subconscious gaiety that leaps up before danger or difficulty. I have not had a moment of depression— that gaiety is outside one's control" (*L*, 733). Terror is converted into joy, "Gaiety transfiguring all that dread," as Yeats writes in his strongest contribution to the sublime (294).

But as Longinus reminds us, the joy of the sublime is ultimately based on an illusion: "It is our nature to be elevated by true sublimity. Filled with joy and pride, we come to believe we have created what we have only heard."[60] The sublime is the momentary illusion that translates hearer into orator, son into father, and elegist into Rocky Face. In Stevens's words, it allows the violence within to conquer the violence without as a matter of self-preservation.[61] This illusion is sometimes dangerously complete—the poet of "The Gyres," for example, may cast too cold an eye on death, inuring himself to violence. He would transform his sad youthful self—like the protesting women of "Lapis Lazuli"—into the erect Rocky Face. We see here and in many versions of the Romantic sublime the same gender coordinates—the male poet's suppression of the elegiac and "feminine" side of his psyche in order to assert a "masculine" heroism. Incorporating the Other (annihilative violence, "numb nightmare," superego on the rampage), the speaker discards the singular pronoun *I*—associated with the earlier, mournful self—and exults instead as a plural identity: "We that look on but laugh in tragic joy." The lyric attempts to deliver the poetic self from the deathly victimage of passive spectatorship (the defeated hearer of Longinus) by converting audience into author, the Rocky Face willing the bloody spectacle it must observe.

The theory of the sublime, as we can already see, helps to explain the intersubjective drama of Yeats's visionary lyrics. Such poems enact the strengthening of the ego by introjection, and yet, in doing so, they admit an "*alien* voice," as Heidegger calls it, that seems to tear the boundaries of the ego, bringing it perilously close to annihilation.[62] We recall that Yeats says of Oedipus, much as Longinus does of the Pythian priestess, that Delphi "spoke through him" (*AV*, 28). Yeats's theory of the mask is a theory of self-transformation through imitation of the not-self, a theory cognate with the sublime in both privileging the subject and violating its integrity: "all joyous or creative energy is a rebirth as something not oneself, something which has no memory and is created in a moment and perpetually renewed" (*Au*, 340). The voice that emerges from the Rocky Face is "not oneself," though its message of reassurance would seem intended to rouse the self to its fullest strength. If "The Second Coming" similarly rehearses death, putting on the power of the repressed father it tropes as rough beast, then it risks destabilizing the self while

trying to achieve stability. Appropriating the violence of the
rough beast for its own aural action and impact, the poem enacts,
in Hertz's phrase, a "transfer of power" typical of the sublime;
but the transfer potentially endangers the integrity of the poetic
self.[63] The "vast image" starts into the poet's mind out of a mind
not his own:

> Surely some revelation is at hand;
> Surely the Second Coming is at hand.
> The Second Coming! Hardly are those words out
> When a vast image out of *Spiritus Mundi*
> Troubles my sight. . . .   [187]

The "Other" of the Yeatsian sublime is that mind beyond our
minds, what Yeats terms *Anima Mundi,* the Daimon, or, occasionally, "the subconscious"; for Kant the Other is the Reason,
for Longinus the divine possessor. Derrida remarks that "as soon
as we no longer know very well who speaks or who writes, the
text becomes apocalyptic," or, we might add, prophetic, curse-
like, or—more generally—sublime.[64] In Yeats's sublime poems,
words and images seem to have an "independent reality," in-
vading the mind from beyond it, each like an "emblem" that
"sails into the sight" (*Myth,* 284; "Coole and Ballylee, 1931,"
244).

Nevertheless, interpretations of the sublime that overempha-
size its threat to the identity of the subject risk turning the
sublime into mysticism, sometimes dressed up in Lacanian
garb.[65] The sublime poet and the mystic share the conviction
that, as Yeats puts it, "the borders of our mind are ever shifting,"
but whereas for the mystic the energy flows in one direction,
from other into self, the sublime poet also reverses the direction,
in a reaction-formation, believing that the self has produced what
it has heard (*E&I,* 28). However much the extra-poetic Yeats
succeeds in being a mystic, the lyric self in his poems is rarely the
passive vessel of the Daimon. Self asserts its prerogatives over
mystic Soul in many more lyrics than "A Dialogue of Self and
Soul," and poetic identity is generated by their agon. Even Soul

does not speak consistently in the rhetoric of self-abnegation but instead opens the dialogue with a favorite Yeatsian command, "I summon," much as the seemingly mystic speaker of "All Souls' Night" repeatedly asserts his dominion with the phrase "I call" (234, 228–29). In a declamatory poem that summons past and future, "To Ireland in the Coming Times," materia poetica is said to come *"from unmeasured mind,"* but the paradox is that the poet's imposed *"measure"* gives access to the measureless Other (50). Without such heroic self-assertion, the poet would remain, like Sappho in Longinus's treatise, broken-tongued, in the same condition as Soul in "A Dialogue of Self and Soul," whose "tongue's a stone," or like Soul in "Vacillation," "Struck dumb in the simplicity of fire!" (235, 252). In the dialectic of the sublime, the poet must rise from this momentary death, the tongue recover from its muteness. By analyzing the formal strategies of Yeats's sublime lyrics, we can concretize this general understanding of the poems' to-and-fro between psychic annihilation and assertion, terror and joy.[66]

Structure, Imagery, Sound, and Rhetoric

Because the Yeatsian sublime often compresses the moments of its dialectic, it does not always follow the clear Kantian stages of assertion of the Imagination, defeat or prosthetic death, and rescue by the Reason, or even the simpler but comparable steps in Burke of terror and joy, in Longinus of daimonic possession and expulsion. Even so, a structural similarity is perceptible in such poems as "The Valley of the Black Pig," "The Second Coming," and the lyrics composing the final movements of "Meditations in Time of Civil War" and "Nineteen Hundred and Nineteen." Each opens with a vision that shatters the sleepy complacency or boundedness of the poetic self, substitutes a more concentrated image for this confused and fragmented vision, and then, having enlarged the boundaries of the ego and totalized reality, drops a veil to separate self from Other.[67] Some of Yeats's sublime poems do not strictly conform to this temporal map. In "Nineteen Hundred and Nineteen," for example, the incubus Artisson—the equivalent of the black pig and the rough beast—"lurches past" only after, and not before, the distancing moment of dropping wind and settling dust (210). Nor do the sublime lyrics easily separate into Kant's categories of the mathematical sublime—incremental and repetitive—and the dynamical sublime—abrupt and singular. Nevertheless, "Leda and the Swan" and "The Cold Heaven" exemplify, with their astonishingly violent openings, the sudden and single moment of rupture characteristic of the dynamical sublime:

> A sudden blow: the great wings beating still
> Above the staggering girl. . . .   [214]

> Suddenly I saw the cold and rook-delighting heaven
> That seemed as though ice burned and was but the more
>   ice. . . .   [125]

A Heideggerian call of conscience blasts through the speaker of "The Cold Heaven," as if it were a thunderbolt out of Longinus, "Until I cried and trembled and rocked to and fro, / Riddled with light." Other poems—for example, "The Magi" and part 6 of "Nineteen Hundred and Nineteen"—are exercises in the mathematical sublime, visionary encounters with an infinite repetition whose formal correlatives are iterative syntax ("With all their . . . / And all their . . . / And all their . . .") and diction ("Violence . . . violence," "round and round") (126, 210).

"The Second Coming" conjoins the mathematical and the dynamical sublime. Opening with the incremental repetitions of the mathematical sublime, the poem pounds in the first line with an insistent dactylic rhythm and envisions a turning and turning without center. As hierarchies and cycles dissolve into an anarchic sameness, the scene of dilation leaves the imagination ever more exhausted by its efforts to totalize:

> Turning and turning in the widening gyre
> The falcon cannot hear the falconer;
> Things fall apart; the center cannot hold;

Mere anarchy is loosed upon the world,
The blood-dimmed tide is loosed, and everywhere
The ceremony of innocence is drowned;
The best lack all conviction, while the worst
Are full of passionate intensity.   [187]

But the terrifying beast that bursts into the mind in the second stanza seems more the violent father of the dynamical sublime, whom the poet attempts to introject in order to quell. This crisscrossing of the mathematical and the dynamical sublime should not surprise us, since even Kant does not distinguish between them with consistency. They also converge in "The Magi," a poem that represents an exhaustive repetition of a quest:

Now as at all times I can see in the mind's eye,
In their stiff, painted clothes, the pale unsatisfied ones
Appear and disappear in the blue depth of the sky
With all their ancient faces like rain-beaten stones,
And all their helms of silver hovering side by side,
And all their eyes still fixed, hoping to find once more,
Being by Calvary's turbulence unsatisfied,
The uncontrollable mystery on the bestial floor.   [126]

The repetition of the quest is duplicated within the poet's mind, the poet holding within "the mind's eye" the questers' "eyes still fixed." Out of the lyric's enactment of their rhythmical appearance and disappearance, which creates the mathematical sublime's texture of "on and on," erupts the last line's unpredictable and "uncontrollable mystery."[68]

In a passage worthy of Longinus or Kant, Yeats describes this dynamic of the sublime: "Does not all art come when a nature, that never ceases to judge itself, exhausts personal emotion in action or desire so completely that something impersonal, something that has nothing to do with action or desire, suddenly starts into its place, something which is as unforeseen, as completely organised, even as unique, as the images that pass before the mind between sleeping and waking?" (*Au*, 222). The Imagination collapses and the Reason starts into place with its transcendental knowledge of the infinite. In some of the visionary poems of a more cryptic sort, such as "Veronica's Napkin" and "Conjunctions," Yeats presents the images alone without the collapse of interpretation that gives rise to them. But in the sublime lyrics, the rough beast and the uncontrollable mystery shatter the texture of the repetitive mental act of attempting to grasp reality. To recur to our generic categories, the Yeatsian sublime arises when one "exhausts . . . desire" in quest-romance or its temporal inverse, elegy. The mind can no longer strain toward libidinal objects: "I think that we who are poets and artists, not being permitted to shoot beyond the tangible, must go from desire to weariness and so to desire again, and live but for the moment when vision comes to our weariness like terrible lightning" (*Myth,* 340).[69] A Longinian flash, the sublime rips unpredictably through Yeats's mournful cycles of desire, the mind transported beyond its objects. Like the rough beast that follows upon the vertiginous rotations of "The Second Coming," an "insolent fiend" lurches into view at the end of "Nineteen Hundred and Nineteen" only after the mind has wearied itself in the effort to hold onto the horses' breaking circle of movement (210).

Whirling, gyring, spiring—the Yeatsian sublime often bolts out of such rhythmic and repetitive movement. In "The Wild Swans at Coole," the poet tries to count the swans, setting in motion the mental operation that Kant describes as the mathematical sublime:

> The nineteenth autumn has come upon me
> Since I first made my count;
> I saw, before I had well finished,
> All suddenly mount
> And scatter wheeling in great broken rings
> Upon their clamorous wings.   [131]

The repetitive act of counting collapses as the swans mount above the poet, transporting his mind with an intimation of incalculable aggregates. These broken rings reappear as the widening gyre and reeling desert birds in "The Second Coming" and as the breaking equestrian courses in "Nineteen Hundred and Nineteen." The movement is sublime because it sets in motion the circle of Coleridgean formalism and breaks it apart.

For Yeats, this figure is emblematic of eternal recurrence, a concept he shares with Nietzsche but which he modifies to allow for temporal variation. One of the most important historical links between Yeats and the theory of the sublime is, in my view, Nietzsche's *ewige Wiederkehr*.[70] Nietzsche generally avoids the term *sublime*, or *das Erhabene*, but he does occasionally use it to describe tragedy, as when he says that the sublime "subjugates terror by means of art."[71] Further, I should like to suggest that his notion of eternal recurrence is a version of the mathematical sublime, though he would never admit such a debt to Kant. For both Nietzsche and Kant, the intuition arrives suddenly; it comes from the failure to constellate reality into higher and higher aggregates; it is an intuition not subject to empirical tests; and it is a revelation of the infinite that is at once empowering and terrifying. Nietzsche and Yeats both take much pride in their ability to reconcile themselves to eternal recurrence; Yeats announces in "A Dialogue of Self and Soul":

> I am content to live it all again
> And yet again, if it be life to pitch
> Into the frog-spawn of a blind man's ditch,
> A blind man battering blind men. . . .   [236]

Here the poet imagines eternal recurrence in a personal rather than a historical sense and arrives at a view of it that approximates Freud's repetition compulsion, another modern version of the mathematical sublime. The poet wills his endless return to the blindness of inorganic matter. But this affirmation of the eternal, autochthonous return is also compensatory. The kinship between eternal recurrence and the sublime should help us see that even though both Yeats and Nietzsche think that their belief in recurrence indicates their release from the spirit of revenge, or ill will toward time, it is in fact an illusion that allows them to think they have transcended time, that they can live an infinite number of lives, and that they have therefore escaped the threatening scythe of the father beyond all fathers.

Unlike Yeats or Nietzsche, Freud literalizes the threatening scythe of the father, and even though we may not agree with his reduction of all death anxiety to the repressed fear of castration, we may still assent that these two anxieties are psychologically linked.[72] Many of Yeats's sublime lyrics contain apotropaic images of decapitation, or what psychoanalysis considers its unconscious correlative, castration. Heads without any clear connection with their bodies can be found in a number of these poems. "The Magi" have "ancient faces like rain-beaten stones" out of which their eyes stare fixedly (126). Such a Rocky Face reappears in "The Gyres," where it is a totemic reminder of the paternal law of necessity, and thus also an apotropaic emblem of the Medusan fate. This mask and the general theory of the mask in Yeats—the severance of being from self-identity—may be in part mediations of castration anxiety. At the end of "Nineteen Hundred and Nineteen," the head of Robert Artisson also looks petrified, "his great eyes without thought / Under the shadow of stupid straw-pale locks," and it "lurches past" with the automatic movement of the rough beast in "The Second Coming" (210). Both incubus and beast have the same blank gaze and nightmarish dissociation of head from body. The late plays *A Full Moon in March* and *The King of the Great Clock Tower* feature castrative beheadings as their principal symbolic action. In "The Second Coming," the "head of a man" is fixed onto a "lion body" (187). The image encodes simultaneously the aggressive, repressed father and the castration that has threatened the son. Rhetorically, it is a violation of decorum, for it has much in common with the example that Horace considers at the beginning of the *Ars poetica*: "If a painter should decide to join the neck of a horse to a human head, and to lay many-colored feathers upon limbs taken from here or there, so that what is a comely woman above ended as a dark, grotesque fish below, could you, my friends, if you were allowed to see it, keep from laughing?"[73] The sublime breaks through decorum and the wholeness of the beautiful. It is a rough beast that, as the seer of "The Second Coming" puts it, "Troubles my sight."

It may also trouble the ear. The rhythms, phonemic patterns, and rhetorical figures of the Yeatsian sublime produce the impression of formlessness breaking through form or, in Yeats's terms, of Transfiguration occurring paradoxically within an aesthetic of Incarnation (*L*, 402). Although Yeats uses the word *sublime* sparingly, he borrows Castiglione's notion of *sprezzatura*, or "recklessness," a pre-eighteenth-century category for the nonrational in art that anticipates the concept of the sublime.[74] The very strictness of Yeats's tightly controlled aural patterns makes rhythmic variations seem all the more reckless. His few comments on the subject accord with the Longinian doctrine that insistently repetitive rhythms can make the auditor ecstatic, in a transport beyond the normal bounds of the ego. But the sublimity of this mathematical pounding accelerates when, at the end of his later iambic lyrics in this mode, Yeats obtrudes into the speech rhythm a polysyllabic word that contains a dactylic cadence, varying the predictable sequence: *punishment, turbulence, uncontrollable, terrible, Bethlehem, indifferent, darkening, monuments, unfashionable, glittering*.[75] This intrusion of rhythmic change often coincides with the sudden heightening of alliterative resonances, especially the voiced stops *b, g,* and *d*: "beauty is born," "Bethlehem to be born," "drifts upon a darkening flood," and so on.[76] These apparently dark sounds help to produce the effect of boundless power and mystery thudding into existence:

> . . . and stricken
> *By* the injustice of the skies for *punishment?*
> ["The Cold Heaven," 125]

> Being by *Calvary's turbulence* un*satisfied,*
> The uncon*trollable* mystery on the *bestial* floor.
> ["The Magi," 126]

> Are changed, changed *utterly:*
> A *terrible beauty* is *born.*   ["Easter, 1916," 182]

And what rough *b*east, its hour come round at last,
Slouches towards *Bethlehem* to be *b*orn?
> ["The Second Coming," 187]

We are *b*lest *b*y everything,
Everything we look upon is *b*lest.
> ["A Dialogue of Self and Soul," 236]

*B*efore the in*different b*eak could let her *d*rop?
> ["Leda and the Swan," 215]

Where the swan *d*rifts upon a *darkening* flood.
> ["Coole and Ballylee, 1931," 245]

That *d*ay *b*rings round the night, that *b*efore *d*awn
His *g*lory and his *monuments* are *g*one.   ["Meru," 289]

> . . . and all thin*g*s run
On that un*fashionable g*yre a*g*ain.   ["The Gyres," 293]

Their eyes mid many wrinkles, their eyes,
Their ancient, *glittering* eyes, are *g*ay.
> ["Lapis Lazuli," 295]

The endings of these lyrics also exemplify the many rhetorical
figures that Longinus associates with the sublime: the rhetorical
question emphasizing the momentary quality of emotion arising
from the occasion, asyndeton hindering the reading while pressing it onward, anaphora combining with asyndeton to force
meaning to leap ahead, and so forth. As Longinus says of Demos-
thenes, "His order becomes disorderly, his disorder in turn ac-
quires a certain order."[77] These formal strategies combine to
hurry the mind out of form, reaching toward what Yeats calls,
echoing Shelley's epithet for the west wind, the "uncontrollable."[78] In the early Yeats, the poetic quest for "disembodied
beauty" falls short of the sublime, lacking the complementary
impulse in the later Yeats to "create form" and work through it
(*L,* 402).

The Curse

Yeats's later lyrics sometimes carry recklessness to the violent extreme of the curse. Exaggerating certain features of the sublime, the curse can help us to analyze further its psychic and rhetorical structure. In their eagerness to assume the voice of the aggressive father, poems like "The Gyres" and "Under Ben Bulben" seem to will the destruction they contemplate. Indeed, many of the poems of tragic joy draw on the curse modally. We should keep this broad affinity in mind as we look at more direct manifestations of the curse in Yeats's prose and poetry. His curses reveal the destructive urge, or death drive, at work in the poetics of the sublime.

Both Allen Grossman and Hugh Kenner discuss "The Fish" as an instance of the Irish genre of the curse, but the curse appears in many other lyrics, essays, and stories.[79] The older Yeats entitles a treatise *On the Boiler* out of fondness for a mad ship's carpenter who, from a boiler, would denounce his neighbors and the wicked times. In another late self-portrait, as we have seen, Yeats calls the cursing Oedipus his "new divinity." As early as the story "The Crucifixion of the Outcast" (1897), Yeats celebrates the curse. Mistreated at a monastery, a gleeman sets a tub upside down under his window and mounts it to "sing a bard's curse on the abbot" (*Myth,* 150). Lest the gleeman teach the curse to children and robbers, the abbot decides to crucify him. For the monks, the curse typifies poetic speech because of the way it violently and unpredictably transforms reality. If left alive, the gleeman would curse whenever "the mood to curse would come upon him," his soul, path, and purpose as unfixed as the wind (*Myth,* 151, 153). But while the curse is a spontaneous and direct speech act, it is also, as Geoffrey Hartman observes, one of the oldest kinds of formalized speech.[80] However sudden and unpredictable the urge to curse, the speakers seem possessed by a language and passion beyond themselves, as in the other modes of the sublime.

Yeats's first full-fledged curse in rhyme appears in the story "Red Hanrahan's Curse" (1897). A young girl who must marry an old man asks Red Hanrahan for help because she understands the curse to be the poet's instrument for fulfilling the *lex talionis*: "when it is people of this earth that have harmed you, it is yourself knows well the way to put harm on them again" (*Myth*, 240). Models of tragic gaiety for the wild old wicked Yeats, Oedipus and King Lear wish on those who have hurt them an equivalent pain of thanklessness or destruction. The young girl in Yeats's story inadvertently wounds Red Hanrahan by telling him he is old, so that his curse represents in part an attempt to recover from this subversion of his potency. Like the aging Lear and Oedipus, Hanrahan curses to regain and dramatize his masculine potency and aggressiveness. Seeing an old and gap-winged eagle and noting that it resembles himself, Hanrahan goes on to curse ceremoniously not only his old, oedipal fathers but also himself:

> The poet, Owen Hanrahan, under a bush of may,
> Calls down a curse on his own head because it withers
>   grey;
> Then on the speckled eagle-cock of Ballygawley Hill
> Because it is the oldest thing that knows of cark and
>   ill. . . .   [*Myth*, 243]

Implicitly, the curse distances the poet Hanrahan from his aged, objectified self, a self that the poem groups with old Paddy Bruen, old Shemus Cullinan, old Paddy Doe, and with an old eagle, an old yew, and an old pike. But even though the curse distances Hanrahan from the impotence of old age, it identifies him with its destructive power. As Hanrahan curses the oedipal father, he also assumes the voice of the father, and thus the very act of cursing transforms him into the object of his curse. Here as in the other modes of the sublime, the relation of poet to father is simultaneously one of identification and aggression. By cursing, the poet comes dangerously close to turning himself into the agent of death to avoid becoming its victim. But Hanrahan's curse backfires: his presumption in adopting the voice of the father brings down on him the fatherly "Old Men," as well as "Old Age and Time and Weariness and Sickness" (*Myth,* 245). To gain the power of the curse, Hanrahan risks paying the cost of self-destruction.

Written during the painful series of losses and crises of the middle period, "The Fascination of What's Difficult" (1909–10) may be Yeats's most compelling absorption of the curse into lyric, and it is a paean to the sublime. Like Hanrahan and Lear, the speaker of this poem begins his denunciation in a moment of impotence, the blockage or proleptic death that sets the sublime in motion:

> The fascination of what's difficult
> Has dried the sap out of my veins, and rent
> Spontaneous joy and natural content
> Out of my heart.   [93]

Sprezzatura has been lost, but even as the poet begins to describe his deadness, he starts to recover from it, for the trope of rending is itself a sublime figure of dislocation. It transforms the destructive power of difficulty into the figurative violence of the poem.

> There's something ails our colt
> That must, as if it had not holy blood
> Nor on Olympus leaped from cloud to cloud,
> Shiver under the lash, strain, sweat and jolt
> As though it dragged road metal.

By packing four verbs into a rhythmically overloaded line (where even the single noun, *lash,* almost seems verbal), Yeats continues to convert his suppression into the poem's mounting intensity. He pictures Pegasus, his own imaginative power, as trapped under the weight of form and the everyday.[81] But instead of remaining underneath these oppressive forces of constraint, the poet is suddenly "on" top of them:

> My curse on plays
> That have to be set up in fifty ways,

On the day's war with every knave and dolt,
Theatre business, management of men.

In the curse the poet brings to a culmination his effort to regain power. By willing destruction on others, he defines himself, restores his sovereignty, and even seems to transcend the bland bourgeois world of commerce. But this curse, like Hanrahan's and like the protagonist's in *Prometheus Unbound*, is also a self-curse, for it falls partly on his own work. The curse ritually enumerates its intended objects, and yet it also seems spontaneous and sudden, an influx of power after blockage. This impression is heightened by the asyndetons and by the diversity of the curse's objects. The poem ends with a full restoration of the poet's strength:

I swear before the dawn comes round again
I'll find the stable and pull out the bolt.

Counter to the repetitive revolutions of the sun, the poet asserts his own unpredictable and violent energy of self-disclosure—the energy he has just unleashed in this very poem.

Such curses represent a spontaneous overflow of powerful feelings, but the feelings they discharge often seem to belong more to Thanatos than to Eros. In the section of "Meditations in Time of Civil War" entitled "My Descendants," the poet curses, in an extraordinary act of anticipatory vengeance, the home of his offspring if they should degenerate:

May this laborious stair and this stark tower
Become a roofless ruin that the owl
May build in the cracked masonry and cry
Her desolation to the desolate sky.   [203]

The passage offers a sublime image of fragmentation, but it purchases its sublimity with a rhetorical act that is partly self-destructive. Like Lear, the poet defines his own potency by willing the ruin of his kin; yet he attacks them by way of the totemic tower—the very emblem of the poet and of the book of poems to which this curse belongs. The object of aggression is thus a figure for the self, much as the uncanny sky is for the owl that cries to it. Another of Yeats's birds with an uncanny shadow-self leaps into the sky in "Nineteen Hundred and Nineteen," prefiguring apocalyptic completion and stirring the poet to will the ruin of his own work:

> The swan has leaped into the desolate heaven:
> That image can bring wildness, bring a rage
> To end all things, to end
> What my laborious life imagined, even
> The half-imagined, the half-written page;
> O but we dreamed to mend
> Whatever mischief seemed
> To afflict mankind, but now
> That winds of winter blow
> Learn that we were crack-pated when we dreamed. [209]

Writing is a veil between the poet and the final integration with reality. The poet's rage would assimilate him to the destructive force of the winter wind, erasing his words and his world. Attempting to evade death, the poet identifies with it. The transcendental impulse of the sublime is ultimately apocalyptic and self-destructive—a rage not only against formal order but also against the self and language.

Prophecy, Apocalypse, and the Politics of the Sublime

Another modality of the sublime, prophecy has long been thought to be related to the curse, and it too can help us to interpret tragic joy in Yeats. Twice in *Richard III* Shakespeare tellingly misremembers Queen Margaret's earlier "prophecies" as "curses."[82] As James Kugel remarks in his analysis of Hebraic prophecy: "The prophet's speech had always been *powerful*, effective; it could be said of him what was said of the soothsayer Balaam ben Be'or, 'those whom you bless are blessed, and those whom you curse are cursed' (Num. 22:6)."[83] As speech acts that simultaneously announce and transform the shape of reality, prophecy and the curse unite the word with divine authority, the transcendental signifier. But whereas the curse is more obviously intended to alter the world by disfiguring it, the central difficulty about prophetic utterance, and about Yeats's prophetic lyrics, is the relation between passive witness and active transformation. In the tropes of Shelley's "Defense of Poetry," a document that Yeats quotes extensively and approvingly, is the prophetic poet "mirror" or "legislator"? In the imagery of the sublime, is he the defeated son or the violent father? In a poem such as "Leda and the Swan," is the speaker like Leda a vessel or like Zeus an aggressor? The rhetoric of prophecy draws on both strands of figure, hoping to turn the interpreter of reality into its creator, just as the Longinian sublime converts the passive listener into a heroic orator. Yeats objects to war poets like Wilfred Owen because "passive suffering is not a theme for poetry" (*Ox,* xxxiv). Envisioning a brutal and war-torn world in "Lapis Lazuli" and "The Gyres," Yeats holds down his own "femininity," passivity, and pathos; but such prophetic poems are sublime and not fanatical only insofar as they inhabit the psychic and rhetorical space of both witness and legislator, victim and aggressor. In other words, "passive suffering" *is* in fact a "theme for poetry" in Yeats, but our access to it is by way of reaction-formations—Yeats's attempts to override it.

Kant warns, however, that the sublime may become fanaticism if one goes "mad with reason," or, in the terms of Freud's *Group Psychology and the Analysis of the Ego,* if one allows the heroic father or politician to replace the superego.[84] We have already seen that Yeats's lyric transformations of the curse approach such an extreme. Other late lyrics also come dangerously close to celebrating the fanaticism of complete identification, such as the third of the "Three Songs to the Same Tune." The apocalyptic impulse in Yeats sometimes approaches this extreme as well; it shares the alchemist's "consuming thirst for destruction" of the world and the "half-written page," the longing for a complete integration of self with "the desolation of reality" (*Myth,* 269–70; *P,* 289).

Another group of Yeats's visionary lyrics approaches the sublime but strays from its true dynamic. If we think of apocalypse not as conflagration but as the disclosure and totalization of reality, Yeats writes many lyrics that assume an apocalyptic perspective toward history—the panoramic or god's-eye view that Whitaker contrasts with the dramatic in Yeats's writing. Although such poems as "The Valley of the Black Pig" and "Two Songs from a Play" reach toward the sublime in their vastness of perspective, they are in a prophetic mode that so distances itself from the drama of history that it loses any sense of contingency and vulnerability—historical qualities allied with the sublime as against the aesthetic necessity of the beautiful.[85]

These poems illustrate what we might call Yeats's prophetic binarism, for they arrange history according to binary oppositions, much like the mythic mind in Lévi-Strauss.[86] In the extraordinary early note to "The Valley of the Black Pig," Yeats sets up a series of paradigmatic opposites—light/dark, winter/summer, sterility/fruitfulness—a dualistic tendency reflected too in the poem's neat division into four lines of violence and four of recovery and prayer:

> The dews drop slowly and dreams gather: unknown
>   spears
> Suddenly hurtle before my dream-awakened eyes,
> And then the clash of fallen horsemen and the cries
> Of unknown perishing armies beat about my ears.
> We who still labour by the cromlech on the shore,
> The grey cairn on the hill, when day sinks drowned in
>   dew,
> Being weary of the world's empires, bow down to you,
> Master of the still stars and of the flaming door. [65–66]

The poem's reduction of the apocalyptic battle to "unknown" sounds heard at a distance suggests that prophetic binarism has allowed the poet to control and miniaturize the violent scene all too well, helping him to adopt the invulnerable perspective of the fatherly "Master." Much later, "Two Songs from a Play" also defeats the sublime terror of violent upheaval by condensing history into antithetical pairs: Virgo/Spica, Athena/Dionysus, Mary/Christ.[87] The prophetic binarism of these poems evokes but muzzles the sublime, their poetics of miniaturization inuring Yeats to the ruptures of history. A similar conjuring but distancing of the sublime can sometimes be seen in the synchronistic aesthetic of Yeats's modernist contemporaries Eliot and Pound, as also in *A Vision*. Insofar as *A Vision,* like some of Yeats's prophetic lyrics, compresses history into the controlled binary patterns of a miniature, it accords with the beautiful. But insofar as it emphasizes violent transformations, abrupt confluences of the human and the divine, dizzying rotations between eternally recurring and infinitely expanding antinomies, it approximates a sublime vision of history.

What is the political form of the sublime in Yeats? As we have seen, the psychological structure of the sublime can lead toward identification with the violent father and, ultimately, with the death drive; hence, it helps to explain the attraction that authoritarianism held for the older Yeats. Although the kinship between Yeats's later politics and the psycholinguistic structure of his sublime remains unremarked, Yeats's "flirtation" with the extreme right continues to generate much scholarly interest.[88] But we may still have the lingering suspicion that Yeats's abhorrent political views are not the sole political potentiality of the Yeatsian sublime or of the sublime in general. Stephen Spender claims that Yeats's apocalyptic poems, such as "The Second Coming," were an important source of inspiration for the "intellectual Left" of his own generation.[89] How is that possible? Maybe we should look at the literary precedents for the Yeatsian sublime to find out more about its political parameters, asking whether its violence is part of a larger poetic impulse to use a violence within to counteract the violence without. If so, then much of what we are inclined to condemn in these lyrics might logically entail a con-

demnation of the sublime as a whole. As pacifists we may well
choose to reject the sublime altogether, but can we legitimately
reject Yeats's sublime because of its violence and inhumanity, as
Bloom does, and still praise the violence and inhumanity of
earlier versions?[90] To get at these questions, we might consider
first some precedents for Yeats's disturbing exultation in war.[91]
Many of Longinus's examples of the sublime describe combat or
bloodshed, and Kant argues not only that we venerate the soldier
because "his mind is unsubdued by danger" but also that "war
itself . . . has something sublime in it."[92] Perhaps in this context
the praise of war and the warrior in "Under Ben Bulben" is less
astonishing, though for many (as for me) no less deplorable:

> You that Mitchel's prayer have heard
> 'Send war in our time, O Lord!'
> Know that when all words are said
> And a man is fighting mad,
> Something drops from eyes long blind
> He completes his partial mind,
> For an instant stands at ease,
> Laughs aloud, his heart at peace. . . .   [326]

Even the hero's moment of "peace" is couched in a rhetoric that is
potentially martial: "at ease." Here, the sublime is inextricable
from the death drive, the hero's "partial mind" resembling the
"half-written page" of "Nineteen Hundred and Nineteen"; both
must be destroyed in the search for apocalyptic wholeness, a
reunion, in Freud's reduction of the sublime, with inorganic
matter.[93] If the mind is always partial because it is never complete
until extinguished, and if writing is always half-written because it
never absorbs that which it signifies, then Yeats's apocalyptic
sublime aggressively attempts to overcome the structure of deferral and desire inherent within thinking and writing.[94]

Shelley and Blake in verse no less than Longinus and Kant in
prose reveal the inescapable connection between the sublime and
violence. In *Prometheus Unbound*, Shelley tries to transcend the
attraction of poetic violence by decontextualizing the sublime

curse and making it an echo, but the force of the work's Lear-like rhetoric arises in the first act from Prometheus's willing "endurance" of violence. Similarly, the Witch of Atlas, whom Yeats invokes at the beginning of "Under Ben Bulben," observes strife and suffering, yet "little did the sight disturb her soul."[95] Yeats suppresses this side of Shelley when he derides him for being "terrified of the Last Day like a Victorian child" (*E&I*, 420). Even as Nietzsche commends the tragic poet's "joy in destroying," Blake, in his prophetic poem *America,* celebrates Orc's "fiery joy" in violent change.[96] And though we may regret that the Rocky Face knows only the word *Rejoice,* this word echoes through the end of *The Four Zoas* in response to total destruction. If we recall the "irrational streams of blood" in "The Gyres" and compare them with the streams of blood in "Night the Ninth," it seems hard to share Bloom's view of Yeats's tragic joy as uniquely "inhumane":[97]

> Into the wine presses of Luvah howling fell the Clusters
> Of human families thro the deep. the wine presses were filld
> The blood of life flowd plentiful. . . .[98]

The poem appropriates the power of the scene's violence, sharing the apocalyptic joy of Luvah's sons and daughters, not the merely human dismay:

> How red the sons & daughters of Luvah how they tread
>   the Grapes
> Laughing and shouting drunk with odors many fall
>   oerwearied
> . . . .
> But in the Wine Presses the Human Grapes Sing not nor
>   dance
> They howl & writhe in shoals of torment in fierce flames
>   consuming
> In chains of iron & in dungeons circled with ceaseless
>   fires

> In pits & dens & shades of death in shapes of torment &
> woe
> The Plates the Screws and Racks & Saws & cords & fires
> & floods
> The cruel joy of Luvahs daughters lacerating with knives
> And whip[s] their Victims & the deadly sports of Luvahs
> sons[99]

These "Victims" are sacrifices to the sublime, their pain essential to the joy assumed by the sons and daughters of Luvah and by the poem itself. In many versions of the Romantic sublime, not just Yeats's, the moment of gaiety presupposes the pain or death from which it rises.

Some recent works on literary apocalypses and prophecies assert that these sublime modes are inherently consistent with politically radical revolution. Derrida remarks, "Nothing is less conservative than the apocalyptic genre."[100] Others, such as Gary Shapiro, have argued that the sublime has strong affinities with fascism.[101] No doubt the political form of the sublime's tendency toward fanaticism is authoritarianism. No doubt, too, the sublime as a vision of history privileges violent ruptures of the sort we associate with revolution (despite Burke's apparently contradictory dislike for the French Revolution). The sublime, in other words, is neither "left" nor "right," though both the left and the right can appropriate it. The "Beautiful Necessity" Emerson praises at the end of the essay "Fate" and the similar "Power" Shelley invokes in "Mont Blanc" might be used for either fascist celebrations of force or radical visions of a force that can "repeal / Large codes of fraud and woe."[102] The sublime does not accommodate easily centrist or pacifist politics, but it does not therefore belong to fascism.[103] Yeats's lyrics of tragic joy turn the sublime in a reactionary direction: in "The Gyres" the speaker celebrates destruction because it ushers in a feudal political order, and in "My Descendants" he curses the home of his offspring if they should lose their inherited nobility. But these political views have no exclusive relation to the Yeatsian sublime or to the sublime generally, any more than the Heideggerian sublime is intrinsically fascist—even though fascism, partly by adopting the Romantic sublime for its own purposes, proved an ideology attractive to both Yeats and Heidegger. Because the sublime can rouse us from the blind and timid politics of the everyday and grant us the "courage," as Kant calls it, to face our own deaths with anticipatory resoluteness, it is potentially an instrument of radicalism, even in Yeats.

Two plays illustrate how the Yeatsian sublime admits of a wider political appropriation than we might assume and how Spender's generation could therefore read the lyrics against the grain of Yeats's own authoritarian views. In *The King's Threshold,* Yeats acknowledges the subversive potential of tragic joy. Having deprived the poet Seanchan of his traditional rights, the king compares his own institutional bonds with the anarchic sublimity of verse:

> But I that sit a throne,
> And take my measure from the needs of the State,
> Call his wild thought that overruns the measure,
> Making words more than deeds, and his proud will
> That would unsettle all, most mischievous,
> And he himself a most mischievous man.   [*VPl,* 261–62]

Seanchan's poetic thought is measureless, breaking through all form, and thus dangerous to the hierarchies of state. His laughter is an energy that defies all boundaries, even the final boundary of death. He declares in his final taunt: "King! King! Dead faces laugh" (*VPl,* 310). In the play Yeats also links the sublime to a repugnant racial theory of mastery by the "white-bodied," but, again, it is not inherently and exclusively connected to such views (*VPl,* 301). In *The Unicorn from the Stars,* the peasants interpret Martin's sublime vision of the apocalypse as a prophetic call for revolution and for the destruction of their oppressors—the English Law and enslaving Church (*VPl,* 684–85). The play turns against such an interpretation of the apocalypse, Martin thinking in the end that the destruction must be ethical and internal.

Critics often distinguish between the conservatism of the internal apocalypse and the revolutionary orientation of the external apocalypse.[104] But in this play, Yeats shows that the tropes for the outer and inner apocalypse, as for the natural and psychological sublime, can be translated into each other. If we regard death as the occasion of the sublime, the movement from inner to outer becomes more intelligible, since death is neither one nor the other. And perhaps we should be more aware that Yeats's play conceives of radical action as a potential articulation of the sublime, if not the one it prefers. On the basis of such revisionary readings, Spender could go so far as to claim that the communist "apocalyptic vision" was compatible with Yeats's.[105] Even though he and other poets of the thirties would ultimately reject Yeats's apocalypses, and even though Yeats will never be a hero of the left, the Yeatsian sublime may still be susceptible to the kind of transvaluation that Auden describes in his elegy for Yeats:

The words of a dead man
Are modified in the guts of the living.[106]

3

"MAN'S DIRTY SLATE"

The Self-Elegy

It is indeed impossible to imagine our own death; and whenever we attempt to do so we can perceive that we are in fact still present as spectators. Hence the psycho-analytic school could venture on the assertion that at bottom no one believes in his own death, or, to put the same thing in another way, that in the unconscious every one of us is convinced of his own immortality.
—Sigmund Freud
  "Thoughts for the Times on War and Death"

Read your own obituary notice they say you live longer. Gives you second wind. New lease of life.
—James Joyce
  Ulysses

It may be "impossible to imagine our own death," but poets frequently try to.[1] Like many an epic poet, Yeats meanders among the dead in *A Vision*. Like many a Decadent poet, he projects erotic deaths onto various dramatic personae, such as the jester in "The Cap and Bells" and the stroller in *The King of the Great Clock Tower*. With fewer precedents, he also writes a large and splendid group of poems explicitly about his own death, from "The Tower" to "Man and the Echo." Literary critics often reserve their highest praise for attempts by poets to imagine their own deaths—an activity in which Yeats may out-strip all rivals. Helen Vendler, for example, says of Stevens, Paul de Man of Verlaine and Mallarmé:

To write in a posthumous voice means to make the supreme imaginative act of imagining oneself dead, one's desires ended, one's record of utterance of feeling complete, one's structures of feeling obsolete and gutted.[2]

Like all true poets, Verlaine is a poet of death, but death for Mallarmé means precisely the discontinuity between the personal self and the voice that speaks in the poetry from the other bank of the river, beyond death.[3]

Yeats also bespeaks the completed life and work in a "posthumous voice." Taking on a "voice" from "beyond the other bank of the river," he often creates a deathlike discontinuity between the living self and the testamentary self. But why such extravagant praise from two very different critics for this "supreme imaginative act," characteristic of "all true poets"? Is it that our own death is indeed unimaginable, making these poetic achievements seem miraculous? If so, then the general reluctance of critics to analyze how Yeats concocts such miracles is understandable. Is it that critics have found consolation in the poetic performance and survival of death? If so, then let us set out in search of such consolations in Yeats's self-elegies—but with a critical eye to the stratagems and tricks by which they seem to accomplish the "impossible."

Of course Yeats imaginatively rehearses his death not only in the self-elegy but in both of the major generic groups that we have been interpreting—though at a certain protective remove. In the elegies, he uses the other's death to practice his own, warding off the threat of dispersal that accompanies the act of mourning, simplifying himself through an intensity of self-contemplation. In the poems of tragic joy and the sublime, he represents death and destruction on an apocalyptic scale, welcoming this panorama of ruin as a test of his heroic self-confidence.

But Yeats also writes a distinct kind of poem in which his own death is the overt subject. I am calling this kind of poem the self-elegy because of its reflexive stance—a term indicative of the form's central perplexity; namely, that the mourning "self" seems to coexist with the dead "self."[4] The prefix "self" may seem not only paradoxical but also redundant. Don't all elegists, like Milton, Gray, and Shelley, "turn" to lament their own destined urns? At a purely psychological level, this observation is accurate, but it fails to do justice to the rhetorical and dramatic uniqueness of a form in which the poet's own death is explicitly the central occasion. Yeats does not invent the self-elegy—witness the epigrammatic self-epitaphs of Raleigh, Coleridge, and Swift, the satiric "Verses on the Death of Dr. Swift," and the death poems of Keats, Dickinson, Whitman, and Christina Rossetti. As mourning rites decay in the twentieth century, and as the technologies of war, medicine, and information increasingly dehumanize death, the self-elegy achieves more prominence. Yeats, Lawrence, and Stevens cultivate the form, bequeathing it to Auden, Lowell, Plath, Berryman, Larkin, and others. This genre includes poems often viewed as among Yeats's best: "The Tower," "Vacillation," "A Dialogue of Self and Soul," "The Circus Animals' Desertion," and "Man and the Echo." Presenting Yeats's dance before death at its most vigorous and complex, these lyrics call for close reading—the task of the second part of this chapter. In the first part I explore the modes intertwined within Yeats's self-elegies, such as invocation, epitaph, and ekphrasis.

Although Yeats's self-elegies sometimes adopt a declamatory voice and cast derision on death ("I declare," "Swear," "pass by!"), they are fraught with an underlying dread. They seek to represent the poet as the master of death, choosing that which resists all choice. But when the rant clears and the declarations of immortality falter, these lyrics give us access to the painful questions concealed by such histrionics:

What shall I do with this absurdity[?]   [194]

When all that story's finished, what's the news?   [247]

What is there left to say?   [304–5]

What do we know but that we face
One another in this place?   [345]

MODES OF SELF-MOURNING

Poems of Transition

Yeats wrote a number of poems about his development, most of them during his middle period, such as "A Coat" (1912) and "The Fisherman" (1914). In these works, he aggressively separates himself from the dead, as in some of his elegies; only the dead are now his former selves—selves from which he seeks deliverance. Such poems belong to the broadly self-elegiac tradition of such autobiographical lyrics as the "Intimations Ode," a work that Wordsworth grouped among his "Elegies and Epitaphic Pieces." They may seem to be more about "growing up" than "growing old" (to echo Trilling on the "Intimations Ode"); but they schematize the career so that growing old is a fortunate matter of growing up—an evolution that defends the poet against merely withering into old age.[5] "A Coat" is the obvious example of a poem of transition, and it starkly displays the mode's rhetorical structure. Much as Yeats the elegist fights off the overbearing dead, Yeats the self-elegist delivers himself from the ghost of his own youth and measures his distance from it:

I made my song a coat
Covered with embroideries
Out of old mythologies
From heel to throat;
But the fools caught it,
Wore it in the world's eyes
As though they'd wrought it.
Song, let them take it,
For there's more enterprise
In walking naked.   [127]

Renunciation is a primary gesture of the poem, in keeping with the elegiac ascesis of Wordsworth's ode:

> We will grieve not, rather find
> Strength in what remains behind. . . .[6]

Grieving still less than Wordsworth, Yeats finds strength in the naked song that remains behind. He promises a surrender of former indulgence and excess for a new austerity, demonstrating the new simplicity by rhyming, with unusual starkness, three times on "it." The colloquial contractions of the poem's second half—"they'd," "there's"—also signal the new plainness. And this second half substitutes a "doric" vocabulary of monosyllables for the earlier polysyllables—words that mimic the surrendered ostentation ("embroideries," "mythologies"). Even the word "enterprise," while rhythmically alluding to these front-loaded dactyls, is shorter by a syllable; the leaner word signifies the ethos of self-reliance that will govern the new art.

The poem delineates the transition from past to present as a literary shift from Romantic to modern; but the poem's family resemblance to such autobiographical lyrics as the "Intimations Ode" suggests that this very example of Yeats's newfound modernity is itself Romantic in structure, relinquishing youth's dreamy innocence for a chastened maturity. Here and elsewhere in *Responsibilities,* Yeats promises to give up his "embroideries" and embrace a "language really used by men"—as Wordsworth describes his "plainer" style, supposedly unadulterated by ornament.[7] But Yeats's myth of "modernization" resumes a tradition that precedes even Romanticism. Herbert, for example, consigns his florid linguistic selves to the grave, closely anticipating the ethos and language of Yeats's poem. In the second "Jordan," he chastises himself for the inventive "metaphors" with which he formerly would "clothe" his sentiments—embellishments he calls the "broider'd coat" in "The Forerunners."[8] Yeats's rhetorical strategy for defining the new language is also negative, since to describe the tropes and tactics of the new style would be to admit that it too is a poetic style. The middle segment of "A

Coat" prepares for the break by calling attention to the old style's inauthenticity. After all, if other poets could borrow the language and pretend "they'd wrought it," then it must be arbitrary in relation to the author—its referent. The final apostrophe ("Song, let them . . .") establishes by contrast the reflexive self-sufficiency of the new style: the song addresses the song. The self-apostrophe is a figure for the authenticity of the new relationship between the writer and his song—an authenticity that affirms itself, however, chiefly by negation.

By representing his past and present as different styles (the embroidered and the plain), Yeats can seem to control their relationship and, thus, how he changes over time. In the proem to *The Hour-Glass,* Yeats similarly identifies himself closely with the "song" he refashions:

> The friends that have it I do wrong
> When ever I remake a song,
> Should know what issue is at stake:
> It is myself that I remake.   [551]

By merging with his poems, Yeats repairs loss: as his artifacts, he can be shaped, manipulated, improved. Time is reversible for a self no longer thrown ineluctably toward death.

But who is this "self" that crafts poetic selves? How can it be coextensive with its products and yet be their artisan? And what is the price of associating oneself with one's written counterparts? The first entry in *Estrangement,* recorded not long after this proem's publication, puts the difficulty in these terms: "Neither Christ nor Buddha nor Socrates wrote a book, for to do that is to exchange life for a logical process" (*Au,* 311). By identifying himself with his language in "A Coat" and "The Friends That Have It . . . ," Yeats grants himself a metamorphic flexibility that would seem to protect him from decay and death. But as he suggests in the diary entry, this objectification is, oddly enough, a kind of self-murder: it exchanges life's spontaneity for the deadness of the word. To evade death in its final form, Yeats pays the price of this linguistic death. Later, in "The Circus Animals'

Desertion" and "The Tower," he worries that the protective cathexis of verse and the correlative internalization of death have betrayed him to a death in life. Blanchot states this problem of autobiographical language in a provocative way. "When I speak: death speaks in me. . . . I say my name, and it is as though I were chanting my own dirge: I separate myself from myself, I am no longer either my presence or my reality, but an objective, impersonal presence, the presence of my name, which goes beyond me and whose stone-like immobility performs exactly the same function for me as a tombstone weighing on the void."[9] In "A Coat" and other lyrics of transition, Yeats measures his development by alienating himself from his earlier selves, fixing on them a series of valedictory inscriptions. He wagers that death as the discontinuity between selves is preferable to death as nonexistence.

To interpret these poems exclusively as elegiac texts, however, would not allow for their modal complexity. "A Coat," "The Fisherman," "An Acre of Grass," and other self-elegiac lyrics of transition also draw on the topos of authorial self-surpassal, a topos perhaps most familiar from the traditional invocation. Developing the mode initiated by the alternative beginning of the *Aeneid,* they define the poet by marking the stages of his career: *"Ille ego, qui quondam gracili modulatus avena / carmen. . . ."* It is this *quondam* (formerly) that distances the present enterprise from the previous discourses of the poet—a verbal partition resumed in Spenser's "whilome," Milton's "erewhile," and the Romantic lyric pervasively.[10] Responding in part to the increasingly marginal and vulnerable status of the modern poetic career, Yeats repeats this rhetorical gesture of self-separation and self-definition more often than his predecessors. Throughout his poetry and prose, he tries to author the death of his previous selves, as if he might win ultimate authority over himself and over death. This before-and-after topos is also embedded in such forms as the palinode, the recantation, and the moment of girding to a more serious task (Virgil's *paulo maiora canamus* of the Fourth Eclogue). In "The Spur," Yeats sharply distinguishes old age from youth to make gain out of loss:

> You think it horrible that lust and rage
> Should dance attendance upon my old age;
> They were not such a plague when I was young;
> What else have I to spur me into song?   [312]

Yeats's muses are neither goddesses nor holy light, but like his predecessors, he draws on forces of inspiration unavailable to him during the innocence of youth. In "The Fisherman," he ridicules his former aesthetic practice and its intended audience, while envisioning compensatory alternatives to both:

> Maybe a twelvemonth since
> Suddenly I began,
> In scorn of this audience,
> Imagining a man . . .
>
> . . . .
> A man who does not exist,
> A man who is but a dream;
> And cried, 'Before I am old
> I shall have written him one
> Poem maybe as cold
> And passionate as the dawn.'   [148–49]

Like Milton in the third invocation of *Paradise Lost*, Yeats wants a "fit audience . . . , though few," feeling himself "with dangers compassed round."[11] This general resemblance also extends to Milton's sonnets on the loss of youth, "How Soon Hath Time" and "When I Consider How My Light Is Spent," since Yeats evaluates the career against the horizon of old age ("'Before I am old'"). Even more than lust or rage, death is the plague that spurs Yeats into song.

Yeats often uses gender to distinguish the various phases of his career. Typically, his revised self is emphatically male, the poet suppressing what he represents as his femininity to win a hard, cold, masculine identity. In a letter of 1901, he tells Fiona Macleod that he is, in his new style, making "everything hard and clear"; a year later, he boasts to Lady Gregory: "My work has got far more masculine. It has salt in it" (*L*, 358, 397). Rebelling against "the prevailing decadence" of the period and of his own youthful verse, Yeats wants to exorcise the nineties' image of the "unmanly" male poet—the poet characterized by "sentiment and sentimental sadness, a womanish introspection" (*L*, 434). "I accuse myself of effeminacy," he later declares (*E&I*, 519). Yeats's poems of tragic joy would transform the "sensitive body" into invulnerable stone: from the effeminate boy to the Rocky Face in "The Gyres," and from the frightened women to the stone China-men in "Lapis Lazuli." The self-elegies of transition also presuppose these gender-coordinates. In "A Coat," the youthful style is clothed with feminine "embroideries," whereas the new song will walk "naked," having cast off its protective sheath. Yeats designates the rugged fisherman as a *man* no less than five times; this lexical repetition almost becomes incantatory as the poem works up to its final image of the cold dawn—an image borrowed, appropriately, from his father (*E&I*, 523). Yeats habitually uses the word *cold* for the aim of his exercises in self-overcoming: resisting "that overcharged colour inherited from the Romantic movement, I deliberately reshaped my style, deliberately sought out an impression as of cold light and tumbling clouds" (*Au*, 48; 138, 184). Like the images of salt, ice, and stone that he uses to describe the remade self, coldness implies an anti-Romantic im-personality and strength—a masculinity that he says is as "hard, cold and invulnerable" as "steel" (*AV*, 160). In his self-revisions he tries to act out Nietzsche's dictum: "Praised be what hard-ens!"[12] Yeats is not the period's only poet to represent literary maturation as the suppression of the feminine and soft in favor of the masculine and hard; T. E. Hulme foretells the modernist aesthetic of Pound and Eliot, who try to outgrow "damp" poetry that is always "moaning or whining" and write poetry that is "all dry and hard."[13]

Yeats explicitly mythologizes his development as a growth away from the feminine in "Lines Written in Dejection"; but here and in the self-elegiac "Wild Swans at Coole," that growth is a lamentable fall. In these works Yeats adheres more closely to the overriding melancholy of many Romantic farewells to youth, such as the "Intimations Ode" and "Tintern Abbey":

When have I last looked on
The round green eyes and the long wavering bodies
Of the dark leopards of the moon?
All the wild witches, those most noble ladies,
For all their broom-sticks and their tears,
Their angry tears, are gone.
The holy centaurs of the hills are vanished;
I have nothing but the embittered sun;
Banished heroic mother moon and vanished,
And now that I have come to fifty years
I must endure the timid sun.   [145–46]

This last line foreshadows the poet's dejected attempts to accept old age in a later self-elegy, "The Circus Animals' Desertion": "I must be satisfied with my heart," "I must lie down" (346, 348). The speaker of "Lines Written in Dejection" mourns that maturation has necessitated his estrangement from the maternal, a change that may rehearse atavistically the shift from the pre-oedipal to the oedipal. In the subtle equivocation over whether the mother moon has "vanished" of her own accord or instead been "Banished," the poet obliquely hints that perhaps he has himself caused the alienation he laments. The lost mother moon is associated with magic, mystery, and bodily rhythm ("long wavering bodies"). In Yeats's mythology of origins, she is akin to Henry More's *Anima Mundi* and Wordsworth's "immortal sea," and she also resembles the pre-oedipal mother of psychoanalysis, the mother before the child distinguishes itself from her through symbolic language (*Myth*, 346). Like Wordsworth, who resignedly casts the "sober colouring" of his eye on the sun, Yeats grieves that only the sun remains with its fatherly rationalism and realism, and that the very different light of the mother moon and the imaginary women associated with it "are gone." But that they and his earlier self *are gone*, that they have opened by their absence a space for the mourning mind to fill—this is for Yeats the precondition that makes possible self-elegiac song and self-remaking.

Written a year later in 1916 and with comparable nostalgia, "The Wild Swans at Coole" is also a lament over estrangement from a self passionately attached to the feminine: nineteen years ago at Coole he was desperately in love, but "All's changed" (131–32). We know, of course, that the biographical Yeats was at this time mourning his loss of desire for Maud Gonne. In the self-elegy Yeats replaces the once productive distance from the beloved (a distance that generated his early love lyrics) with the similarly productive distance from his youthful self. Now the imagination dwells the most not upon a woman lost but on a self lost—a self whose imagination dwelled the most upon a woman lost. Yeats defines his present identity by contrast with the swans that betoken his youth (his former love and hope): from the implied opposites, we surmise that *he* is *now* weary, companionless, and old, that he has lost hope for new passions and conquests:

> *Un*wearied *still,* lover by lover,
> *They* paddle in the cold
> Companionable streams or climb the air;
> *Their* hearts have *not* grown old;
> Passion or conquest, wander where *they* will,
> Attend upon *them still.*

But the painful breech between his past and present selves, between his former longing and his current dispassion, is not without consolation. Although this stanza was once the last, Yeats revised the poem to close with a compensatory vision. In the transition to what is now the final stanza, the swans subtly change from emblems of his lovesick youth and its desires into figures for his creative maturity and its hopes:

> But now they drift on the still water,
> Mysterious, beautiful;
> Among what rushes will they build,

By what lake's edge or pool
Delight men's eyes when I awake some day
To find they have flown away?

Redescribed in aesthetic terms ("Mysterious, beautiful"), the swans come to resemble the very object of mystery and beauty that the poet has just fashioned. Like the poem, they will soon leave the compass of his vision to delight other eyes in ways he could never predict. Overcoming the sad thought of loss, Yeats celebrates indirectly his aesthetic gain. Once again, the miseries of self-division have given rise to the joys of self-creation.[14]

Self-Epitaphs: Speaking from Beyond the Grave

Since development as a poet is for Yeats partly a movement from the feminine to the masculine, many of the self-elegies without the dejection of these poems also share their gender determinants. A second group of self-elegies defines the poet not in relation to a past self he has outgrown or lost but in relation to his anticipated death; and it endows this postmortem self with the authorial voice of the father. No discourse in Yeats's lyrics is more harsh, paternal, and aggressively masculine than this self-epitaphic one, especially in "Under Ben Bulben." That late declamatory testament articulates in an extreme form the dynamic of self-separation that we have been tracing in the poems of transition. In its psychic action it also resembles Yeats's curses and apocalypses. As in those modes, the poet internalizes destructive authority to quell it, ruthlessly suppressing his own "filial" and "feminine" vulnerabilities.

"Under Ben Bulben" resounds with commands, and the first one—"Swear"—grants the voice of the dead father to the speaker, specifically the dead father who berates Hamlet from beyond the grave (325). The abrupt invocation of the Witch of Atlas is less puzzling than it might be if we remember her indifference to the misery, strife, and death that plague humankind.[15] As if handing down the law to undutiful adolescents, the voice demands:

Poet and sculptor do the work
Nor let the modish painter shirk
What his great forefathers did. . . .   [326]

Ventriloquizing the dead forefathers, the injunctive rhetoric obscures the real question of authority that puts such pressure on
the work—namely, the relation of the poet to death's ultimate
authority. And yet, the anxiety in these hysterical efforts at command is palpable: "Swear," "Swear," "do," "Nor let," "Bring,"
"Make him," "run on," "learn your trade," "Sing," "Scorn,"
"Sing," "Sing," "Cast," "Cast," and "pass by!" These "arrogant
imperatives," as Ellmann calls them, reverse the relation of power
that haunts this testament, even though many critics have been
content to take at face value the poet's protestations that death is
no more than a "brief parting" by which a man "completes" his
mind and "can accomplish fate" (325–26).[16] In another self-
portrait, Yeats himself prepares the way for a hermeneutics of
suspicion that would mistrust the bravado: "There one that ruffled in a manly pose / For all his timid heart" ("Coole Park,
1929," 243). The depiction of the muscular gravediggers, who
"thrust" the dead with sharp spades, chiastically inverts the relation between the strength of death and the vulnerability of life.
The famous exhortation,

Cast a cold eye
On life, on death . . . ,

wishfully establishes a relation of freedom with death, as if it were
the poet's eye that actively chose or refused death, and not the
unavoidable, inscrutable, cold gaze of death that chose the term
of life.

This is not the first testament in the Yeats canon to desire a
reversal of authority. Already in "To Ireland in the Coming
Times" (1892), earlier labeled an "Apologia," the speaker ar-
rogantly calls himself a *"brother"* among his poetic fathers—
Davis, Mangan, Ferguson. And then, as if that were not au-
dacious enough, he makes the oedipal boast that his *"rhymes more*

than their rhyming tell" (50). The claim to be not *"less"* but *"more"* knowledgeable than his predecessors once again takes us back to the invocation, particularly to Milton's assertion that his subject is "Not less but more heroic" than Homer's or Virgil's.[17] Indeed, Yeats can help us to compare and contrast the career narratives in the invocation and the self-epitaph. Let us recall an important progenitor of the self-epitaph, the inscription on Virgil's tomb:

MANTUA ME GENUIT, CALABRI RAPUERE, TENET NUNC
PARTHENOPE; CECINI PASCUA, RURA, DUCES.[18]

Like the supposed invocation to the *Aeneid,* this supposed self-epitaph divides the career into a progression with three stages; but unlike the invocation, it locates its own discourse outside the personal history. Although the poetic career becomes a very different notion by the twentieth century, the rhetorical strategies by which Yeats defines it are comparable. His self-elegies of transition situate their own commentary at the latest moment of a life ("It is myself that I remake," "What else have I to spur me into song?"), whereas the more strictly self-epitaphic discourse seems to have passed beyond the life. Probably reflecting a greater professional insecurity about being a poet, Yeats canonizes himself more often than his predecessors. Disentangled from the life, his self-epitaphic rhetoric can effectively aspire to autocanonization. Such is the modal emphasis toward the end of "Coole and Ballylee, 1931," when the poet suddenly seems to levitate above his own existence, retrospectively defining his career and his affiliations by contrast with the decaying times:

> We were the last romantics—chose for theme
> Traditional sanctity and loveliness. . . .   [245]

Two poems later in the volume is Yeats's translation of Swift's formal self-epitaph; it is a similarly indignant self-definition, especially with Yeats's addition of an epithet to Swift's unmodified *"viator"*—"World-besotted traveller" (246). In both "To Ireland in the Coming Times" and "The Municipal Gallery Re-visited," the poet projects himself into *"the dim coming times"* and, looking back on himself, supplies us with the canonizing words we are to pronounce over him: "say my glory was I had such friends" (51, 321). In the disturbing estrangement of such self-epitaphic discourse from the speaker, Yeats dons the mask of the dead to speak of the living; and so his exercises in prosopopoeia might be thought of as exaggerating the discontinuous or allegorical structure concealed within the autobiographical lyric.[19]

The final, self-epitaphic section of "Under Ben Bulben" opens gaps among various "selves." Drawing to its close, this uncanny ending makes two violent rhetorical leaps. First, Yeats suddenly seems to step outside of his body and outside of time, commemorating and canonizing himself:

> Under bare Ben Bulben's head
> In Drumcliff churchyard Yeats is laid,
> An ancestor was rector there
> Long years ago; a church stands near,
> By the road an ancient Cross.
> No marble, no conventional phrase,
> On limestone quarried near the spot
> By his command these words are cut. . . .   [327–28]

Who speaks these lines? Perhaps a *genius loci* since, in accordance with epitaphic tradition, the voice depicts the scene; perhaps no one, for the words represent themselves as dryly impersonal; but surely not the living Yeats. In a poem reverberating with injunctions, this stanza purports to record and not merely foretell how one such injunction has been posthumously realized: "By his command these words *are* cut." Then, at yet another remove and through another mask, a different voice intones the final self-epitaph: "Cast a cold eye. . . ." Because of these layers of prosopopoeia, the final discourse seems abstracted from the life of the poet, as if spoken by his now disembodied but empowered voice, a voice from a timeless nowhere beyond the grave.

Yeats names himself only twice in his poetry: in the introduction to the tomb inscription of "Under Ben Bulben" ("In Drumcliff churchyard Yeats is laid"), and in the earlier inscription for the tower, "To be carved on a Stone at Thoor Ballylee." In both cases, the self-naming relies on the structures of inscription and prosopopoeia. As in "A Coat," the authenticity of the poet's self-relation can only be established through a prior moment of self-estrangement:

> I, the poet William Yeats,
> With old mill boards and sea-green slates,
> And smithy work from the Gort forge,
> Restored this tower for my wife George;
> And may these characters remain
> When all is ruin once again.   [190]

The inscription contrasts its own permanence with the expected ruin of everything else, almost gleeful that it will persist amid destruction. It points to itself with a demonstrative or deictic adjective—"these"—as if its self-relation were obvious and un-problematic. But which characters are "these characters"? The characters "To be carved" on the tower? If so, then the word "these" must be proleptic and cannot be immediately proximate to its referent, at least within the temporal framework of a title that merely predicts such a carving.[20] Even if the characters cut in stone at the tower could refer exclusively and directly to them-selves, their confidence would be misplaced, since the poet can hope only that the written, replicable "characters" of the verse would outlast catastrophic ruin. Like the poet's epitaph, these lines bear such authority not because of an immediate relation to themselves or to the living author but because of the absence of either one of these; hence their apparent power over death. The reader may well credit this power since the words themselves seem to speak from beyond an individual history, from beyond the tomb. Instead of confirming the autobiographical self-iden-tity supposedly characteristic of Yeats's lyrics, the moments of self-naming indicate a prior structure of self-alienation—the rhe-torical structure upon which the fiction of lyric self-identity is founded.

Like the speakers of both inscriptions, the speaker of the lyric entitled "Death" seems to escape any dread about mortality. True, he initially grants dread and hope much importance, for these imaginative rehearsals of death seem to distinguish humans from animals:

Nor dread nor hope attend
A dying animal;
A man awaits his end
Dreading and hoping all;
Many times he died,
Many times rose again.   [234]

But the speaker goes on to applaud the transcendence of all dread, apparently emboldened by this ambiguous reference to dying and reviving (whether in the imagination or in actual reincarnation). Anticipating the self-epitaph in "Under Ben Bulben," he suggests in the verb *cast* a nonchalance before death, a heroic posture that reverses the relation between death and its victim, between murderers and their prey—in this case, the recently assassinated Kevin O'Higgins:

A great man in his pride
Confronting murderous men
Casts derision upon
Supersession of breath;
He knows death to the bone—
Man has created death.

Thus, the poem distinguishes three orders of being according to their attitudes toward death: the animal (lacking all hope and dread), the human (dreading and hoping all), and the great man (feeling but conquering all dread and hope). Schopenhauer applauds such "contempt for death," saying that if we could see deep enough, we would imitate nature and "regard life or death as indifferently as does she."[21] Even though "Under Ben Bulben," "Death," "To be carved . . . ," and "The Gyres" claim such indifference toward death, the stresses and strains of their clamorous rhetoric, together with the dread they occasionally name and other poems more openly describe, betray a mood that could hardly be termed "indifferent."

Two late lyrics, "What Then?" and "The Apparitions," exemplify the opposite from Yeats's epitaphic mode. A phrase in "The Apparitions" may help us to think critically about the hero of "Death," who "Casts derision" upon mortality: "there is safety in derision" (344). The poem also uncovers the terror that underlies the assertions of "joy" in such poems as "The Gyres" and "Under Ben Bulben":

> When a man grows old his joy
> Grows more deep day after day,
> His empty heart is full at length
> But he has need of all that strength
> Because of the increasing Night
> That opens her mystery and fright.
> *Fifteen apparitions have I seen;*
> *The worst a coat upon a coat-hanger.*

Tragic joy is here seen as a defensive energy, an old man's weapon for defeating the fear of nothingness. As Yeats puts it in a discarded stanza of "The Circus Animals' Desertion":

> Even at the approach of the un-imaged night
> Man has the refuge of his gaiety.[22]

In "The Apparitions" death is not the "brief parting" of "Under Ben Bulben"; it is absence, the unknown, the void. The triviality and concreteness of the coat hanger lend emphasis to the abstract Night, suggesting that death is at a terrifying remove from the imagination's reach.[23] In "Under Ben Bulben" and other epitaphic poems, Yeats celebrates death as the occasion for completing a narrative about himself, looking down vertically on his horizontal development. But this illusion of "perfection" is subjected to subtle ridicule in "What Then?" (302). When the old man decrees, "The work is done," only the "boyish plan" has been brought to completion, and so the brutal question persists, "*'What then?'*" Yeats's best self-elegies vacillate between the au-

thorial confidence of the epitaphic mode and the corrosive questioning of these more frightened lyrics. I review the course of this
vacillation in some longer poems after exploring another important mode of the Yeatsian self-elegy, as well as the theory of self-
mourning in *A Vision*.

Ekphrasis: The Artifact as Memento Mori

In a number of self-elegiac poems, Yeats anticipates
and mourns his approaching death in the mirror of a visual
artifact. Defining ekphrasis as the literary mode that presents an
artifact as its ostensible subject, I hope to show that Yeats develops two versions of ekphrasis and that in both of them he
centers his meditation on death.[24] How can we account for
Yeats's recurrent conjunction of the visual artifact with self-
mourning? Why should Yeats's finest ekphrastic lyrics—"The
Municipal Gallery Re-visited," "Lapis Lazuli," and the Byzantium poems—foreground the issue of the poet's mortality?

To get at these difficult questions, we need a genealogy of the
ekphrastic self-elegy. Already in *The Greek Anthology,* the ekphrasis is sometimes a tomb inscription that describes the visual artifact to which it is attached. In this way, ekphrasis is related even
in its earliest form to death and to epitaphic discourse or prosopopoeia.[25] But it is not until the Romantic reinterpretation of
the form that ekphrasis and the poet's mortality become inextrica-
bly linked—in Wordsworth's "Elegiac Stanzas on Peele Castle,"
for example, where Beaumont's painting of an unchanging castle
becomes a tombstone both for the poet's youthful self and his
drowned brother, or Keats's "Ode on a Grecian Urn," where the
burial urn will remain cold and indifferent even while old age
wastes the poet, his generation, and his successors. Intimations of
mortality and reflections on art remain linked in such Victorian
lyrics as Browning's "My Last Duchess" and D. G. Rossetti's "On
Leonardo's Virgin of the Rocks," and this connection persists
after Yeats in such modern ekphrases as Auden's "Musée des
Beaux Arts," Stevens's "Poems of Our Climate," Jarrell's "Knight,

Death, and the Devil," and Ashbery's "Self-Portrait in a Convex Mirror." These modern ekphrases preserve the Romantic association of the visual image with the reality principle—whether by reason of its fixity (Wordsworth's castle), its decay (Shelley's wrecked collosus in "Ozymandias"), or its nonhumanity (Keats's cold urn). Yeats plays an important role in this tradition, elaborating the Romantic inversion of the classical immortality topos and deepening the Romantic preoccupation with the poet's own death in ekphrastic poetry.

In some of the ekphrastic self-elegies, such as "The Municipal Gallery Re-visited" and "Lapis Lazuli," Yeats dissociates his own written artistry from the mute and limited visual image. The icon becomes in such poems a painful reminder of the poet's finitude. Directly countering the classical topos *ut pictura poesis,* these lyrics extend the struggle between poet and visual image evident already in Wordsworth's annoyance with the realistic panoramas or "spectacles" that he sees in London, and continuing to Ashbery's battle with Parmigianino's self-portrait. This type of ekphrasis takes the poet's confrontation with the unthinkable otherness of death and stages it as a confrontation with the accessible otherness of the visual arts. In "The Municipal Gallery Re-visited," Yeats begins to distinguish his own work from the insufficiency of the graphic arts by asking a question about Mancini's portrait of Lady Gregory: "where is the brush that could show anything / Of all that pride and that humility[?]" (320). His question corrects Synge's excessive praise of the portrait—" 'Greatest since Rembrandt,' according to John Synge." This impatience with Synge's hyperbole may displace a deeper undercurrent of impatience with the visual arts: the portrait of Synge encountered at the end of the poem is the work of Yeats's father, although the identity of the painter is undeclared in the lyric. For Yeats, Synge became inextricable from this portrait: "When I try to recall his physical appearance, my father's picture in the Municipal Gallery blots out my own memory" (*Au,* 284). Even though Yeats was fond of much of his father's and brother's work, he also tells of the youthful effort "to break away from my father's style" in painting, and he writes with humiliation about his father's never-finished works (*Au*, 54).[26] This accident of Yeats's personal history—that he waged the oedipal struggle against a painter and his works—would lead him to heighten the implied Romantic troping of the visual artifact as the father, limitation, death. Already in Wordsworth, Beaumont's painting of Peele Castle, "Cased in the unfeeling armour of old time," is a totemic emblem of Necessity. But Wordsworth says he has "submitted to a new control," bowing to the painting's image of fate, whereas Yeats subtly rebels against the paintings in the Municipal Gallery.[27] The portraits, as we saw earlier, depend for their existence on the poet's imagination: Yeats finds in them the "terrible and gay" Ireland he has himself created, and he constitutes Synge's image poetically before he allows the playwright a separate, painterly existence. By the end of the poem, the paintings of the dead friends are ciphers through which we are to "judge" Yeats after his death and grant him his "glory"—and ciphers through which he anticipates and mourns his own annihilation.

In spite of his well-known interest in the graphic arts, Yeats sometimes betrays a different attitude, describing these arts much as he describes the "Body of Fate" in his system. Occasionally he condemns painting for pressing on the mind a universe of death. He explains that he "hated" works by one painter because his art was "too much concerned with . . . the minutely observed irregularity of surfaces"; similarly, Wordsworth is irritated by "mimic sights that ape / The absolute presence of reality"—the deadening reality that is no more than "tuft, stone, scratch minute" (*Au*, 106).[28] Blake more than Wordsworth shapes Yeats's resistance to realistic painting, but both predecessors contribute to the general aesthetic that would lead Yeats to reject entrapment by the empirical eye—an aesthetic that Yeats makes more overtly agonistic. Appropriately, a "death's head" appears in a picture in "Demon and Beast"; for Yeats, painting itself can be a death's head (186).

The inference that Yeats often associates the visual artifact with death and the father may help us to understand why he uses

a cracked medallion to mediate his relationship with death in
"Lapis Lazuli." We have already seen that this poem, exceptional
in its interweaving of many modes, internalizes tragic drama,
participates in the dynamic of the sublime, and resumes the carpe
diem song, the happy death, the ruins tradition and others. Its
Shakespearean exercises in heroically encountering one's own
death also suggest that it is self-elegiac, preoccupied ultimately
with the poet's death. This becomes more evident in the last two
ekphrastic stanzas, where the poet defines his imagination in
relation to a work of art. His cool, detached report of the medallion's surface appears at first to allow some respite from the earlier
bombardment and wreckage. The orderly configuration of the
stone—emphasized by numbers ("Two," "third," "third") and
spatial indices ("behind," "Over")—seems to promise the refuge
from time of the East's hierarchical stability:

> Two Chinamen, behind them a third,
> Are carved in Lapis Lazuli,
> Over them flies a long-legged bird
> A symbol of longevity;
> The third, doubtless a serving-man,
> Carries a musical instrument.   [295]

In Yeats's Orientalist haven, the reliable social and semiotic structures mirror one another: the servingman is subordinate to his
masters, the bird subordinate to its meaning. As in traditional
ekphrasis, the visual artifact consoles by its subordination of all
parts to the law of totality. The language of the poem momentarily takes on a lapidary stillness and objectivity, each pair of lines
built as a complete syntactic unit on the earlier pair.

But in Yeats, such imitations of spatial order seldom endure—
as we know, for example, from the violent disruption of the
crystalline vision of Lissadell in the elegy for the Gore-Booth
sisters. The final stanza of "Lapis Lazuli" unleashes on the stone
the double temporality of physical decay and the poet's spontaneous imaginings:

Every discolouration of the stone,
Every accidental crack or dent
Seems a water-course or an avalanche,
Or lofty slope where it still snows
Though doubtless plum or cherry-branch
Sweetens the little half-way house
Those Chinamen climb towards, and I
Delight to imagine them seated there;
There, on the mountain and the sky,
On all the tragic scene they stare.
One asks for mournful melodies;
Accomplished fingers begin to play.
Their eyes mid many wrinkles, their eyes,
Their ancient, glittering eyes, are gay.   [295]

Like Wordsworth's Peele Castle or Keats's Elgin marbles and Grecian urn, the carving is a memento mori in stone. But Yeats's response to the stone is more assertive: Wordsworth subjugates himself before the painting, and Keats avows that the urn can express a tale "more sweetly than our rhyme."[29] However light the tone of the stanza, the poet responds forcefully to this emblem of his own finitude, as if to defeat its paternal message of limitation. He imaginatively displaces the marks of time—the discolorations, cracks, and dents—with the self-begetting images of the mind—water-course *or* avalanche *or* lofty slope with snow. Associated with regenerative water and the coming spring, these immaterial possibilities supplant the deathly, literal marks on the stone's surface. In its internal time the mind spins out poetic possibilities that seem to surmount the external time that brings decay.

The synaesthetic panoply of the poet supersedes the merely visual stone—corpselike and mute. His conjurings appeal not only to the eye but to the nose—an unseen plum or cherry-branch "Sweetens" the house—and to the ear—the musician plays "mournful melodies." Although this show of poetic prowess goes back ultimately to Homer's "narrativization" of the shield of Achilles, the immediate precursor of the poem is the "Ode on a Grecian Urn." Verbal echoes demonstrate this link: "branches," "sweet," "little," "mountain," "melodies," and the repetitions of "or."[30] But there is more of an effort to outdo the visual artifact in Yeats's ekphrasis than in Keats's. Yeats gives very little space to reporting the stone's surface before embarking on his own imaginings, whereas Keats begins to move beyond the urn's surface only with the imaginary altar and town of the last scene—if even there. Decay has not left Yeats's stone "unravish'd," like Keats's seemingly eternal urn. Inverting the ekphrastic topos that the artwork is eternal, Yeats uses its fragmentation to renew his imaginative life, violating the literal surface with a figurative display that signifies his recovery from the threatened impotence of the poem's beginning. This substitution of figurative life for the marks of death is, as always in elegy, only partial; the poet acknowledges the inevitability of loss: despite his protestations of gaiety, the melodies are "mournful," the scene "tragic," and the faces wrinkled. In attempting to surpass the faded and fissured stone, the poet cannot entirely succeed in the self-elegiac work of transfiguring an emblem suggestive of his own bodily decay.

"Lapis Lazuli" is not the only one of Yeats's lyrics to overturn so flagrantly the twin principles of classical ekphrasis—the association of the artifact with immortality and with closure. In "Meru," closure is an ideological "illusion" by which civilization "is hooped together"; but caverned far from such illusion, the mountain hermits know that humanity's fragile "monuments" are neither eternal nor self-contained (289). In its first stanza "Nineteen Hundred and Nineteen" echoes the iterative lament of all elegy for things that "are gone"—iconic artifacts in bronze, stone, ivory, gold, and olive wood (206). They had seemed in peacetime to be indestructible handiwork, but they "burn" and "break" like everything else we hold dear: "Man is in love and loves what vanishes" (207–8). As J. Hillis Miller observes, the figures of the poem violently revolve without center;[31] this de-centered movement might be seen as a deliberate flouting of ekphrastic norms of closure. Indeed, the poet mocks not only the deluded Horatian attempt to "leave some monument behind" *(monumentum aere perennius)* but also the cognate attempt to totalize:

> We pieced our thoughts into philosophy,
> And planned to bring the world under a rule. . . .   [207]

"Meru" echoes and expounds this last phrase; it asserts that such aesthetic necessity—dear to traditional ekphrasis—is a consoling delusion that wards off the harsher necessity of ruin, death, "the desolation of reality":

> Civilization is hooped together, brought
> Under a rule, under the semblance of peace
> By manifold illusion. . . .   [289]

To follow out one implication of this metaphor of "rule," the artwork's subordination of all parts to the whole resembles ideology's reconciliation of all contradictions in a comedic "reality." But in "Meditations in Time of Civil War," as in a number of Yeats's anticlassical ekphrases, the violence of war shatters the illusions of closure and permanence—a dissolution reproduced by the poem's succession of architectural tropes, from the "escutcheoned doors" and "polished floors" of restful eighteenth-century houses to the "loosening masonry" and "broken stone" of the tower (201, 204–5). In spite of the current critical tendency to associate poetic closure with death, closure in the ekphrastic tradition signifies above all the transcendence of death, from Homer and Horace to the Neoclassicists; and it is this illusion of transcendence that Yeats's lyrics, with their shattered monuments and cracked emblems, question. We need not draw the conclusion, however, that Yeats surrenders himself in these ekphrastic moments to his own finitude. By dramatizing his heroic ability to face decay, Yeats paradoxically seems to exempt himself from it.

I have wanted to suggest that in many of his ekphrastic lyrics, Yeats rehearses death in the ruin of the artifact, as if to master death by repeatedly challenging himself to embrace fragmentation. Indeed, many of these lyrics belong both to the ekphrastic tradition and to the ruins tradition. But in some lyrics the artifact does not decay. Sato's sword is, in accordance with classical ekphrasis, "a changeless work of art" (although Yeats modifies the traditional image of the imperturbable *deus artifex* by giving him "an aching heart" ["My Table," 202–3]). Moreover, in such poems as "Under Ben Bulben" and "The Statues," art structures desire, and it defeats the threat of formlessness and dispersal. A timeless refuge from mortality, Yeats's Byzantine artifice owes much to classical ekphrasis. In "Sailing to Byzantium," the Horatian "Monuments of unageing intellect" promise transcendence of generation and decay (193). Artifice eternalizes the poet, as one expects in ekphrasis.

Nevertheless, death also plays a part in this more traditional mode of Yeatsian ekphrasis, especially in the Byzantium poems. "Sailing to Byzantium" complicates the ekphrastic bifurcation of the mortal and artificial worlds by representing the transition from one to the other as a kind of death. The discontinuity between these worlds draws death away from its final position to a moment internal to the aesthetic ritual. If he wishes to escape death, the poet must die into art. He bids the sages of the Byzantine mosaic:

> Consume my heart away; sick with desire
> And fastened to a dying animal
> It knows not what it is; and gather me
> Into the artifice of eternity.   [193]

As in the elegiac rite taken up in "Parnell's Funeral," the consumption of the dying poet's heart immortalizes him. To the extent that the sages and the artifice figure the poet's own aesthetic power, the poet is represented as mourning and consuming himself. The golden bird of the final stanza—whose ironic significance has been overemphasized—is the elegiac apotheosis of the self-mourned poet; it resumes the Miltonic and Keatsian tradition that will lead to Stevens's self-apotheosis as bird in the

late self-elegy "Of Mere Being." Thus, even when the Yeatsian
artwork shares in "the artifice of eternity," it still occasions the
poet's rehearsal of death and dying. A number of high Romantic
poems already represent dying and creating in terms of each
other, but especially close to "Sailing to Byzantium" is Keats's
Fall of Hyperion. Ascending the purgatorial steps to inspiration,
the poet is told by Moneta, the priestess of art:

> "Thou hast felt
> What 'tis to die and live again before
> Thy fated hour. That thou hadst power to do so
> Is thy own safety; thou hast dated on
> Thy doom."[32]

Even more than delay it, Yeats would annul the fated hour by
drawing death within his self-elegies, transforming it into a stage
in the process of artistic self-sacrifice and self-renewal. He develops Keats's aesthetic rite of death by combining it with its
alchemical correlative: Aherne concludes after the alchemical experience of melting into a vision, "I passed into that Death which
is Beauty herself" (*Myth*, 277).

"Byzantium" is another ekphrastic self-elegy that traces the
process of purgation—except that it now runs the process back-
wards. In an unusual reversal of the elegiac sequence, Yeats first
represents the apotheosis of the dead as breathless ghost or bird
of "changeless metal," and then follows them back to the original
state of blood, mire, and mortality (248). The flames that purge
the dead spirits of their complexities are the self-elegist's transformative powers, simplifying through intensity, burning away the
accidents of the chaotic life. Yeats says that after illness (a frightening bout of Malta fever) "I warmed myself back into life with
'Byzantium,'" much as, after an earlier illness, he wrote "Sailing
to Byzantium" "to recover my spirits" (*P*, 600; *L*, 718). We are
accustomed to reading "Byzantium" as an allegory of the aesthetic process, but it might also be read as an exercise in self-
mourning. In this regard, it resembles Yeats's other ekphrastic
lyrics, about which we may now draw some general inferences.

The artifact has two roles in the wars Yeats wages on death. In the first, he externalizes death by projecting it onto an artifact that is either fixed and limited (the portraits of the Municipal Gallery) or ruined and decaying (the lapis lazuli). He dissociates his poetry from the vulnerable and literal surface of the visual artifact. In the second mode, Yeats internalizes death by locating it within the aesthetic process; it becomes the moment of transition from one world to the next, when the poet dies into the agony of the creative dance. In both versions of ekphrasis Yeats weaves his rite of self-mourning, his desire to master the absolute strangeness of death, around the lesser strangeness of visual artifice.

"The Soul in Judgment"

Before we suspend our focus on the lyrics, it may be useful to review our analysis of the self-elegy thus far. The self-elegies of transition, such as "A Coat," depict the poet in the process of remaking himself; they associate him with a language that is malleable, subject to continual revision. The epitaphic self-elegies, such as "Under Ben Bulben," represent the poet as a voice that has survived death and continues to intone from beyond the grave. In both of these modes, the trajectory of the poet's development is away from "feminine" vulnerability to invulnerable coldness and hardness. In the ekphrastic self-elegies, Yeats sometimes dissociates the temporality of his own poetic play from the mute stillness of the visual-image-as-death, and he sometimes portrays his own creative activity as a ritual of dying into the permanent aesthetic world. In all of these self-elegies, he rehearses death, transforming it into a moment or image accessible within poetry.

But Yeats rehearses death not only in verse. He wanders across the great divide in many stories, romances, and discursive writings, above all in *A Vision*. The formidable section of *A Vision* called "The Soul in Judgment" has been read by Vendler as a description of the creative process and by other critics as a literal map of Yeats's afterlife.[33] Both views are helpful, but I would like to outline a third possibility: it may also be read as an allegory of dying. With this interpretation of "The Soul in Judgment," I introduce some preliminary concepts for analyzing Yeats's finest self-elegies.

The *Tibetan Book of the Dead* notwithstanding, it may seem odd to regard Yeats's description of what happens *after* death as an indirect and idealized account of what happens *before* death. But a poet's imaginative vision of death is often built on what the living know by metonymy of death—namely, dying. Nor should it surprise us to find that this section of *A Vision* can be read as an allegory for both creative writing and for idealized dying, since they are often interchangeable tropologies in Yeats. The intricate distinctions between the stages of the afterlife need not entangle us here; Yeats is neither Blake nor Dante, and we would do well to avoid oversystematizing his system. He himself implies that his system is a mode of defense, though he claims to be describing Flaubert: "We feel too that this man who systematised by but linking one emotional association to another has become strangely hard, cold and invulnerable, that this mirror is not brittle but of unbreakable steel" (*AV,* 160). Penetrating the occult armor, we notice that a number of nonesoteric motifs recur in Book III: purification, repetition, mastery, and detachment. Yeats uses these concepts to describe one's psychological relation to the image of one's life. Thus, "The Soul in Judgment" may be read as Yeats's veiled account of what is traditionally called mortification, for it illustrates how the mind transforms itself and separates itself from its earlier natural state, though in Yeats's version it is the mind, not God, that masters the life. Self-mastery and self-transformation occur as the mind exhorts itself, in Paul's words, "Mortify [*mortificate*] what is earthly in you" (Col. 3:5). The very title of the section might remind us of the traditional scene of judgment during the soul's final hour.[34] Recalling the life, fitting its pieces into a whole, purifying it, judging it, and repenting, the individual finally gains mastery over the life, freedom from its accidents and evils, and courage to face death.

In one of the most important passages of *A Vision* Yeats writes:

> In the *Dreaming Back,* the *Spirit* is compelled to live over and
> over again the events that had most moved it; there can be
> nothing new, but the old events stand forth in a light which
> is dim or bright according to the intensity of the passion that
> accompanied them. They occur in the order of their inten-
> sity or luminosity, the more intense first, and the painful are
> commonly the more intense, and repeat themselves again
> and again. In the *Return,* upon the other hand, the *Spirit*
> must live through past events in the order of their occur-
> rence, because it is compelled by the *Celestial Body* to trace
> every passionate event to its cause until all are related and
> understood, turned into knowledge, made a part of itself.
> All that keeps the *Spirit* from its freedom may be compared
> to a knot that has to be untied or to an oscillation or a
> violence that must end in a return to equilibrium. [*AV,* 226]

The psychological acuity of the passage has been largely missed
because of the failure to grasp it as an analysis of self-mourning.
Like a Shakespearean hero before the moment of death, Yeats's
Spirit reviews the most intense experiences of its life, purges them
of the trivial and the circumstantial, and fits them into an aesthetic totality, before finally gaining its freedom. As when the
poet prepares for the ultimate encounter in "The Tower," "The
Circus Animals' Desertion," and "Man and the Echo," the
mourning mind rakes over the most passionate experiences of the
life, gradually detaching itself from them and fortifying itself. As
in "A Dialogue of Self and Soul" (there are direct verbal parallels
here) and "Vacillation," the mind can transform affect into
knowledge only by tracing the chain of causality that links each
passionate event to its origin.

The psychological activity of "The Soul in Judgment" is similar
to the recathexis and decathexis of one's life in Freud's description
of mourning, or the attempt to reconstruct and affirm one's life as
a totality in Heidegger's description of anticipatory resoluteness.
Freud expresses this process in terms of a psychic economy, as we
can see by modifying his concept of the "lost object" to include the

anticipated loss of the self—a form of loss that he often neglects. Withdrawing its attachments to the lost object, the mind slowly carries out the orders of reality-testing: "They are carried out bit by bit, at great expense of time and cathectic energy, and in the meantime the existence of the lost object is psychically prolonged. Each single one of the memories and expectations in which the libido is bound to the object is brought up and hyper-cathected, and detachment of the libido is accomplished in respect of it."[35] Yeats's poems of self-mourning focus more directly than most such Romantic lyrics on the events and accomplishments of the poet's life, hypercathecting and ultimately decathecting them. In several stages of its meditative progress, the Spirit's primary activity is repetition. In the Phantasmagoria, for example, the mind is able "to exhaust . . . emotion"; this is the stage when the life is "completed, for only that which is completed can be known and dismissed" (230). Similarly, in Heidegger's understanding of anticipatory resoluteness, Dasein keeps *repeating itself,* able at last to "'take back' everything," and attaining its "authentic potentiality-for-Being-a-whole."[36] In Yeats as in Heidegger and Nietzsche, this reconstruction of the life as a totality justifies it, makes of it an aesthetic whole, and ultimately frees it from categories of good and evil (*AV,* 232). Once the Spirit has been "purified" through repetition and reconstruction, the life *disappears*—in one of Yeats's favorite terms for the results of self-mourning (*AV,* 223–24). Much like authentic Dasein in Heidegger, and much like the mind after successful mourning in Freud, the Spirit in Yeats works through its grief for itself and finally becomes "free"—"All memory has vanished" (*AV,* 233). By stripping down these other descriptions of mourning and relating them to Yeats, I do not wish to obscure differences: Heidegger's analysis is part of a project in fundamental ontology, Freud's a description of economic redistributions in the unconscious. Nor would Yeats want to have anything to do with either account. But by bringing these alien texts into play with *A Vision,* we may release certain insights from their concealment in the esoteric trappings of Yeats's system.

If we read Book III of *A Vision* as an allegory of self-mourning, we must acknowledge that it describes this psychological process in wishful terms. It offers only one side of Yeats's view of dying—the more idealized side—whereas the poems are much more alive to the complexities and contradictions of self-mourning. In *A Vision* the individual can see his or her experience as a whole; this whole magnificently collapses in some of the lyrics—for example, when the rabbit's cry shatters the "one clear view" at the end of "Man and the Echo" (346). The overwhelming effort of the self-elegies is to fit the life into "a completed arc," but they can also be quite skeptical about such completeness. As Yeats states in *Estrangement*: "We artists . . . are, as seen from life, an artifice, an emphasis, an uncompleted arc perhaps. Those whom it is our business to cherish and celebrate are complete arcs. Because the life man sees is not the final end of things, the moment we attain to greatness of any kind by personal labour and will we become fragmentary, and find no task in active life which can use our finest faculties. . . . We see all [Romeo's] arc, for in literature we need completed things" (*Au*, 321–22).

Writing about oneself would surely complicate this dichotomy between the uncompleted arc of one's continuing life and the fictive character's completed arc. If poets need completed things, and yet their subject becomes the necessary incompleteness of their own lives, then as a genre, the self-elegy will be especially torn between closure and fragmentation. "It is even possible," Yeats states, "that being is only possessed completely by the dead" (*E&I*, 226). But since death alone unites becoming with "being," Yeats's self-elegies vacillate between a desire to keep life's horizon open and a desire to achieve the totality of being that comes with death.

POEMS OF SELF-MOURNING

Having multiplied and distinguished generic contexts for reading Yeats's self-elegies, we should also recognize the larger cultural and historical forces that would incline a late Romantic poet to mourn in the lyric his anticipated death. As we saw earlier, technological warfare informs Yeats's effort to construct heroic self-images out of his lyric encounters with death. Social and economic transformations, propelled in Ireland by the rise of a new middle class, further enhanced the lyric's promise as a space in which Yeats could establish his individuality against the backdrop of death. Like Wordsworth in the "Preface" to *Lyrical Ballads,* Yeats worries that life in cities "deafens or kills the passive meditative life" (*E&I,* 41). He also claims that the pressure of scientific "externality" is usurping the space of the mind; and he rebels against "the growing cohesiveness" of a world with "everybody thinking like everybody else" (*E&I,* 189; *Ex,* 423). The interiority of the lyric meditation on death, then, might offer refuge from the "pushing world" of the city, from the objectivity of science, and from the educational and economic leveling of differences among individuals (*E&I,* 224). As Adorno argues, the Romantic lyric defines its subjective being as something opposed to the reification of the marketplace, and as Adorno's examples indicate, the lyric self is therefore left in solitude before the approach of annihilation.[37] It invokes this annihilation, in turn, to intensify its condition of solitude. The self-elegiac lyric becomes a privileged space in which poets like Yeats, Rilke, and Stevens can invent their individuality in the mirror of death—an individuality antithetical to the debased self-as-object of the marketplace. Economically marginal, the late Romantic poet desperately attempts to sequester death as that which is emphatically his or her own, irrevocably beyond the ownership of the market.[38]

Furthermore, religion has traditionally regulated the dying person's responses to death; and Yeats, "very religious" but deprived since childhood of his youthful Protestantism, "made a new religion, almost an infallible church of poetic tradition" (*Au,* 77). The poetic traditions of Romanticism—itself a displaced Protestantism—function for Yeats much like religious codes for preparing to die; but his self-elegies fuse the divinity and death traditionally confronted in religious meditation:[39]

Now his wars on God begin;
At stroke of midnight God shall win.

[*"The Four Ages of Man,"* 288]

Yeats's self-elegies also bear traces of older religious traditions, such as *ars moriendi* and mortification; attempting to discover individuality in the mirror of death, they modernize the medieval notion of *speculum mortis,* which has been traced back to the eleventh century.[40] Yeats helps to transfer these practices and ideas from their more rigid codification in the religious sphere to the idiosyncrasies of the poetic. But by calling attention to Yeats's reliance on these cultural forms, and on various psycho-rhetorical devices, I hope to make clear that such preexisting structures shape his responses to death, including his impressively solitary struggle with its menace. No matter how personal Yeats's self-elegies become, they participate in larger patterns of human defense against mortality. And no matter how secular, they share with religion the often unconscious aim of rehearsing death to defeat it.

"The Tower"

Remolding the traditional iconography of the cosmic trial before death, Yeats delegates to himself all judicial roles— almighty judge, prosecutor, defense attorney, and plaintiff. This further internalization of the ultimate trial scene is evident as late as "Man and the Echo," where the poet relentlessly questions himself about his evil deeds, "stands in judgment on his soul," and then "dismisses all" (346). Already in the first major self-elegy, "The Tower" (1925), death harries the poet, pressing him to summon himself before himself, question, judge, and defend himself, justify, and ultimately surrender himself. Such multiplication of selves is a characteristic element of Yeats's self-elegiac defense against death. But death still threatens to retain its inscrutable power, so over the course of this self-elegy, Yeats devises other means of annexing death, such as showing it to be a product of words.

Writing after having suffered an illness and high blood pres-

sure, Yeats grapples in "The Tower" with how to acknowledge
death and dying and yet be their master. Let us begin to read the
poem closely with special attention to its responses to dying—
not in the narrow sense of the final agony but in the broader sense
of a gradual deathward decline. The poet laments old age and
skillfully dissociates himself from it:

> What shall I do with this absurdity—
> O heart, O troubled heart—this caricature,
> Decrepit age that has been tied to me
> As to a dog's tail?   [194]

By his willingness to stare at the fact of old age, apparently
without defenses, Yeats beguiles the reader. In his initial question, "What shall I do with this absurdity . . . ?" he already grants
himself authority over dying, as if he could determine its course,
dispose of old age as he wished. The poet's self-division is symp-
tomatic of the splitting of the ego characteristic of melancholia.[41]
More to the point, it is a rhetorical gesture that usefully implies
that the "I" of the poet is separable from the dying "absurdity." If
bodily decrepitude has merely "been tied" to the poet, then it is
no more than a detachable superfluity. And if the dying body has
the same relation to the poet as a "caricature" to an original, then
surely the speaker may live on without the shrunken simulacrum.

The poem goes on to prove the independence of the "Imagination" from the dying body by expounding high Romantic
arguments. Like Blake's Imagination returning from the Gates of
Death, Yeats's imagination has grown "stronger & stronger as
this Foolish Body decays."[42] The imagination gains strength by
being alienated from Ben Bulben, fishing, the natural world,
apparently contradicting the logic of the "Intimations Ode." But
the verb that Yeats uses to characterize the imagination—"expected"—belongs very much to the Wordsworthian concept of
the "Imagination," whose home is not with the visible, perish-
able world, but with "expectation," with "something evermore
about to be."[43] Yeats does concede that the imagination and the
body have at least some relation:

It seems that I must bid the Muse go pack,
Choose Plato and Plotinus for a friend
Until imagination, ear and eye,
Can be content with argument and deal
In abstract things; or be derided by
A sort of battered kettle at the heel.   [194]

Paraphrase almost makes these lines a Coleridgean bow to theology at a time of dejection: unless the poet gives up verse and embraces philosophy to mortify both the imagination and the senses, he will be unable to shut out the painful awareness of old age and death. But even as Yeats grudgingly accepts the project of mortification, his rhetoric again inverts the relation of ascendancy between himself and death: banishing the Muses and electing the philosophers, he superimposes willed action and choice upon his fate.

The primary rhetorical and psychic action of the poem is gradually to strengthen this inversion of death and choice, dying and decreeing. Having made limited concessions to being the bodily victim of old age, the plaintiff soon assumes the roles of judge and cross-examiner, or, in another vocabulary, magus and medium:

I pace upon the battlements and stare
On the foundations of a house, or where
Tree, like a sooty finger, starts from the earth;
And send imagination forth
Under the day's declining beam, and call
Images and memories
From ruin or from ancient trees,
For I would ask a question of them all.   [194–95]

Pacing upon the battlements and reflecting on mortality, Yeats would have us believe he is the new hero of Elsinore. His pose recalls a faintly ridiculous habit of his youth—"sometimes walking with an artificial stride in memory of Hamlet" (*Au*, 55). Dramatic posturing helps to get under control the self-centered pathos of the earlier section. The poet who had seemed trapped under the burden of old age now rises on a tide of active verbs: "pace," "stare," "send," "call," "ask." The potential victim has transformed himself into a magisterial questioner and summoner. In a more traditionally religious poem, such as "At Algeciras—a Meditation upon Death," God is the "Great Questioner" at the *hora mortis;* here, it is the poet himself (246).

Because the three memories conjured by the poet apparently lack a common denominator, they have caused much interpretive confusion. Once we recognize the self-elegy's underlying attempt to reverse the poet's passive relation to death and dying, we see that these disparate events all signify the poet's desired power over fate. In each case, language causes death or violence, as if to illustrate the proper chain of command between the poet and death. Mrs. French's *words* beget a violent act—the servant's clipping of a farmer's ears. Raftery's *song* leads to a death—the farmer's drowning in the bog during a futile search for the celebrated Mary Hynes. The Raftery story exemplifies the transformative power of verse: "So great a glory did the song confer" that men were "maddened by those rhymes" (195). Yeats's own *stories* of Red Hanrahan drive him to the supernatural women who terrify him and eventually condemn him to death.

But this last death is repressed in the self-elegy. Yeats has adduced two episodes as examples of the word's dominion over death, but in the movement toward the third such parable, death asserts itself over his unfolding words. Recounting the first time when Hanrahan goes to the imposing supernatural women, Yeats suddenly breaks off the narrative:

Hanrahan rose in frenzy there
And followed up those baying creatures towards—

O towards I have forgotten what—enough!   [196]

The thought of Hanrahan's inability to respond to the women is evidently too close to the terror of death that underlies the poem. The self-elegy screens out Hanrahan's all-too-relevant death—his

shameful impotence before the women and his later condemnation to death—with the somewhat forced but reassuring imagery
of dauntless military heroes, Yeats's predecessors in the tower.
Although Hanrahan is latently connected with the stories of Mrs.
French and Raftery by his association with death, the poet prefers to cast him as a promiscuous "lecher." As if to demonstrate a
semidivine strength, Yeats shows off his ability to manipulate
Hanrahan as a puppet. He brags,

> And I myself created Hanrahan
> And drove him drunk or sober through the dawn. . . .
>
> . . . .
>
> He stumbled, tumbled, fumbled to and fro. . . .   [196]

Once again, the poet—"troubled" and "derided" by intimations
of death—now positions himself as the one who does the troubling and deriding. His invulnerability to death seems dependent
on his capacity to deal death and violence to others—"For if I
triumph I must make men mad" (196).

We might pause further over the third death in the sequence of
memories, the death that is signified by a gap in the poem, or,
more literally, by a dash, a stanza break, a repetition, and a
nervous interjection: "towards— // O towards I have forgotten
what—enough!" The hounds lead Hanrahan toward a trial of
strength, a trial restaged in this very lyric's scene of judgment
before death, except that now the poet-figure has securely oc-
cupied all available roles. To understand the full significance of
this blank in the poem, we must recall that at the end of another
story, "The Twisting of the Rope," Yeats already recapitulates
Hanrahan's ritual trial. In this second version of Hanrahan's
encounter with the queen-woman and her associates, the women
deliver the verdict of death-in-life so energetically excluded from
the poem because too near its immediate anxieties: "he will find
no comfort in the love of the women of the earth to the end of life
and time, and the cold of the grave is in his heart for ever. It is
death he has chosen; let him die, let him die, let him die" (*Myth*,
233). No wonder the dying poet has "forgotten" what Hanrahan

encounters. Worried about the death that follows upon physical decrepitude, Yeats is unwilling to face directly this other kind of death—the living death of the love poet. In Yeats's dichotomous mythology of "the life" and "the work" (246), the full antithesis to a "life" of experiential and erotic fulfillment is often the death-like alienation that generates a poet's "Words," as in the poem that bears that title:

> I might have thrown poor words away
> And been content to live.   [90]

The two ritualistic trials of Hanrahan, in which he proves himself "weak" by his inability to rouse the beautiful queen-woman, suggest not only the castration anxiety that Freud equates with the fear of death but also the ominous possibility that the poet must be "castrated" to be productive, cut off from women that he may write about them (*Myth,* 221). Evading this thought, the poet of "The Tower" attempts to find in such severance from women one of the compensations of old age. Because both Raftery and Homer were "blind," they could construct ideal women that would make all men mad (195). So too the third love poet's blindness to woman—making her always the "woman lost"—is less a fearful death than the eternal life of the "imagination" (197). Unless we recognize the latent interconnection in the poem between the love poet's "death" and the physical "death" of old age, the relation between the poet's two questions is unreadable:

> Did all old men and women, rich and poor,
> Who trod upon these rocks or passed this door,
> Whether in public or in secret rage
> As I do now against old age?
>
> . . . .
>
> Does the imagination dwell the most
> Upon a woman won or woman lost?   [197]

As he awaits the final death of the body, the poet wonders obliquely whether it has been worth being dead alive—worth trading life for the death-in-life of the imagination.[44]

We later reach the culmination of the effort to invert the relation between the poet and death. So far, every step toward an acknowledgment of death has been checked by a countermovement
toward denial. Now the poet grants that the time has come to
write his will; but here again, the act of writing the will becomes,
happily, less a concession to death than a defiance of its authority:

> It is time that I wrote my will;
> I choose upstanding men
> That climb the streams. . . .
>
> . . . .
>   I declare
> They shall inherit my pride,
> The pride of people that were
> Bound neither to Cause nor to State,
> Neither to slaves that were spat on,
> Nor to the tyrants that spat. . . .   [198]

The juxtaposition of "will" and "choose" brings out the root
sense of the term "will"—a statement of one's choices from
beyond the grave. In keeping with his self-epitaphic mode, Yeats
asserts his power even in death to choose, to dictate, to decree.
He allows that he is dying, but in that rhetorical miracle so
characteristic of Yeats, he achieves an active relationship of freedom toward death, as if inscribing and circumscribing that which
resists all such determination. The inheritors whom he chooses—
proud people "Bound" to no one—similarly refuse subservience
to any superior power; they resemble him at this moment of
apparent choice. But one has to wonder why the poet would
need to work up such declamatory rant if his power over death
were as certain as he claims.

Having glanced at himself in the image of a swan singing "his
last song," the poet soon reaches a new level of bravura about
being death's author:

> And I declare my faith:
> I mock Plotinus' thought
> And cry in Plato's teeth,

Death and life were not
Till man made up the whole,
Made lock, stock and barrel
Out of his bitter soul,
Aye, sun and moon and star, all,
And further add to that
That, being dead, we rise,
Dream and so create
Translunar Paradise.   [198]

The rhetoric of defiance leads us back to a distant literary ances-
tor: Milton's Satan. Like Satan, the poet would defy the Father,
but now the god defied is death. "The mind is its own place, and
in itself," Yeats proclaims, can make a life of death, a death of
life.[45] This refusal to mortify the visionary or the sensible faculties is a Romantic declaration of "faith" in the eternal imagination. But the word "faith" is hyperbolic, for if this were a secure
faith, the poet would be unlikely to protest so much. In this
stanza, he attempts to override the terrifying discontinuity between life and death by means of a "whole" or an "all" that would
incorporate both terms. He selects a curious though commonplace image for this totality, and it needs to be explicated: "lock,
stock and barrel."[46] Why use a tripartite gun to represent the
imagination's superiority rather than, say, leaf, blossom, and
bole? The power in question here is the poet's power over death,
and the gun suggests that "man" makes for himself the power to
deliver death, just as the destructive words of the poet earlier
figure his desired sovereignty over death.

    As the self-elegy modulates into a darker mood, everything
that Yeats has declared to be man-made, controllable, or insignifi-
cant, creeps back into the purview of the troubled mind:

Now shall I make my soul,
Compelling it to study
In a learned school
Till the wreck of body,
Slow decay of blood,

Testy delirium
Or dull decrepitude,
Or what worse evil come—
The death of friends, or death
Of every brilliant eye
That made a catch in the breath—
Seem but the clouds of the sky
When the horizon fades;
Or a bird's sleepy cry
Among the deepening shades.   [199–200]

As Jeffares observes, the first line means, in Irish usage, "to prepare for death," but its suggestion of remaking the soul is also an apt description of *how* the poet prepares for death in this self-elegy.[47] He has attempted to prepare for death by making the soul into a stronger soul—making it sovereign over death and dying. This self-strengthening allows the poet finally to decathect his past, his body, and his friends, conceding at last that decay and death may be beyond the dominion of the imagination. Having reviewed and reassimilated his life and attachments, he can now, as at the end of several of the self-elegies, surrender them. The final image of the sleepy bird fading out of view is an elegiac figure for the disappearance of the poet and his friends. This image, together with the image of the clouds in the sky, rejoins a tradition of Romantic self-valediction that leads from the end of "To Autumn," where "gathering swallows twitter in the skies," to the end of "Sunday Morning," where pigeons,

> in the isolation of the sky,
> . . . .
>   sink
> Downward to darkness, on extended wings.[48]

"A Dialogue of Self and Soul"

We have seen various discontinuities between voices in the self-elegies. In "The Tower," for example, the poet strad-

dles the gap between the vulnerable, aging victim and the testamentary, postmortem judge. In "A Dialogue of Self and Soul"
(1927), Yeats schematizes the relation between these discourses
by mapping them onto opposed characters in a psychomachia. As
before, the splitting of this melancholic "man" is a response to the
crucial given of the poem: he is "Long past his prime" (235). The
two speakers set forth opposed programs for dying. According to
the Soul, dying should be regulated by a Yeatsian version of
mortification: one must concentrate on the "darkness" of death,
imitating as nearly as possible that future state. In contrast, the
Self is provoked by dying to reaffirm natural existence. The Self
reviews the life not to deny the imagination and the senses but to
reassert their ultimate worth. Yet, any general statement of each
persona's views misses the deeper function of the poem's dramatic configuration. In my view, the binary pair, Self/Soul, is a
consoling and defensive alternative to the more troubling pair,
Life/Death. By referring the nondramatic opposition of being
and absence to two perspectives within the human subject, the
poem draws an unthinkable binarism into the penumbra of articulate experience.[49]

We begin our examination of the poem's struggle with death
by trying to determine the function of the Soul in the self-elegy.
The Soul's rhetoric is typical of meditative poems of mortification. Commanding the mind to focus on the difficult way to
purification—reminiscent of the "steepe" way to Hierusalem in
Spenser—the Soul enacts this ascent through ever higher and
more distant images of death, from the broken battlement to the
breathless air and the hidden pole.[50] In the paradox shared by
earlier poetic versions of the ars moriendi, the poet commands
his mind to "Set" and "Fix" upon that which can be neither
located in space nor limited by trope:

> Fix every wandering thought upon
> That quarter where all thought is done:
> Who can distinguish darkness from the soul?   [234]

Traditionally, such poets as Herbert and Proctor would "mark" or "see" concrete images of death, specifically its refuse: ashes, bones, and skulls.[51] Less restrictive, Yeats's spatial figure—"That quarter where all thought is done"—still places death and circumscribes it. The Soul's aim is to think nothingness, achieving an anticipatory union with it. But the Soul proves itself trope-bound; it subverts its aim by "wandering" from stair to battle-ment, air to star, the pole to the quarter—trope insinuating itself into each attempt to get beyond trope. And in its larger structure the poem continues to disrupt the Soul's aim of mortification, "wandering / To this and that and t'other thing"—a wandering dramatized by the to-and-fro movement between Self and Soul (235). Even the poem's dramatic form vindicates the Self.

Although it fails, the Soul's attempt to assimilate "darkness" and the "night" is another manifestation of Yeats's desire to introject death. If no one "can distinguish darkness from the soul," then death is no longer alien and unknowable but a human impulse toward self-annihilation. Canceling moral and epistemological binarisms (which make poetry possible), the Soul's achievement of inner death is beatific:

> . . . man is stricken deaf and dumb and blind,
> For intellect no longer knows
> *Is* from the *Ought,* or *Knower* from the *Known*—
> That is to say, ascends to Heaven;
> Only the dead can be forgiven;
> But when I think of that my tongue's a stone.   [235]

Nevertheless, with the Soul's every step toward death, the Self refastens its grip on life. This rhythm of the poem resembles the inner battle between Eros and Thanatos that Freud describes, a resemblance that follows from both writers' internalization of death: "It is as though the life of the organism moved with a vacillating rhythm. One group of instincts rushes forward so as to reach the final aim of life as swiftly as possible; but when a particular stage in the advance has been reached, the other group jerks back to a certain point to make a fresh start and so prolong the journey."⁵² In spite of the Soul's drive toward death, the Self keeps fixing its attention on the blatantly phallic sword, its scabbard bound with "embroidery, torn / From some court-lady's dress" (235).

What does this movement and countermovement suggest about the underlying relation between the two speakers? Although Bloom correctly observes that there is no overt dialogue between the speakers, their relation offers solace because, unlike the relation between the poet and death, it allows for interchange and reciprocity.⁵³ The Soul comments moralistically on the Self's preoccupation with "love and war," and the Self responds to the Soul largely in terms suited to the Soul. Just as the image-bound Soul differs from the Self less than it would have us believe, so too the Self differs from the Soul less than may be initially apparent. True, the Self sets its own language of the body ("my knees," "court-lady's dress," "Heart's purple") against the Soul's abstract "scorn," and sets its rhetoric of history ("centuries," "tattered," "faded," "Five hundred years ago") against the Soul's ahistorical "darkness." But the Self is also anxious to answer the Soul's exclusive claim to the sacred—Sato's blade is "consecrated"— and to timeless endurance—the blade is "still as it was . . . / Unspotted by the centuries." Moreover, the last stanza is the Self's direct, secular counterpart to the spiritual beatitude, a beatitude that left the Soul's tongue a stone: casting out "remorse," the Self is flooded with "sweetness" (236). These underlying links between the contrasting speakers signify the poem's quiet replacement of the unmediable opposition between death and life with a difficult but mediable opposition between two perspectives on death and life.

This substitution of Soul/Self for Death/Life is not the poem's only masterful trick, as we see from the Self's primary achievement in the second half of the poem. Briefly stated, the Self convinces itself and us that it has heroically accepted and defeated the challenge of death, when it has done nothing of the kind. Instead, the Self brilliantly, and slyly, replaces death with its

antithetical opposite, making us think that its acceptance of life is
a stirring feat of the utmost courage. Let us trace the evolution of
this turn in the lyric, a psycho-rhetorical inversion that has been
obscured by excessive submission to Yeats's metaphysic of reincarnation. Whether or not we recall the biographical seed of the
poem—Yeats's battle with an illness that congested his lungs and
left one bleeding—the Soul's attempt at mortification and its
suggestion that the poet is "Long past his prime" make us expect
that the Self too will have to respond to death. Therefore, when
the Self rebuts the Soul's promise of deliverance "from the crime
of death and birth" by claiming the right "to commit the crime
once more," the crime in question may well seem to be "death"
rather than "birth." But by the second section of the poem, the
substitutive progression is complete, from death, to death and
birth, and finally, to birth and life:

> A living man is blind and drinks his drop.
> What matter if the ditches are impure?
> What matter if I live it all once more?
> Endure that toil of growing up;
> The ignominy of boyhood; the distress
> Of boyhood changing into man;
> The unfinished man and his pain
> Brought face to face with his own clumsiness. . . .
>
> [235–36]

Of course the dying poet is willing to "live it all once more"!
Blindness is the only lingering indication here that the living man
being embraced is a substitute for the occluded dead man—the
real problem in the poem. And yet, for these rites of self-mourning
to move us, we must possess at least an unconscious awareness
that death as death—not rebirth into life—is the fundamental
occasion of the stanzas, though they triumphantly repress it. The
poet "dreams back" (in Yeats's terminology), "hypercathects" (in
Freud's), or "repeats" (in Heidegger's) the painful stages of
growing up. He recasts them into a qualified totality—a narrative
that ends in an "unfinished man." The narrative achieves a com-

pleteness sufficient for self-forgiving to take place, the self-forgiving that comes when the life can be read as the composite of all its parts. If "Only the dead can be forgiven," then Yeats implies in the declaration "forgive myself the lot!" that he may have taken a postmortem perspective on himself as a complete but dead man.

Replacing the necessity of death with the chosen act of mourning his life, Yeats chants:

> I am content to live it all again
> And yet again, if it be life to pitch
> Into the frog-spawn of a blind man's ditch,
> A blind man battering blind men;
> Or into that most fecund ditch of all,
> The folly that man does
> Or must suffer, if he woos
> A proud woman not kindred of his soul.   [236]

The joyous energy and heroic rhetoric of this stanza so seduce us into forgetting death (earlier the "darkness" where "all thought is done") that we momentarily believe the poet has fought and won the ultimate battle. Yet the poet facing death is doubtless willing to embrace life again. And he is doubtless willing, above all, to embrace "that most fecund ditch of all"—the frustrated love that is one of the most fecund sources of his poetry. The image of diving into a generative, womblike ditch is bound to be more consoling than the image it subliminally replaces—falling into a lifeless grave. The poem's extraordinary internalization and repression of death make possible the ecstatic freeing of libido at the end, as we saw in chapter 2. Yeats triumphs by making us believe that in choosing to live again, he has accepted death; and that in choosing the Self over the Soul, he has embraced his finitude. Freud, whose mythology of the drives may also represent an effort to internalize and master death, states precisely the achievement of this self-elegy: "Here again there has been a wishful reversal. Choice stands in the place of necessity, of destiny. In this way man overcomes death, which he has recognized intellectually. No greater triumph of wish-fulfilment is conceivable. A choice is made where in reality there is obedience to a compulsion."[54] What is chosen in Yeats's poem is not a thing of terror but the most desirable thing of all for a man "Long past his prime"—life itself.

"Vacillation"

In both "The Tower" and "A Dialogue of Self and Soul," Yeats mourns his life by reviewing it and shaping it into a coherent self-image—a stronghold against dispersal. The re-cathexis of self in "Vacillation" (1931–32) follows the temporal pattern that Yeats mythologizes as "the *Return*," in which "the *Spirit* must live through past events in the order of their occurrence": the worldly ambition of youth, the midlife crisis of "the fortieth winter," the brief ecstasy of his "fiftieth year," and so forth (249–253). But Yeats superimposes on the apparent linearity of the narrative, with its onward rush toward death, a to-and-fro movement between what we have come to know as the Self and the Soul, carpe diem and contemptus mundi, tragic joy and self-pity. He attempts to show that death and life are no more than opposing human responses to them: sorrow and affirmation. Once again bifurcating the self, Yeats sets the lively interchange between selves against the impossibility of dialogue with death. Reinforcing the odelike turn and counterturn between affective stances, he moves the poem back and forth between antithetical images. Take, for example, the mediating dialectic between flame on the one hand—*brand, flaming breath, glittering flame, body . . . blazed, sunlight, Isaiah's coal, the simplicity of fire*—and foliage on the other—*green / Abounding foliage, lush leaf, Lethean foliage, branches of the night and day*. These ritualistic oscillations in stance and image are the self-elegy's structural defense against headlong movement toward the fated endpoint.

Elsewhere, Yeats defines "the form of . . . life itself": it "turns, now here, now there, a whirling and a bitterness"—a turning or troping common to both life and poetry (*AV*, 52). Title and form align this poem with life, but death is its point of departure:

> Between extremities
> Man runs his course;
> A brand, or flaming breath,
> Comes to destroy
> All those antinomies
> Of day and night;
> The body calls it death,
> The heart remorse.
> But if these be right
> What is joy?   [249–50]

This initial bifurcation already diminishes death by making it a perspective of the terrified body, known to the grieving heart as remorse. If we have any doubts that the destructive "brand, or flaming breath" is an image for death, the abundance of literary associations can help us out. Partly an inversion of Jahweh's life-endowing breath, the image alludes principally to both the "flaming brand" that shuts Adam and Eve into a world of mortality and out of their happy seat, and to the "brand from heaven" that Lear promises for anyone that parts him from Cordelia.[55] But from this bleak initial intimation of finitude, the poet turns to an elegiac quest for consolations—for sources of the "joy" that is Yeats's characteristic reaction-formation against anxiety.

The poem's counterassertion against death is based upon the two substitutions we teased out of Yeats's other self-elegies, although they are developed here with a baroque multiplicity: the substitution of a mediable binarism for the binarism of death and life, and the substitution of choice for fate:

> A tree there is that from its topmost bough
> Is half all glittering flame and half all green
> Abounding foliage moistened with the dew;
> And half is half and yet is all the scene;
> And half and half consume what they renew,
> And he that Attis' image hangs between
> That staring fury and the blind lush leaf
> May know not what he knows, but knows not grief.   [250]

Let us consider the first type of substitution. In the earlier stanza the brand or flaming breath comes to destroy all antinomies; but now it is no more than one side of an antinomy—the flaming top of the miraculous tree of the *Mabinogion* (*E&I*, 176). Instead of the negation of all contraries, death has become merely a positive "half," and both halves "renew" rather than destroy one another. Moreover, the poet fastens on top of this consoling image two more images that mediate death and life: a dying and reviving god, Attis, and a poet-priest who uses Attis' effigy to enact death and resurrection.[56] These rows of mediable opposites override ever more completely the underlying, unbridgeable binarism of existence and nothingness. As Lévi-Strauss argues, the rows of opposites grow "spiral-wise," seeking by repetition to overcome a fundamental contradiction.[57] The second substitution—choice for fate—is also visible in this stanza. As Yeats knew from Frazer, both Attis and the priest who imitates him castrate themselves.[58] This self-immolation allows the potential victim of death to believe momentarily that he is himself willing and controlling his own final destruction. Alfred Nutt, another comparative anthropologist familiar to Yeats, says that the participant in such a ritual felt himself temporarily "pass out of the mortal into the immortal"—the aim of what Yeats calls "the little ritual of his verse" (*E&I*, 202).[59]

Performing a rite that seems to incorporate death into life, the priest "knows not grief." He possesses the manic joy, the release from mourning and melancholia, sought by the poet. But in the next section of the poem and in several later stanzas, the poet lapses into the bitter animosity of melancholia. Contrary to the visionary mode, the tone now becomes homiletic, angry, and sarcastic, as the speaker offers not only ironic advice—"Get all the gold and silver that you can, / Satisfy ambition"—but also humorless, misogynist "maxims"—"All women dote upon an idle man . . ." (250). These attacks disguise self-pity, much in the manner of Lear's curses, and Lear is appropriately echoed again when the speaker reflects on the insufficiency of "children's gratitude or woman's love."[60] Miraculously transforming this bitter-

ness over being unloved into the seemingly joyful relinquishment
of women, the poet-warrior joins the company of such Zarathus-
tran "men as come / Proud, open-eyed and laughing to the tomb"
(250). Free from desire, the poet can start to fulfill his self-
exhortation: "Begin the preparation for your death." Self-suf-
ficient, he can test every work of his "hands" by the standards of
the male warrior ethos.

But soon, the proud denials of dependency bring to the surface the vulnerabilities they would suppress:

> Things said or done long years ago,
> Or things I did not do or say
> But thought that I might say or do,
> Weigh me down, and not a day
> But something is recalled,
> My conscience or my vanity appalled.   [251]

The anger toward the world has turned inward. Instead of surrendering everything unheroic and laughing to the tomb, the
poet is haunted by shameful memories of inadequacy. The triple
repetition, "said or done," "do or say," "say or do," mimetically
suggests the rotations of words and actions in his guilty conscience.

The alienation of the poet from his own words and deeds
reverses not only his Nietzschean affirmations of his "work" but
also his manic repossession of himself through his own book:

> My fiftieth year had come and gone,
> I sat, a solitary man,
> In a crowded London shop,
> An open book and empty cup
> On the marble table-top.
>
> While on the shop and street I gazed
> My body of a sudden blazed;
> And twenty minutes more or less
> It seemed, so great my happiness,
> That I was blessed and could bless.   [251]

The moment of narcissistic beatitude in this poem is a moment of freedom from anxiety about death (the "brand" that he dreads) and from the melancholic self-division akin to death (his regret for earlier words and deeds). Yeats describes this experience in *"Anima Mundi"*: "At certain moments, always unforeseen, I become happy, most commonly when at hazard I have opened some book of verse. Sometimes it is my own verse when, instead of discovering new technical flaws, I read with all the excitement of the first writing. Perhaps I am sitting in some crowded restaurant, the open book beside me, or closed, my excitement having over-brimmed the page. . . . I have no longer any fears or any needs; I do not even remember that this happy mood must come to an end" (*Myth,* 364–65). The prose version brings out two elements of the experience: that reading his own verse is the most important instance; and that the self-communion banishes time and fear. The secular transcendence therefore presupposes the estrangement of the poet from his own words—the ordinary condition from which he is momentarily released. It also presupposes the predominance of "fears," the poet always grieving for his projected self-loss. Directed backward to the past and forward to death, this psychic energy is suddenly made superfluous when the poet achieves transparent access to himself through his own words. Freud observes that melancholia has the remarkable "tendency to change round into mania," and Yeats formalizes this tendency in the many turns and counterturns of his self-elegy.[61] The poem's ritualistic oscillation harnesses the frightening nonrelation between being and nonbeing to contrary affects within the mind.

The lyric justifies its supersession of mourning and melancholia by making the counterintuitive claim that all song surrenders the past to oblivion:

From man's blood-sodden heart are sprung
Those branches of the night and day
Where the gaudy moon is hung.
What's the meaning of all song?
'Let all things pass away.'   [252]

Song bids farewell to all external reality because the heart contains the source of reality within itself. The antinomies that spring from the human heart are, by implication, not only "night and day" but also the principal binarism that underlies the poem—death and life. Like the moon hung between night and day, this song mediates what seemed at the outset to be an insuperable contradiction, humanizing and internalizing it.

The next stanza confirms the interiority of death and life in its stichomythia between Heart and Soul. Miniaturizing the dialogue of Self and Soul, it presents a choice between the mute eternal life gained by mortification and the poet's inevitable lot—secular existence. The poet's answer is again predictable. But what has happened to death? What about the brand that hangs over all such antinomies? True, the final response of the poet is to accept the necessity of his own death,

> though heart might find relief
> Did I become a Christian man and choose for my belief
> What seems most welcome in the tomb. . . .   [252]

But the poem's conversion of death into a mere "half" of life and displacement of death and life onto other antinomies have so effectively canceled the initial image of the "brand, or flaming breath" that death hardly seems worrisome after all. Concerned at the time of writing the poem that he might "take to religion," Yeats uses his own poetic ritual to master dread, rendering traditional belief superfluous (L, 788). For these reasons, the poet can maintain in the last stanza a tone much like Herbert's—self-assured and whimsical before death—even as he bids Christian salvation farewell. In spite of all the heroic protestations of *amor fati*, he also seems at the poem's close to back into a belief in immortality. He accepts, above all, Christian miracles that are emblematic of a triumph over death and decay:

> The body of Saint Teresa lies undecayed in tomb,
> Bathed in miraculous oil, sweet odours from it come,
> Healing from its lettered slab.   [252]

As in the earlier self-elegies, the poet succeeds in making us believe that he has courageously resigned himself to death, when he has instead erased the whole question of death. He has replaced the image of his own threatened body with Saint Teresa's undecaying body, healing the anticipatory wound of death by means of his own lettered slab.

"The Circus Animals' Desertion"

In the self-elegies we have discussed so far, reflexivity is a governing trope. In the mirror of death, or speculum mortis, Yeats invents his self-relation. But we might ask what distinguishes Yeats's self-elegiac use of this consoling trope from its many Romantic incarnations, particularly when we reach a poem that is obviously of high Romantic descent, "The Circus Animals' Desertion" (circa 1937–38). Although this poem derives from such Romantic songs of "Despair" (an earlier draft's title) as the "Intimations Ode" and "Dejection," these odes disguise a pivotal question of literary self-mourning—namely, the relation of poets to their own work—whereas Yeats's self-elegy brings it to the fore. By recasting the figure of self-relation as his relation to his own writing, Yeats departs from much Romantic practice but joins the broader tradition of authorial self-valedictions. From a modern poet's perspective, the tradition would have to include not only the invocations we have noted but also Chaucer's dismissal of his secular works in the "Retraction," Herbert's melancholy valediction "Farewell, sweet phrases, lovely metaphors," and the Romantic reading of Prospero's vow, "I'll drown my book."[62] Yeats's review of three works as synecdoches for his oeuvre closely prefigures Stevens's self-elegiac reconsideration of

That poem about the pineapple, the one
About the mind as never satisfied,

The one about the credible hero, the one
About summer. . . .[63]

For Yeats and Stevens, the consoling review of one's work leads, nevertheless, to a painful awareness of discontinuity in time and to questions about the human cost of such defensive attachment to one's own language. Has the price of defeating death's finality been a life of death? Yeats guiltily acknowledges:

> Players and painted stage took all my love
> And not those things that they were emblems of.   [347]

Stevens asks with astonishing directness:

> I wonder, have I lived a skeleton's life,
> As a disbeliever in reality,
>
> A countryman of all the bones in the world?

As in the literary testaments of Chaucer, Herbert, Stevens, and others, Yeats gazes down vertically on the work of a lifetime, hoping to fulfill the self-injunction of a rejected stanza: "prepare to die." To understand the completed work, he must disentangle himself from the necessarily mystified act of composition:

> I sought a theme and sought for it in vain,
> I sought it daily for six weeks or so.
> Maybe at last being but a broken man
> I must be satisfied with my heart, although
> Winter and summer till old age began
> My circus animals were all on show,
> Those stilted boys, that burnished chariot,
> Lion and woman and the Lord knows what.   [346–47]

The phrase "old age" takes us back to "The Tower," but there the author distances himself from the "caricature" of the body, whereas he now withdraws his psychic investments from his poems or "circus animals." Yeats indicates his remove from his works with the dismissive phrase "the Lord knows what," implying that he does not. He elevates himself above his creations by reducing them to mechanical, toylike figures, pleasing only to the immature mind. However painful, the self-parody is also solacing; it transforms literary impotence from a torment into a measure of the poet's maturity.

The recathexis and decathexis of memories in "The Tower," of the stages of growing up in "A Dialogue of Self and Soul," and of moments of dejection and bliss separated by ten-year intervals in "Vacillation," is rewound in this poem around three of the poet's narrative and dramatic pieces: *The Wanderings of Oisin, The Countess Cathleen,* and *On Baile's Strand.* According to Bloom, we ought not to demur at Yeats's choice of these "three crucial works."[64] But what is the principle of selection? Why should the poet who considers himself primarily a craftsman of lyrics steer away from his shorter poems? Unlike his lyrics, his longer stories allow him to demonstrate an ascendancy over himself. Yeats suggests that, at the time of composition, these longer works permitted him to imagine he was getting outside himself; but now he is anxious to overcome that pretense and resubjectivize their meaning. Now he can strip his stories of their apparent self-sufficiency by showing them to be covert lyrics—subjective and expressive—which have all aspired to be like the present work. In his apparent state of weakness, he can lay claim to the power of self-demystification. By reinterpreting his work, Yeats does much more than the first question implies:

> What can I but enumerate old themes,
> First that sea-rider Oisin led by the nose
> Through three enchanted islands, allegorical dreams,
> Vain gaiety, vain battle, vain repose,
> Themes of the embittered heart, or so it seems,
> That might adorn old songs or courtly shows;
> But what cared I that set him on to ride,
> I, starved for the bosom of his faery bride?   [347]

Having lost the ability to sublimate and 'fictionalize' desire, the poet demonstrates several compensatory powers. One is the power of literary exegesis, for he decodes the specific, "allegorical" meanings of the islands. Another is self-psychoanalysis: he interprets the formal "shows" and heroic quests as disguises for his narrative's real wish-fulfillment—the fulfillment in fantasy of his longing for a "faery bride." To counter the danger of the imagination's death, he also displays his continuing prowess by manipulating and satirizing his earlier work. Having delighted in bullying the diminished Hanrahan in "The Tower," he now makes the heroic Oisin another puppet, "led by the nose." In "A Coat" he overcomes himself by taking off his embroidered coat of mythologies; now the poet's early language again seems old-fashioned, allegorically estranged from its tenor—the word "adorn" suggesting negatively the authentic inwardness that Yeats habitually seeks in his rites of self-renewal.

But these gestures of demystification may amount to a remystification, since they belong, ultimately, to Yeats's myth of self-remaking. By burying his former selves and generating himself anew, Yeats seems to gain authority over his own dying and reviving. In this poem his self-purgation takes on a specifically psychobiographical form.[65] He offers two psychoanalytic views of his art: the author satisfies an unfocused desire for women by creating and loving his own fiction (Niamh); and, according to the "counter-truth," he uses a fiction to assuage his focused but frustrated desire for a specific woman (Maud Gonne). Both self-analyses present the imagination as compensating for unsatisfied desire:

> And then a counter-truth filled out its play,
> 'The Countess Cathleen' was the name I gave it,
> She, pity-crazed, had given her soul away
> But masterful Heaven had intervened to save it.
> I thought my dear must her own soul destroy
> So did fanaticism and hate enslave it,
> And this brought forth a dream and soon enough
> This dream itself had all my thought and love.   [347]

This story of aesthetically supplanting the beloved is akin to the myth of Pygmalion: the poet devises a representation so good that it blots out the original. Both the poet and the mythical sculptor fabricate an imaginary beloved not to reproduce the inadequate original but to replace it. In Yeats's version of the story, the poet dreams up an ideal woman, rendering the living woman superfluous. Outdone by the verbal construct, the fanatical woman no longer seems to exist. The poet, in effacing her, has appropriated the female power of origination. Ovid's Pygmalion, in love with his own work, has much in common with Ovid's Narcissus; and Yeats also emphasizes that he loves his own dream—a mediating blank through which to channel self-love.[66] The relevance of the mythical subtext to the poem's immediate occasion should be clear: fearing literary impotence and death, the poet pictures himself giving birth to an aesthetic construct that replaces a constraining reality. Within the generic context of the self-elegy, then, the replacement of reality by a liberating dream signifies the author's ability to escape limitation, to manipulate fate, and to effect elegiac substitution.

As self-parody gives way to the greater intimacy of this third stanza and the next, the poet is no longer casting off his work but searching it for compensatory indications of art's independence from reality. "Art is art because it is not nature," according to one of Yeats's favorite maxims (*Au,* 185). The sharper the division between "a dream" and "my dear," between "art" and "nature," between "the work" and "the life," the more the word must be able to persist in the absence of its referent—a referent that is finally in this self-elegy the poet himself:

> And when the Fool and Blind Man stole the bread
> Cuchulain fought the ungovernable sea;
> Heart mysteries there, and yet when all is said
> It was the dream itself enchanted me:
> Character isolated by a deed
> To engross the present and dominate memory.
> Players and painted stage took all my love
> And not those things that they were emblems of.   [347]

The dream, the character, the player, the stage, and the emblem—these elements of artifice all seem to stand outside the personal history. They form a *nunc stans* that is able to "engross the present" and transcend the horizons of past and future. They are "not those things that they" signify; the representations re-place the things re-presented, much as the dream of the beloved occluded the original. By the same logic, this self-elegy represents the "self" only by replacing it with a completed and fictive "char-acter." We recall that Yeats distinguishes between the necessarily "uncompleted arc" of an artist's life and the "complete arcs" of fictive characters. Here, the poet can be both a living fragment and an aesthetic totality only by "killing" himself—by dying of his own will into the artifice of eternity.

The relation between aesthetic completion and the sprawling panoply is the subject of the final stanza:

> Those masterful images because complete
> Grew in pure mind but out of what began?
> A mound of refuse or the sweepings of a street,
> Old kettles, old bottles, and a broken can,
> Old iron, old bones, old rags, that raving slut
> Who keeps the till. Now that my ladder's gone
> I must lie down where all the ladders start
> In the foul rag and bone shop of the heart.   [347–48]

Here, we may think, Yeats is at last trying not to outdo death but to accept it—accept the descent into matter and dispersal, into everything from which aesthetic form has shielded him. And indeed, there is a real difference from earlier poems in the steady gaze at oblivion, the willingness not to hide behind heroic taunts, and the apparent refusal of all transcendence. Having reviewed some of his work's "complete" images, the poet abandons them, joining himself to the incomplete and the temporal—the world in which everything is "Old," "old," "broken," "old," "old," "old." But this descent is itself part of the myth that the poem has carefully structured. Within the context of the poem's bifurcation of work and life, or "emblems" and "things," the poet mytholo-gizes death as the crossing from one to the other, from the signifier to the signified. This aesthetic myth integrates death into the domain of poetic experience: death here means for the poet to join himself with the "things" that have been supplanted by the "emblems" of his poetry, things including the urban and the material. Nor should it surprise us to find a woman—now as "that raving slut"—among the "things" effaced by Yeats's poetry and rejoined in death. Death becomes a linguistic or poetic event, a shift from the figurative to the literal. It is not a movement into an alien terminus but a rejoining of origins—the multifarious world from which the poems "began" before they left it behind. The last word of the poem, "heart," suggests that the task of self-mourning has succeeded indeed, replacing the mortal poet with a traditional elegiac synecdoche.

"Man and the Echo"

There are several contenders for Yeats's definitive death poem. "Under Ben Bulben" had long stood at the end of the "Lyrical" poems, where it seemed a swollen and unsubtle valediction, but the newer editions follow Yeats's design and place "Politics" at the end. By contrast with the rigidly epitaphic discourse of "Under Ben Bulben," "Politics" flouts outrageously the norms of death poetry. *Respice finem,* the tradition had commanded, but Yeats responds that he cannot fasten his thoughts on death and calamity as long as he is still full of desire:

> How can I, that girl standing there,
> My attention fix . . . ?   [348]

The poem deliberately inverts the programmatic meditation on death. Instead of moving from a brief *memory* of the worldly past, to an *understanding* of its errors and temptations, to a final assertion of the *will*—surrendering the world and embracing God—the speaker considers the possibility of moral action only to reject it outright and reassert the sway of lust.[67] Rather than decathect the life, he gives in to what the ars moriendi books had warned was the final temptation of the dying: *avaritia,* the passionate love of persons or things.[68] Dismayed by the overbearing solemnity of "Under Ben Bulben" and the frivolously antifeminist, antipolitical "Politics," recent readers have tended to prefer "Cuchulain Comforted" or "The Circus Animals' Desertion" as *the* death poem. Because most of Yeats's strong poems are in some sense death poems, there are indeed many candidates, but among them, "Man and the Echo" (1938) is assuredly one of the best.

Yeats again adopts the dialogue form, now as the literary device of the echo. Herbert's "Heaven," like Yeats's poem, has both an echo and an eschatological focus. It is the penultimate lyric of *The Temple,* and Yeats wanted his echo-poem to be followed by only two other lyrics. But Herbert uses the echo for entirely different purposes, and the contrasts are telling. The echo in Herbert's poem offers catechistic responses, educating the questioner by leading him to *Light, Joy, Leisure, Ever.* But if Herbert's echo is the voice of God, Yeats's is the voice of God as Thanatos. Its two injunctions lead the questioner not to Light but to final darkness: "Lie down and die," and "Into the night." Many of Yeats's self-elegies, as we have seen, adopt the aggressive and hortatory voice of paternal authority; but here Yeats truncates the role of the rocky voice, preferring Hamlet's uncertain, filial rhetoric to Lear's rant—a preference most obvious in the questions about the afterlife and the allusion to a "bodkin." The major speaker of this poem is not one of Yeats's postmortem voices; he is only a

> *Man.* In a cleft that's christened Alt
>   Under broken stone I halt
>   At the bottom of a pit
>   That broad noon has never lit,
>   And shout a secret to the stone.   [345]

The spatial structure of the scene is noteworthy. Instead of declaiming to us from the broken battlement of the tower or from atop the ship carpenter's boiler, this speaker stands at the *bottom* of a mountain gash, the stony father rising above him vertically, as in the Romantic scenes of oedipal confrontation in "Mont Blanc" and the boating episode of *The Prelude.* Alt bears as its name the Irish word for cliff—a name that also resonates with the Latin *altus* (high, deep, or ancient) and the German *alt* (old). As in "Lapis Lazuli," the speaker defines himself in relation to an anti-self of stone, but now, instead of struggling to overcome the stone, he speaks in the confessional language of a guilty son.

Not a single question makes its way into the muscular and homiletic language of "Under Ben Bulben," but in this poem, all the poet's previous utterances break down into questions— grammatical correlatives for his moral and epistemological in-completeness:

> All that I have said and done,
> Now that I am old and ill,
> Turns into a question till
> I lie awake night after night
> And never get the answers right.
> Did that play of mine send out
> Certain men the English shot?
> Did words of mine put too great strain
> On that woman's reeling brain?
> Could my spoken words have checked
> That whereby a house lay wrecked?
> And all seems evil until I
> Sleepless would lie down and die.
>
> *Echo.* Lie down and die.   [345]

In a vocabulary that for Yeats is unusually simple, often mono-syllabic, the man openly confronts his powerlessness—in par-ticular, his inability to regulate the significances of his own words and deeds. As he withdraws from his past and sees it defamiliar-ized, his actions and statements become ghosts of their former selves, emptied of the stable intentionality that had governed their meaning. Like the de casibus ghosts of Lydgate, Boccaccio, or Shakespeare in *Richard III,* the poet's statements now besiege the mind with guilty questions. His "books & words"—as Yeats puts it in the prose draft—now provoke self-questioning about the destruction they brought in their freedom from his intentions.[69] *Cathleen ni Houlihan* makes him ask if he inspired the leaders of the Easter Rising and inadvertently brought about their execution; his advice to Margot Ruddock prompts him to worry whether he helped to craze her; his unspoken defense whether he could have prevented the destruction of Coole Park. In "The Tower" the poet had been the imperious questioner of his work; now his work questions him. Apparently entombed in historical fact ("done") and statement ("said"), the letter of the past insists in the present, as it "Turns" uncontrollably into something it was not.

In its form, the lyric demonstrates grammatically this frightening drift of the poet's life and work into instability. The echo distorts the poet's subjunctive statement of a wish—"I / Sleepless would lie down and die"—by turning it into a harrowing command—"Lie down and die." The echoic form of the poem, then, articulates the dying poet's anxiety about the future dislocation of his own language, the inevitable troping or turning of reception; "the guts of the living"—to recall Auden's elegy for Yeats—modify and punish the "words of a dead man." Not that this thought of linguistic inheritance is without its consolations. There is even a hint of unconscious self-flattery in the selection of utterances—utterances that allude to many of the poet's other lyrics, utterances that may have altered the course of history or of other people's lives.[70] But by comparison with the attempts in other of the self-elegies to regulate death, this one is particularly open about guilt and vulnerability.

Rejecting the Echo's imperative, the Man justifies his pause before death by explaining the "great work" of self-mourning:

Man.   That were to shirk
    The spiritual intellects's great work
    And shirk it in vain. There is no release
    In a bodkin or disease,
    Nor can there be a work so great
    As that which cleans man's dirty slate.   [345–46]

The poem canonizes itself by proclaiming its own work to be
greater than any other. Neither the extreme of chosen death—"a
bodkin"—nor that of accidental death—"disease"—releases one
from responsibility for this life. The poet attempts to discharge
this responsibility by accepting the destructive consequences of
his words and deeds, an acceptance that might clean the ledger of
his sins. As in the traditional *hora mortis,* penitence might erase
the individual book (or "slate") that lists one's transgressions.[71]
The biblical prayer is now self-addressed: "Wash me thoroughly
from mine iniquity, and cleanse me from my sin" (Ps. 51:2).

Among the stages of purgative self-mourning that Yeats describes, he performs in this poem an intermediary stage—sleepless self-questioning and self-assessment:

> While man can still his body keep
> Wine or love drug him to sleep,
> Waking he thanks the Lord that he
> Has body and its stupidity,
> But body gone he sleeps no more
> And till his intellect grows sure
> That all's arranged in one clear view
> Pursues the thoughts that I pursue,
> Then stands in judgment on his soul,
> And, all work done, dismisses all
> Out of intellect and sight
> And sinks at last into the night.

Echo. Into the night.

That these lines recall "The Soul in Judgment" does not mean
that they are merely about the afterlife; rather, their autodescrip-
tion may suggest that the afterlife is about the kind of self-
mourning enacted by the poem. The lyric steps outside itself to
locate its own activity of restless questioning on a temporal map
of self-mourning: "the thoughts that I pursue" (self-questioning)
are the aftermath of corporeal slumber and the harbinger of self-
judgment. Yeats concurs with Wordsworth that our secular lives

are "a sleep and a forgetting," but he adds that the fear of death awakens "man" from his stupor.[72] First embracing thankfully the senses and then mortifying them, the self-mourning man attempts to arrange his life into a completed object that he may evaluate and relinquish it. Yeats's more self-epitaphic poems situate themselves at the later stages of totalization and judgment, but this one, fortunately, stays within the borders of inquiry. In the final stage of self-mourning, the poet releases his grip on the work—including the present work—and sinks into nothingness.

Just as the conscience of the poet turns his statements into questions, and just as the paternal Echo turns the poet's qualified statements into commands, so too the poet turns the Rocky Face's command in "The Gyres"—"Rejoice"—into a question:[73]

> *Man*.   O rocky voice
>   Shall we in that great night rejoice?
>   What do we know but that we face
>   One another in this place?   [346]

Death literally puts into question the poet's mythologies, rolling *A Vision* into two questions. Instead of offering us "His Convictions," as "Under Ben Bulben" was originally entitled, the poet can only inquire; but even the certainty presupposed by the act of questioning soon dissolves:

>   But hush, for I have lost the theme
>   Its joy or night seem but a dream;
>   Up there some hawk or owl has struck
>   Dropping out of sky or rock,
>   A stricken rabbit is crying out
>   And its cry distracts my thought.   [346]

The rabbit's cry of pain interrupts the deathward meditation. This moment of rupture, as the poet tries to fix his thought on death, suggests that "Man" can only think death indirectly, through trope and turn. We are prepared for the usual resolution to such a meditative lyric by the tripartite division, leading from the first part's *memory* of ill deeds and words, to the attempt at a unifying *understanding* of life in the second part, and, finally, to the expected assertion of *will* when the poet begins his direct colloquy with the rocky voice—the negative God. But the meditation falters, arresting the expected movement toward harmony with the addressee. As in Yeats's other self-elegies, life disrupts the meditative progression toward death, calling the poet back with a cry of suffering. Having attempted to imagine his own death, the poet discovers that he still remains as spectator, the spectator inevitably of another's death. The effort to totalize the life breaks off, when the cry of a fellow victim—whose fate foreshadows his own—permits him to reflect on his own death in the only way that he or anyone can: in the mirror of a death that is not his own. In all the self-elegies, death challenges the poet into rites of rehearsal and acceptance, but this haunting interruption suggests that he can never *own* his own death, that he can know death, if at all, only in distraction.

CODA

The narrative of this book has been dialectical: we began with the pathos of the elegies, then turned to the ethos of the poems of tragic joy and the sublime, and concluded with the combination of these stances in the self-elegies. But within each pole of the dialectic we found another dialectic that complicated this simple scheme. The elegies are often more muted in their expressions of pathos than they are in their heroic affirmations— affirmations of "wit" and "joy," of "terrible beauty" and "glory," all born of death. In some of the elegies, such as "In Memory of Alfred Pollexfen," Yeats counteracts "the submission in pure sorrow" by defining himself over against the dead. In others, such as "Upon a Dying Lady" and "Beautiful Lofty Things," he con-

structs noble images of himself by communing with the dead—
an illustrious fellowship sharply distinguished from the tawdry
world of the living. Similarly, the other pole of the dialectic is
itself dialectical. In the poems of tragic joy and the sublime, we
found pathos inscribed within even the most vehement exulta-
tions. Repeatedly declaring the joy of death in "Lapis Lazuli," the
poet strains to overcome the pity and terror he covertly shares
with the "hysterical women." And even though he recommends
in "The Gyres" that we "laugh in tragic joy," he himself enacts a
poetic rite of mourning for a lost youth and a spent civilization:
"A greater, a more gracious time has gone." Against anxiety these
poems offer a sublime counterassertion of glee, "Gaiety transfiguring all that dread." Thus, each of these large generic groups
incorporates its opposite, "Dying each other's death, living each
other's life" (AV, 68). The self-elegies are the fortunate outcome
of Yeats's vertiginous responses to his own mortality. Although
"Under Ben Bulben" is a clamorous declaration of strength in the
face of death, and "The Apparitions" a pained admission of
uncertainty, the best self-elegies, from "The Tower" to "Man and
the Echo," vacillate between ethos and pathos. That the simple
dialectic should turn out to be more a matter of vacillations
within vacillations is only fitting for the theorist of the gyres—
the poet who had "never thought with Hegel that the two ends
of the see-saw are one another's negation, nor that the spring
vegetables were refuted when over" (AV, 72–73).

But this more complicated picture of vacillations within vacillations risks representing Yeats's poetry of death as all-encom-
passing, a poetry that includes all contraries. To clarify the outer
limits of these vacillations, we might extricate ourselves from
their inner dynamic, setting Yeats against another poet of death:
Wilfred Owen. Elegies, self-elegies, and poems of the sublime—
they have all attested that Yeats held dear what Kenneth Burke
calls one of the major "deflections" of death: "Death as dignifica-
tion."[1] Yeats reacted violently against Owen's work because he
saw in it the less dignified responses to death that his own work
energetically suppresses. His denunciations of Owen's poetry are

well known: "unworthy of the poet's corner of a country newspaper," "all blood, dirt and sucked sugar-stick," "clumsy," "dis-
cordant" (*L*, 874–75). In the introduction to *The Oxford Book of
Modern Verse* he condemns the omitted Owen without naming
him: "passive suffering is not a theme for poetry" (*Ox*, xxxiv).

Passive suffering, I have tried to show, is often a surreptitious
theme for poetry in Yeats; still, important differences remain between the writers, as some of Owen's poetic reactions to Yeats
demonstrate. For even though we usually consider this literary
relationship in terms of Yeats's comments about Owen, Owen
sharply criticized Yeats, particularly in one of his more complex
and disjunctive poems—"S.I.W." Owen's epigraph is from the
play that most clearly foreshadows Yeats's later exercises in tragic
joy: *The King's Threshold*. It includes the monk's observation that
the exalted poet, Seanchan, "has set his teeth to die."[2] This heroic
attitude of anticipatory resoluteness characterizes many of the
mature poems that Owen would never read, such as "The Tower"
and "Lapis Lazuli." But Owen rewrites the epigraph by literalizing Yeats's metaphor; he transfers its referent from a poet's lofty
resolve to a soldier's physical suicide: "With him they buried the
muzzle his teeth had kissed." Preparing for death, the Yeatsian
poet Seanchan, as we recall from earlier in the play, had declared
that "when all falls / In ruin, poetry calls out in joy"; this is the
seed of "Lapis Lazuli" and "The Gyres" (*VPl*, 266–67). But
Owen's poetry calls out in *pity* when all falls in ruin.[3] Moreover,
Owen replaces Yeats's totalizing abstractions (*all, ruin*) with the
felt particulars of a single "wretch": *ruin* for his soldier is the
"torture of lying machinally shelled"; it is "infrangibly wired and
blind trench wall / Curtained with fire, roofed in with creeping
fire." Owen censures Yeats for distancing and blurring violence;
he brings it into focus by placing it in a historical context. Visions
of apocalyptic destruction are often for Yeats the imaginary occasions that allow him to construct courageous images of himself,
as he rehearses over and over his own death. Although Owen's
soldier suffers in isolation, his violent milieu is a social and
political construct, produced by "this world's Powers who'd run

amok." Owen rebukes the heroic ethos of Yeats and Yeats's Seanchan, indirectly associating the fictive poet's elevation of death
over dishonor with the patriarchal cant that sent millions of sons
into battle:

> Father would sooner him dead than in disgrace,—
> Was proud to see him going, aye, and glad.

Trapped by his father's ideology, the soldier prefers to set his
teeth to his gun rather than inflict a wound and get out of
combat:

> He'd seen men shoot their hands, on night patrol.
> Their people never knew. Yet they were vile.
> 'Death sooner than dishonour, that's the style!'
> So Father said.

So Yeats said—for Owen, another kind of father.

In spite of their loneliness, such soldiers in Owen's poetry
typically "die as cattle," deprived of the heroic individuality of a
Yeatsian death.[4] We shall return to the relatively anonymous
death in Owen's work; let us first review and put in context the
apparent individuality of death in Yeats's poems. In such terms,
the narrative of this book could be schematized not as a dialectic
but as a linear progression: from the elegies to the sublime poems
and the self-elegies, death has become increasingly immediate
and solitary, represented finally as the poet's own death. Yeats
struggles to construct his uniqueness against the backdrop of
death, even to represent himself as the lamp casting death as its
mere shadow. But since he must encounter death through trope,
convention, and loss, and since these are known only to the
living, his *own* death can never be his own. He brings this antinomy into crisis, particularly in his self-elegies: however much
death is inalienably his own, it is also inalienably *not* his own, for
it is not his own until he *is* no longer. As one of "the last
romantics," Yeats joins poets from Keats to Dickinson and Plath
in trying to remain unique till the end, ever rehearsing death to
make it his own. According to Blanchot, this cultural manifesta-

tion of a perennial desire "is rooted in a form of individualism which belongs to the end of the nineteenth century."[5] With the exception of a few poems, such as "Reprisals" and "Nineteen Hundred and Nineteen," Yeats resembles Nietzsche, Heidegger, Stevens, and other Romantics in trying to individualize death, suppressing in particular the anonymous death of modern war: "If war is necessary, or necessary in our time and place, it is best to forget its suffering as we do the discomfort of fever, remembering our comfort at midnight when our temperature fell, or as we forget the worst moments of more painful disease" (*Ox*, xxxv). The absurd and banal death of technological warfare could not be the occasion of the final, individual utterance that Yeats took as a model for the lyric—an utterance crammed with meaning and passion, an utterance that recalls Shakespearean heroes and Paterian ecstasy: "amid the great moments, when Timon orders his tomb, when Hamlet cries to Horatio 'Absent thee from felicity awhile,' when Antony names 'Of many thousand kisses the poor last,' all is lyricism, unmixed passion, 'the integrity of fire'" (*E&I*, 240). Even Yeats's Irish airman bespeaks a final illumination, preferring the lonely joy of death to the monotony of life.

Owen has a very different notion of utterance at the brink of death. Instead of summing up like a tragic hero or a Yeatsian visionary, Owen's soldiers speak prefabricated expletives as they die. In "The Last Laugh," this is what they say:

'Oh! Jesus Christ! I'm hit,' he said; and died.
· · · · · · · · · · · · · · · · · · ·
Another sighed—'O Mother,—Mother,—Dad!'
· · · · · · · · · · · · · · · · · · · ·
'My Love!' one moaned.[6]

For Yeats, the heroic, lyrical utterance should demonstrate self-possession and possession of a death uniquely one's own. But Owen's expletives are about others rather than oneself; anonymous, they have nothing unique about them. And they prove ascendancy neither over oneself nor over death. Instead, the

instruments of war are far more expressive than the human beings they vanquish:

> The Bullets chirped—In vain, vain, vain!
> Machine-guns chuckled—Tut-tut! Tut-tut!
> And the Big Gun guffawed.

Chiastically, Owen attributes meaning and expressive power to
the machines, mechanized speech to the soldiers that are their
victims. I am not claiming that Owen's language is "realistic,"
Yeats's "poetic"; if anything, Owen in "The Last Laugh" heightens more than Yeats ever does the deliberate artifice of two poetic
devices—the pathetic fallacy and onomatopoeia. But the contrast
between the two men's aesthetics reminds us that Yeats's poetry
of death, spectacular though it often is, excludes other ways of
constructing death. His work might be thought of as a multifarious elegy for an ennobling and heroic vision of death—a
vision that has become increasingly anachronistic in the modern
period. Yeats fondly repeats Villiers de L'Isle Adam's lofty sentence, "As for living—our servants will do that for us" (*Au*, 203).
Indirectly, the sentence implies, "As for dying—we the masters
will do that for ourselves." Supposedly the great leveler, death is
for Yeats the great ennobler—the last preserve for those repulsed
by what Wilde calls "the sordid perils of actual existence."[7] Owen
closes "Apologia Pro Poemate Meo," "Dulce et Decorum Est,"
and "Insensibility" by challenging civilians to reflect on the horri-
ble deaths they have helped to bring about. But Yeats inverts the
social provenance of the exhortation, memento mori; his remem-
brances of death are intended less for the moral instruction of the
many than for the dignifying reflection of the few.

This notion of the intended reader can help us conclude our
epitaphic "decathexis" of Yeats, for although his poetry sometimes uses death to dignify both poet and reader, at other times it
uses death more to dignify the poet and overwhelm the reader.
Dramatizing his conflict with the final authority of death, Yeats
hopes to convince us that he chooses that which resists all choice,

that he masters that which resists all mastery. When he rhetorically appropriates the authority of death, he sometimes uses that authority to move and even berate us; a disembodied voice declaims from beyond the tomb: "Swear," "do the work," "learn your trade," "Scorn the sort now growing up," "pass by!" Herbert Marcuse reminds us that no domination is complete without the use of death, and Louis-Vincent Thomas argues that the power of death is at the base of all political systems.[8] If we stretch an analogy to say that the relation of the reader to a death poem is a political microcosm, we see that the psycholinguistic power of Yeats's death poetry can sometimes resemble, however distantly, the structure of political domination. This is not true throughout Yeats's poetry of death, which often signals its reliance on death for its own authority and aesthetic life: in such poems as "A Dream of Death," "Lapis Lazuli," and "The Circus Animals' Desertion," Yeats shows us that he depends on death for his poetries of mourning, of joyful assertion, and of self-definition. It is true, however, of poems like "Under Ben Bulben," so I have tried to unravel the rhetorical and psychic structures by which a few such poems grant themselves their power over us. And yet any such attempt at demystification—unpacking the power relation among Yeats, death, and the reader—ends up reinscribing itself in another mystification; for the very focus of this study on death, and its own desire to persuade, must duplicate the sometimes coercive use of death that it tries to interrupt and analyze. "Man has created death," Yeats proclaims, but with its power to dignify, inspire, and tyrannize, death sometimes seems to have created "Man."

NOTES

INTRODUCTION

1 Yeats's "defence of reincarnation," as Richard Ellmann observes, "is scarcely that of a believer"; see *The Identity of Yeats,* 2d ed. (New York: Oxford University Press, 1964), 212. I agree with Ellmann but do not presume to offer anything approaching a full interpretation of Yeats's extra-poetic thoughts on death; the present book is about Yeats's poems and not about his "esoteric philosophy." For a brief reading of Book III of *A Vision,* however, see chap. 3. Among the many books on Yeats and the occult, see George Mills Harper, *Yeats's Golden Dawn* (London: Macmillan, 1974) and his collection *Yeats and the Occult* (London: Macmillan, 1976); see also Kathleen Raine, *Yeats, the Tarot and the Golden Dawn,* 2d ed. (Dublin: Dolmen Press, 1976) and *Yeats the Initiate: Essays on Certain Themes in the Works of W. B. Yeats* (London: Allen and Unwin, 1986); and Graham Hough, *The Mystery Religion of W. B. Yeats* (Totowa, N.J.: Barnes and Noble, 1984).

  For two essays on Yeats and death, see Hugh Kenner, "The Three Deaths of Yeats," *Yeats* 5 (1987): 87–94, and Robert Pack, "Yeats as Spectator to Death," *Affirming Limits: Essays on Mortality, Choice, and Poetic Form* (Amherst: University of Massachusetts Press, 1985), 151–73.

2 As Ellmann remarks of Yeats's famous letter about Rilke and death, "the process of life and death is like the process of making a poem," for both end in the dissolution of the sensuous image (*L,* 916–17); see Ellmann, *Identity,* 213.

3 Harold Bloom, *The Anxiety of Influence: A Theory of Poetry* (New York: Oxford University Press, 1973), 10.

4 Arthur Schopenhauer, *The World as Will and Representation,* trans. E. F. J. Payne (New York: Dover, 1969), 2:463.

5 On Yeats and the Romantics, see Hazard Adams, *Blake and Yeats: The Contrary Vision* (1955; New York: Russell, 1968); Harold Bloom, *Yeats* (New York: Oxford University Press, 1970); George Bornstein, *Yeats and Shelley* (Chicago: University of Chicago Press, 1970) and *Transformations of Romanticism in Yeats, Eliot, and Stevens* (Chicago: University of

Chicago Press, 1976); Robert Langbaum, *The Mysteries of Identity: A Theme in Modern Literature* (Chicago: University of Chicago Press, 1977), 147–247; Carlos Baker, *The Echoing Green: Romanticism, Modernism, and the Phenomena of Transference in Poetry* (Princeton: Princeton University Press, 1984), 149–85; and Patrick Keane, *Yeats's Interactions with Tradition* (Columbia: University of Missouri Press, 1987).

6   Shelley, *Shelley's Poetry and Prose*, ed. Donald H. Reiman and Sharon B. Powers (New York: Norton, 1977), lines 50, 23–24.

7   Mario Praz, *The Romantic Agony*, trans. Angus Davidson, 2d ed. (London: Oxford University Press, 1951), 23–50. For more on Romantic views of death, see Paul H. Fry, "Disposing of the Body: The Romantic Moment of Dying," *Southwest Review* 71 (1986): 8–26; Philippe Ariès, *The Hour of Our Death,* trans. Helen Weaver (New York: Vintage-Random House, 1982), 409–556; and Jacques Choron, *Death and Western Thought* (London: Macmillan, 1963), 156–61.

8   Yeats's discussions of the lyric, from a lecture of 1893, "Nationality and Literature," to "A General Introduction for my Work" of 1937, bear the unmistakable stamp of Pater's "Conclusion" to *The Renaissance* (*UP*1, 266–75; *E&I*, 509–26). Yeats's Romantic view of the lyric would be untenable for a critic like René Wellek, who attacks the attempt to define the lyric in terms of *Erlebnis*—an attempt that extends from Hegel to Käte Hamburger. But the project with which he proposes we replace such definitions—namely, the description of the lyric in terms of its historical traditions—requires, paradoxically, that we recognize the tropes of intensity, inwardness, and death-heightened experience as among the historical conventions that govern the late Romantic lyric. See his *Discriminations: Further Concepts of Criticism* (New Haven: Yale University Press, 1970), 225–52.

9   Wallace Stevens, "Sunday Morning," *The Collected Poems* (1954; New York: Vintage-Random House, 1982), 68. General accounts of death and modern literature include Frederick J. Hoffman, *The Mortal No: Death and the Modern Imagination* (Princeton: Princeton University Press, 1964); Eric Rhode, "Death in Twentieth-Century Fiction," in *Man's Concern with Death*, ed. Arnold Toynbee (London: Hodder and Stoughton, 1968), 160–76; A. Alvarez, *The Savage God: A Study of Suicide* (London: Weidenfeld and Nicolson, 1971); Lawrence L. Langer, *The Age of Atrocity: Death in Modern Literature* (Boston: Beacon Press, 1978); Anthony Libby, *Mythologies of Nothing: Mystical Death in American Poetry, 1940–70* (Urbana: University of Illinois Press, 1984); Ed-

ward Engelberg, *Elegiac Fictions: The Motif of the Unlived Life* (University Park: Pennsylvania State University Press, 1989); and, still more generally, Jacques Choron, *Death and Modern Man* (New York: Collier-Macmillan, 1964).

10 T. S. Eliot, "*Ulysses,* Order and Myth" (1923), rpt. in *Selected Prose,* ed. Frank Kermode (London: Faber, 1975), 178.

11 Julia Kristeva, "The Pain of Sorrow in the Modern World: The Works of Marguerite Duras," *PMLA* 102 (1987): 139; see also Robert Jay Lifton and Eric Olson, *Living and Dying* (New York: Praeger, 1974).

12 The cultural taboo and the resultant "pornography of death" were first diagnosed by Geoffrey Gorer, "The Pornography of Death" (1955), rpt. in *Death, Grief, and Mourning* (Garden City, N.Y.: Doubleday, 1965), 192–99; see also Philippe Ariès, "The Reversal of Death: Changes in Attitudes toward Death in Western Societies," in *Death in America,* ed. David E. Stannard (Philadelphia: University of Pennsylvania Press, 1975), 134–58.

13 For exemplary works that take different critical approaches to death, see Garrett Stewart, *Death Sentences: Styles of Dying in British Fiction* (Cambridge, Mass.: Harvard University Press, 1984); Peter Sacks, *The English Elegy: Readings in the Genre from Spenser to Yeats* (Baltimore: Johns Hopkins University Press, 1985); Arnold Stein, *The House of Death: Messages from the English Renaissance* (Baltimore: Johns Hopkins University Press, 1986); and J. Gerald Kennedy, *Poe, Death, and the Life of Writing* (New Haven: Yale University Press, 1987).

14 Kenneth Burke, "Thanatopsis for Critics: A Brief Thesaurus of Deaths and Dyings," *Essays in Criticism* 2 (1952): 368.

15 Burke, "Thanatopsis," 369; Ludwig Wittgenstein, *Tractatus Logico-Philosophicus* (London: Routledge and Kegan Paul, 1922), 185.

16 Philippe Ariès, *Western Attitudes toward Death: From the Middle Ages to the Present,* trans. Patricia M. Ranum (Baltimore: Johns Hopkins University Press, 1976), 56, 68; see also *Hour,* 409–74. In other respects, I owe much to Ariès's historical analysis of death.

17 In *The Standard Edition of the Complete Psychological Works of Sigmund Freud* (hereafter abbreviated as *SE*), ed. James Strachey (London: Hogarth Press and the Institute of Psycho-Analysis, 1953–74), see, e.g., *The Interpretation of Dreams,* 5:454–55; "The Theme of the Three Caskets," 12:299; *Beyond the Pleasure Principle,* 18:14–17; and *The Future of an Illusion,* 21:19. This aspect of Freud's work is clearly indebted to Schopenhauer: "All religious and philosophical systems are . . . primarily

the antidote to the certainty of death" (*World as Will and Representation*, 2: 463). Similarly, Yeats states, "The makers of religions have established their ceremonies, their form of art, upon fear of death" (*E&I*, 203).

18 See Freud, "Thoughts for the Times on War and Death," *SE*, 14:289; *The Ego and the Id, SE*, 19:58; and *Inhibitions, Symptoms and Anxiety, SE*, 20:130.

19 See Martin Heidegger, *Being and Time*, trans. John Macquarrie and Edward Robinson (Oxford: Basil Blackwell, 1980), 279–311.

20 See the *Phaedrus,* trans. R. Hackforth, in *The Collected Dialogues of Plato,* ed. Edith Hamilton and Huntington Cairns (Princeton: Princeton University Press, 1961), 521; Jacques Derrida, *Of Grammatology,* trans. Gayatri Chakravorty Spivak (Baltimore: Johns Hopkins University Press, 1976), 69; and Paul de Man, *The Rhetoric of Romanticism* (New York: Columbia University Press, 1984), 81. Maurice Blanchot bridges the rhetorical and ontological approaches to death, even as Jacques Lacan bridges the psychoanalytic and the ontological.

21 See Richard Wollheim, *The Thread of Life* (Cambridge, Mass.: Harvard University Press, 1984), 257–59.

22 Genre rather than poetic volume is my primary interpretive context; for recent works that emphasize the volume instead, see David Young, *Troubled Mirror: A Study of Yeats's "The Tower"* (Iowa City: University of Iowa Press, 1987), and Hazard Adams, *The Book of Yeats's Poems* (Tallahassee: Florida State University Press, 1990).

23 Northrop Frye, *Anatomy of Criticism: Four Essays* (Princeton: Princeton University Press, 1957), 247–48.

24 Allen Tate, "Yeats' Romanticism," in *Yeats: A Collection of Critical Essays,* ed. John Unterecker (Englewood Cliffs, N.J.: Prentice-Hall, 1963), 162.

1. THE ELEGY

1 On the distinction between genre and mode, see Alastair Fowler, *Kinds of Literature: An Introduction to the Theory of Genres and Modes* (Cambridge, Mass.: Harvard University Press, 1982), 106–7. For the Miltonic echo, compare the line "And yet anon repairs his drooping head" in "Lycidas," *Complete Shorter Poems,* ed. John Carey (1968; London: Longman, 1971), line 169. The image can be traced back to the death of Pallas in the *Aeneid* and of Gorgythion in the *Iliad*.

2   Vendler raises the question of the group form and briefly alludes to
    Yeats's "uncomplimentary" portraits; see "Four Elegies," in *Yeats, Sligo
    and Ireland,* ed. A. Norman Jeffares (Gerrards Cross: Colin Smythe,
    1980), 216–31. See also Joseph Kishel, "Yeats's Elegies," *Yeats Eliot
    Review* 7 (1981): 78–90.

3   Ben Jonson, "To the Memory of My Beloved, the Author Mr William
    Shakespeare: And What He Hath Left Us," lines 12, 31, 56, 80. Work-
    ing on Yeats, Bloom developed his theory about an analogous struggle—
    the struggle of poets against the crippling power of their often dead
    predecessors; see *Yeats,* 3–22. See also Lawrence Lipking's remarkably
    insightful analysis of elegies for other poets in *The Life of the Poet:
    Beginning and Ending Poetic Careers* (Chicago: University of Chicago
    Press, 1981), 138–79. Celeste Marguerite Schenck describes the "career-
    ist" contests of pastoral elegy in *Mourning and Panegyric: The Poetics of
    Pastoral Ceremony* (University Park: Pennsylvania State University Press,
    1988), 33–53. Such competition, as she argues, is more characteristic of
    male than of female elegists, but combative elegies by Plath and other
    women would obviously complicate this gender distinction; see "Femi-
    nism and Deconstruction: Re-Constructing the Elegy," *Tulsa Studies in
    Women's Literature* 5 (1986): 13, 15.

4   Hans-Georg Gadamer, *Reason in the Age of Science,* trans. Frederick G.
    Lawrence (Cambridge, Mass.: MIT Press, 1981), 74–75. For this em-
    phasis on identification, see Eric Smith, *By Mourning Tongues: Studies in
    English Elegy* (Totowa, N.J.: Rowan and Littlefield; Ipswich: Boydell
    Press, 1977), 3, and Peter Sacks's reading of "In Memory of Major
    Robert Gregory" (*English Elegy,* 270, 288). Otherwise, I am indebted to
    Sacks's superb book.

5   See Thomas Hardy's "The Going," W. H. Auden's "In Memory of W. B.
    Yeats" and "In Memory of Sigmund Freud," Robert Lowell's "Com-
    mander Lowell," Sylvia Plath's "Daddy," and John Berryman's Dream
    Song 384.

6   Richard Eberhardt, introduction to *A Poet to His Beloved: The Early Love
    Poems of W. B. Yeats* (New York: St. Martin's Press, 1985), ix–x. Given
    parenthetically, the above dates and others through 1900 indicate year of
    first publication; dates after 1900 indicate year of composition.

7   For the "consumptive sublime" and an overview of late nineteenth-
    century representations of dead women, see Bram Dijkstra, *Idols of Per-
    versity: Fantasies of Feminine Evil in Fin-de-Siècle Culture* (New York:

Oxford University Press, 1986), 29, 49–63. On the Romantic association of death with beauty and sex, see Praz, *Romantic Agony,* 23–50, and Ariès, *Hour,* 369–81, 392–95.

8 Edgar Allan Poe, "The Philosophy of Composition," *Essays and Reviews* (New York: Library of America, 1984), 19. For an analysis of woman as the absent and absented referent in androcentric culture, see Margaret Homans, *Bearing the Word: Language and Female Experience in Nineteenth-Century Women's Writing* (Chicago: University of Chicago Press, 1986), esp. chaps. 1 and 2. Simone de Beauvoir argues that the definition of woman as the mother, with the power of life and death over the male, and as the other, negated by patriarchy, results in "the alliance between Woman and Death"; see *The Second Sex,* trans. and ed. H. M. Parshley (New York: Knopf, 1953), 165. On Yeats, Dante, and the "sublation" of woman, see Gayatri Chakravorty Spivak, "Finding Feminist Reading: Dante-Yeats," *Social Text* 1 (1980): 73–87.

9 In the next line he also echoes the earlier image of woman as "labyrinth." On the beloved's absence and poetic inspiration in Yeats, see Elizabeth Cullingford, "Yeats and Women: *Michael Robartes and the Dancer,*" *Yeats Annual* 4 (1986): 40, and Patricia Yaeger, "'Because a Fire Was in My Head': Eudora Welty and the Dialogic Imagination," *PMLA* 99 (1984): 959–60. Among works that discuss the representation of women in Yeats, see also Richard Ellmann's preface to the later edition of *Yeats: The Man and the Masks* (New York: Norton, 1979), vii–xxviii; A. Norman Jeffares, "Women in Yeats's Poetry," *The Circus Animals: Essays on W. B. Yeats* (Stanford: Stanford University Press, 1970), 78–102; Gloria Klein, *The Last Courtly Lover: Yeats and the Idea of Woman* (Ann Arbor: UMI Research Press, 1983); Catherine Cavanaugh, *Love and Forgiveness in Yeats's Poetry* (Ann Arbor: UMI Research Press, 1986); and Patrick J. Keane, *Terrible Beauty: Yeats, Joyce, Ireland, and the Myth of the Devouring Female* (Columbia: University of Missouri Press, 1988).

10 See the helpful discussions of titles in John Hollander, *Vision and Resonance: Two Senses of Poetic Form* (1975; New Haven: Yale University Press, 1985), 212–26, and Fowler, *Kinds of Literature,* 92–98.

11 Frank Kermode, *Romantic Image* (1957; London: Routledge and Kegan Paul, 1961), 89.

12 Allen Grossman argues that "Requiescat" is the precursor-poem; see this reading and his general commentary on the early Yeats in *Poetic Knowledge in the Early Yeats: A Study of "The Wind Among the Reeds"* (Charlottesville: University Press of Virginia, 1969), 154.

13 Maud Gonne MacBride, *A Servant of the Queen* (London: Victor Goll-ancz, 1938), 147.

14 Freud, *Die Traumdeutung* (Frankfurt am Main: Fischer Taschenbuch Verlag, 1942), 216. Although published in 1899, this work was dated 1900. For Freud's subsequent analysis of his grandson's *fort/da* (gone/there) game, in which the boy mournfully renounces and seeks the mother, see *Beyond the Pleasure Principle, SE,* 18:14–17.

15 In Lacan's view desire is inextricable from the elegiac language that creates it. See Jacques Lacan, *Speech and Language in Psychoanalysis,* trans. Anthony Wilden (Baltimore: Johns Hopkins University Press, 1981), 84. Schopenhauer anticipates the view that "lack" generates desire, and Yeats echoes him on this point (*Ex,* 430); see *The World as Will and Representation,* 2:539.

16 See Paul de Man, "Image and Emblem in Yeats," *Rhetoric of Romanticism,* 145–238. The translation of the beloved into an emblem is what Derrida calls "metaphorization": "the movement of metaphorization . . . is nothing other than a movement of idealization" ("White Mythology: Metaphor in the Text of Philosophy," *Margins of Philosophy,* trans. Alan Bass [Chicago: University of Chicago Press, 1982], 226).

17 On the male word's "murder" of woman or mother, see Sandra M. Gilbert and Susan Gubar, *The Madwoman in the Attic: The Woman Writer and the Nineteenth-Century Literary Imagination* (New Haven: Yale University Press, 1979), 14–25, and Homans, *Bearing the Word,* 11. Ellmann aptly remarks that young men visited Maud Gonne because "they adored Yeats's images of her; and she died, rather unwillingly, into his poems, which she never greatly liked"; see *Yeats: The Man and the Masks,* xxi.

18 For example, Maurice Blanchot remarks: "For me to be able to say, 'This woman' I must somehow take her flesh and blood reality away from her, cause her to be absent, annihilate her. The word gives me the being, but it gives it to me deprived of being. The word is the absence of that being, its nothingness, what is left of it when it has lost being—the very fact that it does not exist. . . . Of course, my language does not kill anyone. And yet: when I say, 'This woman,' real death has been announced and is already present in my language" (*The Gaze of Orpheus, and Other Literary Essays,* ed. P. Adams Sitney, trans. Lydia Davis [Barrytown, N.Y.: Station Hill, 1981], 42). Regarding death and signification, see also Jacques Derrida, *Speech and Phenomena,* trans. David B. Allison (Evanston: Northwestern University Press, 1973), 40, 54, 93–96, 138, and *Of Grammatology,* 69, 183–84.

19   Freud recalls Schiller's lines: "What is to live immortal in song must
     perish in life" *(Was unsterblich im Gesang soll Leben, / Muss in Leben
     untergehen)*; see *Moses and Monotheism, SE,* 23:101.

20   See John Freccero, "The Fig Tree and the Laurel: Petrarch's Poetics," rpt.
     in *Literary Theory/Renaissance Texts,* ed. Patricia Parker and David Quint
     (Baltimore: Johns Hopkins University Press, 1986), 20–32. Unlike
     Petrarch, Yeats puns on the beloved's real name. In English poetry,
     another precedent is John Donne's pun on his name (Donne/done) in "A
     Hymne to God the Father."

21   I draw here upon Hegel's master-slave dialectic; see G. W. F. Hegel, *The
     Phenomenology of Mind,* trans. J. B. Baillie (New York: Harper and Row,
     1967), 233, 237.

22   For the holograph of "On a Child's Death" (dated here by year of com-
     position) and Ronald Schuchard's commentary, see "Yeats's 'On a
     Child's Death,'" *Yeats Annual* 3 (1985): plate 16, and 190–92.

23   Shelley, *Adonais,* 34.300; Spenser, "Dolefull Lay of Clorinda," part of
     "Astrophel," line 96.

24   Peter Sacks argues that poets rehearse in the elegy childhood episodes of
     self-construction—episodes that include the Lacanian mirror stage, the
     fort/da game, and the oedipal conflict (*The English Elegy,* 8–12).

25   Maurice Blanchot, *The Space of Literature,* trans. Ann Smock (Lincoln:
     University of Nebraska Press, 1982), 95. See also Heidegger's discussion
     of *"freedom towards death"* in *Being and Time,* 308–11.

26   Heidegger, *Being and Time,* 358.

27   See the "Epitaph" toward the end of the *Astrophel* sequence, line 13,
     where Sidney's "race" is his noble lineage. This passage may well have
     been Yeats's source, since just above it is an image reworked in the
     Gregory elegy of the heart doubling its might: the mourner's zeal, care,
     and love "hath doubled more" with Sidney's death (line 8).

28   Since Yeats frequently quotes from Nashe's "A Litany in Time of
     Plague," he probably recalls (in this line on toys and death) Nashe's
     comment on life's "joys": "Death proves them all but toys" (line 4).

29   M. L. Rosenthal and Sally M. Gall, *The Modern Poetic Sequence: The
     Genius of Modern Poetry* (New York: Oxford University Press, 1983), 98.

30   This odd view that Achilles laughs at death derives ultimately from the
     Apology, where Socrates suppresses Achilles' anxiety to make him a fore-
     runner of his own stoicisim (*Collected Dialogues of Plato,* 14).

31 Milton provides "a little ease" for himself and the reader ("Lycidas," line 152).

32 See Thomas R. Whitaker, *Swan and Shadow: Yeats's Dialogue with History* (Chapel Hill: University of North Carolina Press, 1964), 170.

33 Spenser's dedication, "To His Booke," lines 1–2 of *The Shepheardes Calender;* Chaucer, *Troilus and Criseyde,* 5.1786. Instead of being fully content with this noble literary lineage, Yeats feels he must manufacture a repugnant claim to *"blood / That has not passed through any huckster's loin."*

34 For a discussion of place and pastoral elegy, see Ellen Zetzel Lambert, *Placing Sorrow: A Study of the Pastoral Elegy Convention from Theocritus to Milton* (Chapel Hill: University of North Carolina Press, 1976), xi–xxxiv. On language, death, and placelessness, see Blanchot, *Space,* 254–63.

35 Ellmann shows that the poem's "object is not to praise the dead for their superior knowledge," despite the magical trappings, and Bloom remarks that the poet contrasts these "self-ruining quests" with his own literary success; see Ellmann, *Identity,* 175–76; Bloom, *Yeats,* 370.

36 See Georg Simmel, *Conflict [Der Streit]* (1908), trans. Kurt H. Wolff, in *"Conflict" and "The Web of Group-Affiliations"* (New York: Free Press, 1955), 11–123, and Freud, "Mourning and Melancholia," *SE,* 14:250–51. Simmel's views are developed by Lewis Coser, *The Functions of Social Conflict* (New York: Free Press, 1956). See also David D. Gilmore's anthropology of aggression in *Aggression and Community: Paradoxes of Andalusian Culture* (New Haven: Yale University Press, 1987), 10–28.

37 As Ellmann remarks, each poem might have been written by a member of a different religion (*Identity,* 231). Except for "Reprisals" (1920), the Gregory poems were written in 1918.

38 Sacks, *English Elegy,* 265; his view reiterates the sentiment that goes back to Marion Witt's description of the song as "coldly theoretical" and "esoteric" ("The Making of an Elegy: Yeats's 'In Memory of Major Robert Gregory,'" *Modern Philology* 48 [1950]: 114). The simple, generic context is more helpful in interpreting the aesthetic basis of the song than are the usual Platonic explanations, such as in F. A. C. Wilson's *W. B. Yeats and Tradition* (New York: Macmillan, 1958), 200–205.

39 Spenser, "Astrophel," line 11.

40 The exceptionally rich sequence of generic studies of the poem includes Witt, "Making," 112–21; Kermode, *Romantic Image,* 30–42; Marjorie Perloff, "The Consolation Theme in Yeats's 'In Memory of Major Robert

Gregory,'" *Modern Language Quarterly* 27 (1966): 306–22; Bloom, *Yeats,* 193–96; Daniel Harris, *Yeats: Coole Park and Ballylee* (Baltimore: Johns Hopkins University Press, 1974), 126–37; and Sacks, *English Elegy,* 260–98. The ensuing quotation is from Tennyson, *In Memoriam* 1, line 6.

41   Sacks thinks the phrase hints ambiguously at the poet's death (*English Elegy,* 273–74).

42   Shelley, *Adonais,* 21.183; Tennyson, *In Memoriam* 78, line 17; Emerson, "Experience," *Essays and Lectures* (New York: Library of America, 1983), 473. In Shakespeare's revision of the economic trope, payment does not diminish the debt: the poet tells "The sad account of fore-bemoanèd moan, / Which I new pay as if not paid before" (Sonnet 30, lines 11–12).

43   The elegiac transfer of the heart from one person to another recurs in Yeats, from the gesture of casting his *"heart"* into his rhymes for future generations in "To Ireland in the Coming Times" to the lengthier elaborations of the trope in "Two Songs from a Play," "Parnell's Funeral," and "The Circus Animals' Desertion" (51).

44   There is a further irony here, since it was Yeats who had helped Synge in this preparation for death by advising him "to go to a wild island off the Galway coast" (*Au,* 384).

45   Perloff, "Consolation Theme," 309–10, 319–22; for a contrasting view, see the readings by Kermode and Sacks. Perloff also makes the important point that the image of Gregory's combustion exemplifies what Yeats shows in "The Tragic Generation" to be the wrong kind of energy: "violent energy, which is like a fire of straw, consumes in a few minutes the nervous vitality, and is useless in the arts. Our fire must burn slowly" (*Au,* 212).

46   A genetic interpretation might detect, throughout the poem's anxious assertions of this Unity, atavistic traces of Lacan's mirror stage, when the infant imposes upon itself the coherent bodily image it sees in the mirror, controlling the earlier fragmentary self-image of uncoordinated limbs and sensations; see Jacques Lacan, "The Mirror Stage as Formative of the Function of the I," *Ecrits: A Selection,* trans. Alan Sheridan (New York: Norton, 1977), 1–7.

47   Wordsworth, *The Prelude: 1799, 1805, 1850,* ed. Jonathan Wordsworth, M. H. Abrams, and Stephen Gill (New York: Norton, 1979) (1805), 11.257–59.

48   The superlative statement about the portrait has been singled out as "a prime example" of the "embarrassing" emotional excesses of the poem,

even though the speaker clearly disputes it; see Thomas Parkinson, *W. B. Yeats: The Later Poetry* (Berkeley: University of California Press, 1964), 42–43.

49   According to Vendler's fine reading of the Gallery elegy's last stanza, Yeats's portrait is imagined as hanging between Synge's and Gregory's; see "Four Elegies," 230.

50   Divested of this "hatred" and others, the soul "learns at last that it is self-delighting, / Self-appeasing, self-affrighting" (189). See *Poems of Sir Samuel Ferguson,* ed. Perceval Graves (Dublin: Phoenix, 1916), xxviii. The echo may not have been noticed because the shorter version of Ferguson's elegy, commonly reproduced, excises these lines, among others.

51   On many other issues, Yeats was of course sympathetic to Young Ireland; see Dwight Eddins, *Yeats: The Nineteenth-Century Matrix* (University: University of Alabama Press, 1971), 41–78.

52   William Blake, "London," *The Complete Poetry and Prose of William Blake,* ed. David V. Erdman, rev. ed. (New York: Anchor-Doubleday, 1982), line 8.

53   Theodor Adorno, "Lyric Poetry and Society" (1957), trans. Bruce Mayo, *Telos* 20 (1974): 58. For a critique of the distinction between journalistic and literary language, see Marjorie Perloff, "Revolving in Crystal: The Supreme Fiction and the Impasse of Modernist Lyric," in *Wallace Stevens: The Poetics of Modernism,* ed. Albert Gelpi (Cambridge: Cambridge University Press, 1985), 50–51.

54   On Yeats's sense of "social disinheritance," see Terry Eagleton, *Criticism and Ideology: A Study in Marxist Literary Theory* (London: Verso, 1978), 152.

55   On anger and melancholia, see Freud, "Mourning and Melancholia," *SE,* 14:244, and Sacks, *English Elegy,* 21–22, 64–89.

56   Conor Cruise O'Brien claims that in spite of this poem, Yeats was less smitten than excited by Parnell's death, eager to use "Parnell's coffin for a platform" ("Passion and Cunning: An Essay on the Politics of W. B. Yeats," in *In Excited Reverie,* ed. A. Norman Jeffares and K. G. W. Cross [New York: Macmillan, 1965], 217–19).

57   See Simmel, *Conflict,* 91, and Freud, *Civilization and Its Discontents, SE,* 21:108–16.

58   Yeats quotes Goethe's statement on Irish jealousy: "The Irish seem to me like a pack of hounds, always dragging down some noble stag" (*Au,* 211).

59 *Hamlet, The Riverside Shakespeare,* ed. G. Blakemore Evans (Boston: Houghton Mifflin, 1974), 5.1.203–4: "noble dust . . . stopping a bunghole."

60 The elegiac technique of interwoven voices goes back to classical eclogues, such as the singing contest in Virgil's fifth eclogue; Yeats imitates the eclogue in "Shepherd and Goatherd" and at the end of *The King's Threshold.* In Renaissance elegies, ecclesiastical satire plays a prominent role in the genre; elegiac satire returns in eighteenth-century mock-elegies and later in the war elegies of Hardy and Owen, Stevens's "Emperor of Ice-Cream," Pound's *Hugh Selwyn Mauberley,* and Eliot's *Waste Land.* In his elegies, Yeats echoes Renaissance elegies that intermingle satire, lament, and other modes: Donne's "Anniversaries," where each encomium for Elizabeth Drury follows immediately on the heels of a complaint over the sickness, deformity, and disorder of the world; Jonson's Pindaric ode "To . . . Sir Lucius Cary and Sir H. Morison," where some men's drunken lives set off and ennoble the virtuous pair; and "Lycidas," where the satiric, encomiastic, and other modes of discourse are represented as dramatic voices. Compare, for example, the Unity of Being refrains of "In Memory of Major Robert Gregory" with the eulogistic sections of Donne's "First Anniversarie": she "did faithfully compact / And glue all vertues," "draw, and fasten sundred parts in one"; in man, "All faculties, all graces are at home" (lines 49–50, 222, 162). Also compare the descriptions of Gregory's Unity with Jonson's eulogy for Morison: "He stood, a soldier to the last right end, / A perfect patriot, and a noble friend, / But a most virtuous son. / All offices were done / By him. . . ." (lines 45–49).

61 As Ellmann observes, the questioner seems to forget that he is asking questions (*Identity,* 143). Denis Donoghue wonders whether the word *delirium* may qualify Yeats's admiration but concludes that "delirium, in Yeats's context, is a word of praise, as in saying that someone was driven crazed for something he loved" (*We Irish: Essays on Irish Literature and Society* [New York: Knopf, 1986], 22).

62 Thomas Parkinson, *W. B. Yeats, Self-Critic: A Study of His Early Verse* (Berkeley: University of California Press, 1951), 108; Whitaker, *Swan and Shadow,* 152.

63 The cry of the addressee, " 'Some woman's yellow hair / Has maddened every mother's son,' " though too general, usefully assimilates the delirium of the lover, and specifically of the lover-poet writing this elegy, to

the heroic madness of the martyrs. Substituting patriot for "lunatic," Yeats gathers a group that recalls the Shakespearean triad: "The lunatic, the lover, and the poet, / Are of imagination all compact" (*A Midsummer Night's Dream*, 5.1.7–8).

64   See Heidegger's discussion of "idle talk" *(Gerede)* and the concealment of death in *Being in Time*, 211–14. Unfortunately, Heidegger's political affiliations suggest that he did not apply his potentially radical insights to the "idle talk" of nazism—a language that reduced the deaths of its victims to anonymous necessities. As Frank Kermode states, such racist scapegoating is a "fiction of escape which tells you nothing about death but projects it onto others" (*The Sense of an Ending* [Oxford: Oxford University Press, 1967], 39). Heidegger's and Yeats's views on death and "idle talk" are informed by the ideological notion that poetry "can transcend a corrupting 'world' of politics and money"; see Jerome J. McGann, *The Romantic Ideology: A Critical Investigation* (Chicago: University of Chicago Press, 1983), 13.

65   Robert Bly, "Leaping up into Political Poetry," in *Poetry and Politics*, ed. Richard Jones (New York: William Morrow, 1985), 133–34.

66   Adorno, "Lyric Poetry," 61–62, 65.

67   For exhaustive analysis of the line "A terrible beauty is born" and a negative assessment of the poem's politics, see Terry Eagleton, *Against the Grain* (London: Verso, 1986), 173–80. For his early, sympathetic reading of the poem, see "History and Myth in Yeats's 'Easter 1916,'" *Essays in Criticism* 21 (1971): 248–60.

68   Tennyson, *In Memoriam* 7, line 12; W. H. Auden, "In Memory of W. B. Yeats," *Collected Poems*, ed. Edward Mendelson (New York: Random House, 1976), 197.

69   My reading of the poem as allegorical and rhetorically discontinuous runs counter to interpretations of it in terms of symbol; see, e.g., Kishel, "Yeats's Elegies," 87. I use *allegory* here in accordance with its meanings in Walter Benjamin, *The Origin of the German Tragic Drama*, trans. John Osborne (London: NLB, 1977), 159–235, and Paul de Man, "The Rhetoric of Temporality," *Blindness and Insight: Essays in the Rhetoric of Contemporary Criticism*, 2d ed. (Minneapolis: University of Minnesota Press, 1983), 187–228. For Yeats on allegory, see *E&I*, 147.

70   Spenser, "Two Cantos of Mutabilitie," 7.58.515, 7.59.525.

71   Blanchot, *Orpheus*, 40. "The writing of the poem becomes an analogue for the event which is its subject," observes C. K. Stead; but he sees the

analogy differently, arguing that the stone in the third stanza is a metaphor for the poem and the Rising (*The New Poetic* [London: Hutchinson, 1964], 39).

72   Maud Gonne, "Yeats and Ireland," in *Scattering Branches*, ed. Stephen Gwynn (New York: Macmillan, 1940), 27. Elizabeth Cullingford discusses Yeats's influence on Pearse and MacDonagh in *Yeats, Ireland and Fascism* (New York: New York University Press, 1981), 91–95.

73   For the opposite view, see Stead, *New Poetic*, 39. External evidence, discounted by Stead, supports my reading of the stanza: Yeats used the stanza to implore Maud Gonne "to forget the stone and its inner fire for the flashing, changing joy of life"; see her "Yeats and Ireland," 31–32.

74   Adorno, "Lyric Poetry," 62.

75   Sir James Frazer, *The Golden Bough*, abridged ed. (London: Macmillan, 1957), 331–38; Freud, *Totem and Taboo, SE,* 13:54–59, 81–87. Yeats describes his magical use of names (*Au,* 247–48).

76   See Surrey's "Epitaph on Sir Thomas Wyatt."

77   Yeats had described what Eva Gore-Booth dreams as an "Abstract humanitarian dream"; for the earlier drafts of the poem and a discussion of the sisters, see Jon Stallworthy, *Between the Lines: Yeats's Poetry in the Making* (Oxford: Clarendon Press, 1963), 164–76.

78   Shelley, "To Wordsworth," lines 13–14.

79   Wordsworth, "Ode: Intimations of Immortality," line 152. For a discussion of elegiac fire and light imagery—particularly in relation to the ending of "In Memory of Major Robert Gregory"—see Sacks, *English Elegy,* 292.

80   Milton, "Lycidas," line 23.

81   Bly, "Leaping up," 132.

82   Milton, "Lycidas," lines 127–29.

83   Freud, "Mourning and Melancholia," *SE,* 14:244, 251, and *Totem and Taboo, SE,* 13:60. After his father's death, Freud analyzed his own self-reproaches, and out of this self-analysis evolved the theory of the Oedipus complex (*SE,* 1:233; 4:xxvi).

84   See Whitaker's insightful reading of the poem in *Swan and Shadow,* 249.

85   Shelley, *Adonais,* 17.151, 34.36.

86   "Ursprunglicher als jedes *Wissen* darum ist das Schuldig*sein.*" See *Being and Time,* 332; *Sein und Zeit* (1927; Tübingen: Max Niemeyer Verlag, 1984), 286.

87   For a psychoanalytic view of the violence within identification, see Freud, *Totem and Taboo, SE,* 13:142; "Mourning and Melancholia," *SE,*

14:249–50; *Group Psychology and the Analysis of the Ego, SE,* 18:109; and *The Ego and the Id, SE,* 19:28. Freud describes this violence—on the analogue of the consumption of the totemic father to achieve identification with him—as the mourner's cannibalistic introjection of the lost object into the ego. See also Lacan, "Aggressivity in Psychoanalysis," *Ecrits,* 8–29.

2. TRAGIC JOY AND THE SUBLIME

1   See Fowler's discussion of "mode" in *Kinds of Literature,* 106–11.

2   Compare, for instance, their readings of "Lapis Lazuli": Ellmann, *Identity,* 185–87, 193–94; Bloom, *Yeats,* 437–39. For another generally unfavorable and favorable pair of responses to this aspect of Yeats, see Kermode, *Sense,* 98–108, and Denis Donoghue, *Yeats* (Glasgow: Fontana-Collins, 1971).

3   James Joyce, *Ulysses,* ed. Hans Walter Gabler (New York: Vintage-Random House, 1986), 8–9, 21; "Lycidas," line 165. I do not wish to suggest that the personal and literary past are distinct for Yeats: Bornstein argues through much of *Yeats and Shelley* that Yeats's rejection of Shelley is really a rejection of his own early poetry. As for Yeats's youthful pathos, Jon Stallworthy demonstrates the high incidence of the word *sorrow* in the early poetry and its virtual disappearance later on; see his *Vision and Revision in Yeats's Last Poems* (Oxford: Clarendon Press, 1969), 32–34.

4   See, for example, B. L. Reid, *William Butler Yeats: The Lyric of Tragedy* (Norman: University of Oklahoma Press, 1961). For discussions of Yeats, tragedy, and "tragic joy," see Edward Engelberg, *The Vast Design: Patterns in W. B. Yeats's Aesthetic* (Toronto: University of Toronto Press, 1964), 166–75, and C. A. Patrides, "'Gaiety Transfiguring All That Dread': The Case of Yeats," *Yeats* 5 (1987): 117–32. On the related issue of Yeats's heroic types, see Alex Zwerdling, *Yeats and the Heroic Ideal* (New York: New York University Press, 1965), and Michael Steinman, *Yeats's Heroic Figures* (Albany: State University of New York Press, 1983).

5   Gadamer discusses this trend not in sociohistorical but in philosophical terms. See *Truth and Method,* trans. Sheed and Ward Ltd., 2d ed. (New York: Crossroad, 1982), 39–90.

6   Harold Bloom, "The Internalization of Quest Romance" (1968), rpt. in *The Ringers in the Tower: Studies in Romantic Tradition* (Chicago: Univer-

sity of Chicago Press, 1971), 13–35, and Bornstein, *Transformations of Romanticism*, 10–11. Yeats reads the history of literature as a process of internalization, though he claims he would reverse it (*Au*, 130–31).

7   Wordsworth, *The Prelude* (1805), 7.509–16; note to "The Thorn," *Wordsworth's Literary Criticism*, ed. W. J. B. Owen (London: Routledge and Kegan Paul, 1974), 97; and "Preface" to *Lyrical Ballads* (1800), *Wordsworth's Literary Criticism*, 84–85.

8   See Wilde, "The Critic as Artist," *The Artist as Critic: Critical Writings of Oscar Wilde*, ed. Richard Ellmann (Chicago: University of Chicago Press, 1982), 380, and Matthew Arnold (who in the same essay praises the "joy" to be drawn from the best poetry), "The Study of Poetry," *English Literature and Irish Politics*, vol. 9 of *The Complete Prose Works of Matthew Arnold*, ed. R. H. Super (Ann Arbor: University of Michigan Press, 1973), 169, 163. For the impact of Shakespeare's death scenes on Yeats, see Rupin W. Desai, *Yeats's Shakespeare* (Evanston: Northwestern University Press, 1971), 119–32.

9   The idea's importance for Yeats is evident from his earlier and later variations of the same sentence: "amid the great moments, when Timon orders his tomb, when Hamlet cries to Horatio 'Absent thee from felicity awhile,' when Antony names 'Of many thousand kisses the poor last,' all is lyricism, unmixed passion, 'the integrity of fire'" (*E&I*, 240); "The arts are all the bridal chambers of joy. . . . I can hear the dance music in 'Absent thee from felicity awhile', or in Hamlet's speech over the dead Ophelia, and what of Cleopatra's last farewells, Lear's rage under the lightning, Oedipus sinking down at the story's end into an earth 'riven' by love?" (*Ex*, 448–49).

10 Heidegger, *Being and Time*, 331, 435.

11 For the influence of Nietzsche on Yeats, see Eitel Friedrich Timm, *William Butler Yeats und Friedrich Nietzsche* (Würzburg: Königshausen und Neumann, 1980); Otto Bohlmann, *Yeats and Nietzsche: An Exploration of Major Nietzschean Echoes in the Writings of William Butler Yeats* (London: Macmillan, 1982); and Frances Nesbitt Oppel, *Mask and Tragedy: Yeats and Nietzsche, 1902–10* (Charlottesville: University Press of Virginia, 1987).

12 On the Shelleyan echo in the first stanza, see Bloom, *Yeats*, 320, and Bornstein, *Transformations of Romanticism*, 64.

13 Shelley, *Prometheus Unbound*, 1.479. In borrowing the phrase Yeats changes it from plural to singular.

14 Shelley, *Prometheus Unbound*, 1.644.

15   Yeats also writes that in reverie he begins "to dream of eyelids that do not quiver before the bayonet" (*Myth*, 325).

16   Nietzsche, *"The Birth of Tragedy" and "The Genealogy of Morals,"* trans. Francis Golffing (New York: Anchor-Doubleday, 1956), 3.

17   In German, "ein metaphysischer Trost reisst uns momentan aus dem Getriebe der Wandelgestalten heraus" (Nietzsche, *Birth of Tragedy*, 102; *Werke in Drei Bänden*, ed. Karl Schlechta [Munich: Carl Hanser Verlag, 1954], 1:93). Although presented as apolitical, the poem's aestheticization of violence and celebration of the heroic yea-sayer could be seen as aligning its ideology more with the fascists of the day than with their opponents. See Joseph Chadwick's ideology critique of Yeats's aestheticization of violence and its relation to fascism in "Violence in Yeats's Later Politics and Poetry," *English Literary History*, 55 (1988): 869–93.

18   Nietzsche, *The Birth of Tragedy*, 51; *Werke*, 1:48. On Nietzsche's *Artisten-Metaphysik*, see *The Birth of Tragedy*, 9–10; *Werke*, 1:14.

19   Walter Pater, *The Renaissance: Studies in Art and Poetry*, ed. Donald L. Hill (1893; Berkeley: University of California Press, 1980), 190. On the "passing moment" and death, see Yeats's approving quotation of Florence Farr (*E&I*, 349).

20   See Stein, *House of Death*, 23–34. This tradition also has an Irish heritage.

21   See the draft printed in Stallworthy, *Vision and Revision*, 48. On the feminization of grief, see Ariès, *Hour*, 450–54, and Ann Douglas, *The Feminization of American Culture* (New York: Avon, 1977), 240–49.

22   Joyce Carol Oates, " 'At Least I Have Made a Woman of Her': Images of Women in Twentieth-Century Literature," *Georgia Review* 37 (1983): 7. On the rebellion of Nietzsche and Yeats against their own "femininity," see Bohlmann, *Yeats and Nietzsche*, 5–6.

23   Blake, *The Four Zoas*, 64:4–9, 131:31.

24   Friedrich Nietzsche, *Thus Spoke Zarathustra*, in *The Portable Nietzsche*, ed. and trans. Walter Kaufmann (New York: Viking-Penguin, 1976), 430. Wordsworth, "Ode: Intimations of Immortality," lines 176–77.

25   Coleridge proclaims: "We in ourselves rejoice!" ("Dejection: An Ode," line 72); Blake, *The Four Zoas*, 138:6, 8, 21.

26   Wordsworth, "Intimations Ode," lines 169, 198; Coleridge, "Dejection," line 54; Shelley, "Ode to the West Wind," line 60.

27   Frazer, *Golden Bough*, 441, 461.

28   John Dryden, "An Essay of Dramatic Poesy," *The Works of John Dryden*,

ed. H. T. Swedenborg (Berkeley: University of California Press, 1971), 17:35.

29 W. H. Auden, "In Memory of W. B. Yeats," *Collected Poems,* ed. Edward Mendelson (New York: Random House, 1976), 198.

30 Emerson, "Self-Reliance," *Essays,* 271.

31 Vivienne Koch, *W. B. Yeats, The Tragic Phase: A Study of the Last Poems* (1951; Hamden, Conn.: Archon, 1969), 99; Bloom, *Yeats,* 435.

32 Bornstein, *Transformations of Romanticism,* 50.

33 Freud, "Mourning and Melancholia," *SE,* 14:255.

34 Freud, "On Transience," *SE,* 14:306.

35 Freud, *Jokes and Their Relation to the Unconscious, SE,* 8:147. Freud's theory of laughter is a modification of Herbert Spencer's.

36 See, among other poems, "The Sad Shepherd," "The Madness of King Goll," "The Rose of Battle," "Cradle Song," and "An Appointment." For the origin of the commonplace, see Aristotle, "Parts of Animals," *The Complete Works of Aristotle,* ed. Jonathan Barnes, rev. ed. (Princeton: Princeton University Press, 1984), 1:1049; the dictum would have been familiar to Yeats from the discussion of laughter in Castiglione's *Book of the Courtier,* which Yeats read in Hoby's translation (*The Book of the Courtier,* trans. Sir Thomas Hoby [London: Dent, 1975], 137).

37 On the social dimension of laughter, see Kenneth Burke, "Hypergelasticism Exposed" (1941), *The Philosophy of Literary Form: Studies in Symbolic Action* (Berkeley: University of California Press, 1973), 414–18, and John Morreall, *Taking Laughter Seriously* (Albany: State University of New York Press, 1983), 4–19.

38 Mikhail Bakhtin, "The History of Laughter," *Rabelais and His World,* trans. Hélène Iswolsky (Cambridge, Mass.: MIT Press, 1968), 90–92.

39 Nietzsche, *The Gay Science,* trans. Walter Kaufmann (New York: Vintage-Random House, 1974), 207; *Zarathustra,* 153.

40 Bakhtin, "Laughter," 69–70.

41 In Lacan's version of the master-slave dialectic, the slave identifies with the dead master; see *Speech and Language in Psychoanalysis,* 79, 161–70.

42 Bloom alone invokes the sublime to interpret Yeats. But he restricts himself to the sublime of influence and, even while celebrating the transcendence of the human in earlier Romantics, condemns as inhumane the lyrics that for me manifest the Yeatsian sublime. Compare his response to what he calls Yeats's "inhumane nonsense" with his praise for Thomas Weiskel's assertion: "The essential claim of the sublime is that man can, in feeling and in speech, transcend the human." See Bloom,

Yeats, 438, and Foreword to Thomas Weiskel, *The Romantic Sublime: Studies in the Structure and Psychology of Transcendence* (1976; Baltimore: Johns Hopkins University Press, 1986), vii; Weiskel, *Romantic Sublime,* 3. In a later essay on Yeats, Bloom revises his negative view of the Yeatsian sublime but refers dismissively to the position I elaborate here: that the "daemonic or Sublime is thus merely another evasion of the unacceptable necessity of dying" ("Yeats, Gnosticism, and the Sacred Void," *Poetry and Repression: Revisionism from Blake to Stevens* [New Haven: Yale University Press, 1976], 209).

43   Much work has been done to synthesize the sublime, ranging from the classic book of Samuel Holt Monk, *The Sublime: A Study of Critical Theories in Eighteenth-Century England* (1935; Ann Arbor: University of Michigan Press, 1960), to Weiskel, *Romantic Sublime,* 3–33. For the similarities between Longinus and Edmund Burke on the sublime, see Paul H. Fry, *The Reach of Criticism* (New Haven: Yale University Press, 1983), 60–61. I draw on Fry's discussion, which assimilates Kant's mathematical and dynamical sublime to Longinus's version; on Weiskel's synthesis; and on Neil Hertz's interreading of Longinus, Burke, Kant, and Freud in "The Notion of Blockage in the Literature of the Sublime," in *Psychoanalysis and the Question of the Text,* ed. Geoffrey Hartman (Baltimore: Johns Hopkins University Press, 1978), 62–85.

44   Friedrich von Schiller, *"Naive and Sentimental Poetry" and "On the Sublime": Two Essays,* trans. Julius A. Elias (New York: Frederick Ungar, 1966), 210; Iris Murdoch, "The Sublime and the Beautiful Revisited," *Yale Review* 49 (1959–60): 268. For the counterassociation of the sublime with the comic, see the comments on Hegel and Marx of Gary Shapiro, "From the Sublime to the Political: Some Historical Notes," *NLH* 16 (1985): 225–26; and for a genealogy of the comic sublime, see Raimonda Modiano, "Humanism and the Comic Sublime: From Kant to Friedrich Theodor Vischer," *Studies in Romanticism* 26 (1987): 231–44.

45   Longinus, *On Sublimity,* trans. D. A. Russell, in *Ancient Literary Criticism: The Principal Texts in New Translations,* ed. D. A. Russell and M. Winterbottom (Oxford: Clarendon Press, 1972), 478–79.

46   Longinus, *On Sublimity,* 476.

47   For an analysis of the ambivalence of the sublime, see Angus Fletcher, *Allegory: The Theory of a Symbolic Mode* (Ithaca: Cornell University Press, 1964), 243–52.

48   Edmund Burke, *A Philosophical Inquiry into the Origin of Our Ideas of the*

Sublime and the Beautiful, ed. James T. Boulton (London: Routledge and Kegan Paul, 1958), 73.

49 Schiller, "On the Sublime," 198.

50 Emmanuel Kant, *Critique of Judgment,* trans. J. H. Bernard (London: Hafner-Macmillan, 1951), 100–101.

51 Bloom acknowledges Yeats's resistance to the deadening "object-world"; it makes Yeats possibly one of the last "Sublime" poets (*Poetry and Repression,* 209). Bornstein also brings out this antinaturalism in Yeats's visionary poems (*Transformations of Romanticism,* 27–30).

52 Burke's "thesaurus" of the "deflections" of death differs from mine; see "Thanatopsis," 369. Nothing itself, death could be seen as exemplifying and exaggerating the hidden metonymical structure of naming, because death must inevitably undergo translation. A literalist reading of Yeats's myth of the afterlife would, of course, annul the importance of death in any of these forms, but it would also be incapable of explaining his lyrics' ambivalent representation of death as an occasion for courage.

53 Longinus, *On Sublimity,* 473.

54 Longinus, *On Sublimity,* 476.

55 Burke, *Philosophical Inquiry,* 65, 59.

56 Kant, *Critique of Judgment,* 100.

57 Wordsworth, *Prelude* (1805), 6.534–35.

58 Heidegger, *Being and Time,* 320.

59 On the oedipal or pre-oedipal nature of the sublime, see Neil Hertz, "A Reading of Longinus," *The End of the Line: Essays on Psychoanalysis and the Sublime* (New York: Columbia University Press, 1985), 1–20, and Weiskel, *Romantic Sublime,* 91–106.

60 Longinus, *On Sublimity,* 467.

61 Wallace Stevens, *The Necessary Angel: Essays on Reality and the Imagination* (New York: Vintage-Random House, 1951), 36.

62 Heidegger, *Being and Time,* 321.

63 Hertz, "Longinus," 7.

64 Jacques Derrida, "Of an Apocalyptic Tone Recently Adopted in Philosophy," trans. John P. Leavey, Jr., *Semeia* 23 (1982): 87.

65 Suzanne Guerlac's version of Longinus sometimes approaches such a view, though her analysis is generally insightful; see her "Longinus and the Subject of the Sublime," *NLH* 16 (1985): 275–89. With the help of the later Heidegger, Guerlac argues against the affective theory of the sublime because "feeling" obscures the threat of the rhetorical sublime to the subject's self-identity. But Heidegger's analysis of the intersubjective

basis of *Stimmung* (mood), and especially of *Mitbefindlichkeit* (co-state-of-mind), preserves the affective sublime without necessarily endorsing an ideological concept of the self.

66 Whitaker describes these two moments in the early apocalyptic romances as the psychic annihilation of "Rosa Alchemica" and the complementary inflation of "The Tables of the Law," the self-negating Christ and the self-asserting Lucifer (*Swan and Shadow*, 44).

67 As Brenda Webster argues of Yeats's bird and sword, the concentrated image may be thought of as a "talismanic object," a "defense against fears of nothingness and loss of individuality" (*Yeats: A Psychoanalytic Study* [Stanford: Stanford University Press, 1973], 207). It may also be likened to Hertz's moment of "figurative reconstitution" in the sublime after the moment of "disintegration" ("Longinus," 14).

68 Weiskel uses the phrase *on and on* to describe the mathematical sublime (*Romantic Sublime*, 22).

69 For an elaboration of Yeats's central aesthetic tenets on the basis of this passage, see Helen Vendler, *Yeats's "Vision" and the Later Plays* (Cambridge, Mass.: Harvard University Press, 1963), 28.

70 See *AV*, 206; *E&I*, 288. On eternal recurrence, or *ewige Wiederkehr*, in Yeats and Nietzsche, see Bohlmann, *Yeats and Nietzsche*, 57–68.

71 Nietzsche, *Birth of Tragedy*, 52; *Werke*, 1:49.

72 Freud, *Ego and the Id, SE*, 19:58; *Inhibitions, Symptoms and Anxiety, SE*, 20:130.

73 This resemblance is not only rhetorical but also psychological, as we might surmise from the image of a woman with "grotesque" nether parts. See Horace, "The Art of Poetry," trans. Walter Jackson Bate, in *Criticism: The Major Texts*, ed. Bate, 2d ed. (New York: Harcourt Brace Jovanovich, 1970), 51.

74 Samuel Holt Monk, "A Grace beyond the Reach of Art," *Journal of the History of Ideas* 5 (1944): 131–50.

75 Technically, syncope would shorten the prosodical value of some of these examples: *indifferent, darkening*, and *glittering*.

76 Although the older Yeats was fond of such words and such sounds in general, they converge more often at the ends of his later sublime lyrics than they do elsewhere. They intensify and possibly surpass the general stylistic freedom of his verse in this period. The characteristic variations in meter—as in stanza and rhyme—have been amply described and need not be rehearsed here; see Harvey Gross, *Sound and Form in Modern Poetry: A Study of Prosody from Thomas Hardy to Robert Lowell* (Ann

Arbor: University of Michigan Press, 1964), 48–55; Parkinson, *W. B. Yeats: The Later Poetry,* 181–231; and Adelyn Dougherty, *A Study of Rhythmic Structure in the Verse of William Butler Yeats* (The Hague: Mouton, 1973).

77   Longinus, *On Sublimity,* 483, 480–89.

78   Shelley addresses the wind with the apostrophe, "O Uncontrollable!" in the "Ode to the West Wind," line 47.

79   Grossman, *Poetic Knowledge,* 162; Hugh Kenner, *A Colder Eye: The Modern Irish Writers* (New York: Penguin, 1984), 108–10.

80   Geoffrey Hartman, *Saving the Text: Literature/Derrida/Philosophy* (Baltimore: Johns Hopkins University Press, 1981), 130.

81   Remaking himself, Yeats simultaneously converts two antisublime poets into precursors of his sublimity. In "An Essay on Criticism," Pope grudgingly allows for the waywardness of Pegasus and then suggests that there is a semisublimity or "*Grace* beyond the Reach of Art" (lines 150–55). Further, Yeats's verbal pile-up echoes Ben Jonson's satiric "Ode to Himself": "Run on, and rage, sweat, censure, and condemn . . . though thy nerves be shrunk, and blood be cold . . . thy strain" (lines 9–10, 45, 49).

82   Shakespeare, *Richard III,* 3.3.15–18, 5.1.25–27. On Yeats and prophecy, see Jon Stallworthy, "The Prophetic Voice," in *Vision and Revision,* 20–38. Whitaker offers the best analysis of the apocalypse in Yeats; see *Swan and Shadow,* 34–54.

83   James L. Kugel, "Two Introductions to Midrash," in *Midrash and Literature,* ed. Geoffrey Hartman and Sanford Budick (New Haven: Yale University Press, 1986), 81.

84   Kant, *Critique of Judgment,* 116.

85   Hayden White uses the regulative aesthetic categories of the sublime and the beautiful to analyze the discipline of history; see "The Politics of Historical Interpretation: Discipline and De-Sublimation," *Critical Inquiry* 9 (1982): 113–37.

86   Claude Lévi-Strauss, "The Structural Study of Myth," rpt. in *The Structuralists: From Marx to Lévi-Strauss,* ed. Richard T. DeGeorge and Fernande M. DeGeorge (Garden City, N.Y.: Anchor-Doubleday, 1972), 169–81, 193.

87   On miniature and binarism, see Claude Lévi-Strauss, *The Savage Mind,* trans. George Weidenfeld and Nicolson Ltd. (London: Weidenfeld and Nicolson, 1966), 16–33. Ellmann discusses the pairs in "Two Songs from a Play" (*Identity,* 260–63).

88   Discussions of Yeats's relation to fascism include O'Brien, "Passion and Cunning"; Cullingford, *Yeats, Ireland and Fascism*; Grattan Freyer, *W. B. Yeats and the Anti-Democratic Tradition* (Totowa, N.J.: Barnes and Noble, 1981); Chadwick, "Violence in Yeats's Later Politics and Poetry"; and Paul Scott Stanfield, *Yeats and Politics in the 1930s* (London: Macmillan, 1988).

89   Stephen Spender, *The Thirties and After: Poetry, Politics, People, 1933–1970* (New York: Random House, 1978), 5–6, 13.

90   See, for example, Bloom's readings of "The Second Coming," "Lapis Lazuli," and "The Gyres" in *Yeats*.

91   For an overview of Yeats's thoughts on war, see Fahmy Farag, "Needless Horror or Terrible Beauty: Yeats's Ideas of Hatred, War, and Violence," *The Opposing Virtues* (Dublin: Dolmen, 1978), 7–19.

92   Kant, *Critique of Judgment*, 102.

93   Freud, *Beyond the Pleasure Principle, SE,* 18:36–39.

94   Derrida, "Apocalyptic Tone," 87.

95   Shelley, "The Witch of Atlas," 63.545.

96   Nietzsche's phrase is "die *Lust am Vernichten*" (*The Twilight of the Idols,* in *Portable Nietzsche,* 563; *Werke,* 2:1032); Blake, *America,* plate 8, line 3.

97   Bloom, *Yeats,* 434–39.

98   Blake, *The Four Zoas,* 135:36–39.

99   Blake, *The Four Zoas,* 136: 16–17, 21–27.

100 Derrida, "Apocalyptic Tone," 89. See also Terence Allan Hoagwood, *Prophecy and the Philosophy of Mind: Traditions of Blake and Shelley* (University: University of Alabama Press, 1985), 57.

101 Shapiro, "From the Sublime to the Political," 216.

102 Emerson, *Essays,* 967–68; Shelley, "Mont Blanc," lines 16, 80–81.

103 I do not wish, however, to exaggerate the political flexibility of the sublime. The sexual politics of the sublime has traditionally been antifeminist, and we still need a full feminist critique of the sublime as the violent agon of father and son or as a masculine war with danger. For these reasons, as well as for pacifist concerns, one may ultimately decide to reject the sublime altogether. But, in my view, one might also attempt to construct a version of the sublime that would be compatible with certain forms of revolutionary feminism.

104 See, for example, R. W. B. Lewis, "Days of Wrath and Laughter," *Trials of the Word: Essays in American Literature and the Humanistic Tradition* (New Haven: Yale University Press, 1965), 184–235. Douglas Robinson criticizes Lewis's distinction but goes on to argue that the Augustin-

ian, spiritual view is "suited to political conservatives" as against "implicitly revolutionary predictive interpretations"—an assertion that recent fundamentalism in the United States would seem to contradict. See his helpful introductory analysis in *American Apocalypses: The Image of the End of the World in American Literature* (Baltimore: Johns Hopkins University Press, 1985), 17.

105 Spender, *Thirties,* 13.
106 Auden, *Collected Poems,* 197.

3. THE SELF-ELEGY

1 Freud, *SE,* 14:289.
2 Helen Vendler, *Wallace Stevens: Words Chosen Out of Desire* (1984; Cambridge, Mass.: Harvard University Press, 1986), 35.
3 De Man, *Blindness and Insight,* 181.
4 The term has been used by other critics from John Draper to Harold Bloom. Although no comprehensive interpretation of the self-elegy exists, many discussions of elegy touch on the subject. Lawrence Lipking describes a related form: poets' representations of their careers; see *Life of the Poet,* 65–137. Arnold Stein analyzes Renaissance lyrics about one's own death in *The House of Death,* 69–118. Edward Engelberg studies Romantic and post-Romantic laments for the unlived life, primarily in prose works; see *Elegiac Fictions.* Philippe Ariès offers a brief historical account of reflection on one's own death in *Western Attitudes toward Death,* 27–54. The corresponding medieval genre of "Dyenge Well" is usefully described by Nancy Lee Beaty in *The Craft of Dying: A Study in the Literary Tradition of the* Ars Moriendi *in England* (New Haven: Yale University Press, 1970).
5 Lionel Trilling, *The Liberal Imagination: Essays on Literature and Society* (1950; London: Secker and Warburg, 1964), 131.
6 Wordsworth, "Ode: Intimations of Immortality," lines 180–81.
7 Wordsworth, "Preface" to *Lyrical Ballads, Literary Criticism,* 70–71.
8 Herbert, "Jordan" (II), lines 5, 11; "The Forerunners," line 23.
9 Blanchot, *Orpheus,* 43. My discussion of the "specular," "reflexive," and "autobiographical" structure of the self-elegy also draws on de Man's "Autobiography as De-Facement," *Rhetoric of Romanticism,* 67–81. For a discussion of de Man's and Bloom's concepts of self-representation with regard to Yeats's autobiographical prose, see Daniel O'Hara, *Tragic*

Knowledge: Yeats's "Autobiography" and Hermeneutics (New York: Columbia University Press, 1981), 7–51.

10   "I am the one who formerly measured his song with a slender reed" (Spenser, *The Faerie Queene*, 1.1.1.2); Milton, *Paradise Regained*, line 1; see Wordsworth's "Tintern Abbey," "Intimations Ode," and "Prospectus" to *The Recluse*.

11   Milton, *Paradise Lost*, 7.26–27. Yeats writes in "Remorse for Intemperate Speech" that he has "[f]it audience found" (254).

12   Nietzsche, *Zarathustra*, 265.

13   T. E. Hulme, "Romanticism and Classicism," *Speculations* (London: Kegan Paul, 1924), 126–33.

14   This last phrase is Richard Rorty's; see his highly suggestive analysis of self-creation in *Contingency, Irony, and Solidarity* (Cambridge: Cambridge University Press, 1989).

15   Shelley, *The Witch of Atlas*, 62.537–63.552.

16   Ellmann, *Identity*, 191. I am not the first reader to call attention to the poem's rhetoric; see Whitaker, *Swan and Shadow*, 262–68. For negative assessments of the poem, see Kermode, *Sense*, 106, and Bloom, *Yeats*, 466–69. My view that the poem "talks death down" is anticipated by Priscilla Washburn Shaw, *Rilke, Valéry, and Yeats: The Domain of the Self* (New Brunswick, N.J.: Rutgers University Press, 1964), 221.

17   Milton, *Paradise Lost*, 9.14.

18   "Mantua bore me; the Calabrians snatched me away; now Naples holds me; I sang of pastures, the countryside, leaders." As a form, the self-epitaph goes back at least to the works in *The Greek Anthology*.

19   On the relation between prosopopoeia and other lyric tropes, see Paul de Man, "Lyrical Voice and Contemporary Theory: Riffaterre and Jauss," in *Lyric Poetry: Beyond New Criticism*, ed. Chaviva Hošek and Patricia Parker (Ithaca: Cornell University Press, 1985), 57, and "Autobiography as De-Facement." For a discussion of the Romantic epitaph, see Paul H. Fry, "The Absent Dead: Wordsworth, Byron, and the Epitaph," *Studies in Romanticism* 17 (1978): 413–33. For more on Yeats's epitaph, including a review of the relevant scholarship, see James Lovic Allen, *Yeats's Epitaph: A Key to Symbolic Unity in His Life and Work* (Washington, D.C.: University Press of America, 1982). See also Hugh Kenner's perceptive remarks about this epitaph's transformation of the genre: "The Sacred Book of the Arts," *Gnomon: Essays on Contemporary Literature* (New York: McDowell, Obolensky, 1958), 27.

20   Similarly, the last section of "Under Ben Bulben," according to which

"Yeats is laid" in Drumcliff churchyard beside "these words," would not be "true" until after the 1948 return of his remains from France—if even then.

21 Schopenhauer, *World as Will and Representation,* 2:463, 474.

22 For the text of the rejected stanza and critical appraisals of it, see Parkinson, *W. B. Yeats: The Later Poetry,* 174, and Bloom, *Yeats,* 456.

23 See Ellmann, *Identity,* 204. Though Yeats often represents death as male, here it is female. According to some psychoanalysts, we imagine death as a return to the pre-oedipal, and at this stage we cannot distinguish male and female.

24 For discussions of ekphrasis as a critical term, see Leo Spitzer, "The 'Ode on a Grecian Urn,' or Content *vs.* Metagrammar" (1955), *Essays on English and American Literature,* ed. Anna Hatcher (Princeton: Princeton University Press, 1962), 72, 92, and Jean Hagstrum, *The Sister Arts: The Tradition of Literary Pictorialism and English Poetry from Dryden to Gray* (Chicago: University of Chicago Press, 1958), 18. See also Murray Krieger, "The Ekphrastic Principle and the Still Movement of Poetry; or *Laoköon* Revisited," *The Play and Place of Criticism* (Baltimore: Johns Hopkins University Press, 1967), 105–28.

25 Geoffrey Hartman discusses the generic link between inscriptions attached to the objects they commemorate and such Romantic lyrics as Wordsworth's "Lines Left Upon a Seat in a Yew-Tree," in which the inscription is freed from its dependent status; see "Wordsworth, Inscriptions, and Romantic Nature Poetry," *Beyond Formalism: Literary Essays 1958–1970* (New Haven: Yale University Press, 1970), 207–8; see also his *Wordsworth's Poetry, 1787–1814* (New Haven: Yale University Press, 1964), 12, 28.

26 Among the many works stressing Yeats's sympathetic relation to the visual arts, see Giorgio Melchiori, *The Whole Mystery of Art: Pattern into Poetry in the Work of W. B. Yeats* (New York: Macmillan, 1961), and Elizabeth Bergmann Loizeaux, *Yeats and the Visual Arts* (New Brunswick, N.J.: Rutgers University Press, 1986). Though Yeats indisputably held a lifelong interest in the visual arts (a sympathetic interest evident in his more traditional ekphrases), some of his lyrics suggest that a more combative sensibility also underlies this fondness.

27 Wordsworth, "Elegiac Stanzas Suggested by a Picture of Peele Castle, In a Storm, Painted by Sir George Beaumont," lines 51, 34.

28 Wordsworth, *The Prelude* (1805), 7.248–49, 277.

29 "Ode on a Grecian Urn," *The Poems of John Keats,* ed. Miriam Allott (New

York: Longman-Norton, 1970), line 4. For another account of the poem's relation to Romantic meditations on art, see Bornstein, *Transformations of Romanticism*, 89–90.

30 Keats, "Ode on a Grecian Urn," lines 11, 34–35, 43.

31 J. Hillis Miller, *The Linguistic Moment* (Princeton: Princeton University Press, 1985), 347.

32 Keats, *The Fall of Hyperion: A Dream*, 1.141–45.

33 Vendler, *Yeats's "Vision,"* 71–92.

34 See Ariès, *Hour*, 99–110.

35 Freud, "Mourning and Melancholia," *SE*, 14:245.

36 Heidegger, *Being and Time*, 355–56.

37 Adorno, "Lyric Poetry and Society," 59–60.

38 Ann Douglas argues that for similar economic reasons, women and clergymen became the nineteenth-century custodians of death (*Feminization of American Culture*, 240–49). Louis-Vincent Thomas presents the view that capitalist societies lack a place for death (*Anthropologie de la mort* [Paris: Payot, 1976]). In a letter Yeats cites Rilke's notion of the human desire to escape "mass death" (*L*, 917). Even though he goes on to offer his "own philosophy" of death and expresses in another letter annoyance over "one of Rilke's ideas about death," he does not directly dispute this notion of avoiding "mass death" (*L*, 913). For a comparative analysis of Yeats and Rilke, see Shaw, *Rilke, Valéry, and Yeats*, 175–273. Suggesting that Yeats's fascination with death arose from his hatred of the middle class, Seamus Deane asks, "Sexuality and death, posed against the mob and democracy—surely this almost too easily offers another instance of solitude in the face of a mass civilization?" (*Celtic Revivals: Essays in Modern Irish Literature, 1880–1980* [London: Faber and Faber, 1985], 41–44).

39 On the interchangeability of God and death in Yeats, see Ellmann, *Yeats: The Man and the Masks*, 288, and Bloom, *Poetry and Repression*, 214. Drawing on Northrop Frye, Bloom describes Romanticism as a displaced Protestantism in *The Visionary Company: A Reading of English Romantic Poetry*, rev. ed. (Ithaca: Cornell University Press, 1971), xvii–xxv. For a historical treatment of Protestantism and death poetry, see John Draper, *The Funeral Elegy and the Rise of English Romanticism* (New York: New York University Press, 1929). Ariès observes that spiritualism—by means of which Yeats sought communion with the dead—flourished primarily among Protestants; see Ariès, *Hour*, 462. My view of Yeats's self-elegies contrasts with Bloom's argument that for Yeats and

European poets, as against American "solipsists," death is "a social phenomenon essentially"; see "Death and the Native Strain in American
Poetry," *Figures of Capable Imagination* (New York: Seabury, 1976), 99.

40 Ariès, *Western Attitudes toward Death,* 51.

41 Freud, "Mourning and Melancholia," *SE,* 14:246–53.

42 Blake, "To George Cumberland," 12 April 1827, *Complete Poetry,* 783.
Elsewhere, Yeats quotes this famous letter (*E&I,* 138).

43 Wordsworth, *The Prelude* (1850), 6.607–8. Whitaker contrasts Yeats's
"Tower" and Wordsworth's "Intimation's Ode" (*Swan and Shadow,* 196).

44 Indebted to David Lynch, my view that death is the repressed signified
nevertheless modifies his argument that it is Hanrahan's overexcitement
before the women; see *Yeats: The Poetics of the Self* (Chicago: Chicago
University Press, 1979), 17–28. See also Harris, *Coole,* 191.

45 Milton, *Paradise Lost,* 1.254–55.

46 Daniel Harris usefully observes that the rifle is an emblem of the mind's
own violence (*Coole,* 197–98).

47 A. Norman Jeffares, *A New Commentary on the Poems of W. B. Yeats*
(Stanford: Stanford University Press, 1984), 223.

48 Keats, line 33; Stevens, *Poems,* 70. Bloom also notes the parallel with
Stevens (*Yeats,* 352).

49 The logic of my argument is built on two sources: Freud's discussions of
reaction-formations and antithetical terms (see, e.g., *SE,* 12:299) and
Lévi-Strauss's discussions of the structure of myth. Lévi-Strauss observes
that "mythical thought always works from the awareness of oppositions
toward their progressive mediation" ("The Structural Study of Myth,"
188). Yeats's technique of regulating the binarism of life and death by
superimposing upon it dramatic "voices" can be traced back to earlier
lyrics, such as "Ego Dominus Tuus" and "The Phases of the Moon," and
back to Shelley's "The Two Spirits—An Allegory," Marvell's "A Dialogue Between the Soul and the Body," and the inner dialogues of the
Sufi tradition.

50 Spenser, *The Faerie Queene,* 1.10.55.2. Both Spenser and Yeats allude to
the Gospel of Saint Matthew, 7:14.

51 In Herbert's "Church-monuments," the speaker commands himself:
"Mark here below / How tame these ashes are" (lines 22–23); and
Thomas Proctor translates the title of his "*Respice Finem*" with the words,
"See here, the fine" of mortal joys (line 2).

52 Freud, *Beyond the Pleasure Principle, SE,* 18:41.

53 Bloom, *Yeats,* 373.

54 Freud, "The Theme of the Three Caskets," *SE*, 12:299. Freud himself wonders whether the death drive represents an attempt to console himself: "Perhaps we have adopted the belief because there is something comforting in it. . . . It may be . . . that this belief in the internal necessity of dying is only another of those illusions which we have created '*um die Schwere des Daseins zu ertragen* [to bear the burden of existence].'" See Freud, *Beyond the Pleasure Principle, SE*, 18:40.

55 Milton, *Paradise Lost*, 12.643; Shakespeare, *King Lear*, 5.3.22. Bornstein thinks the brand or breath recalls Shelley's fading coal of the imagination (*Transformations of Romanticism*, 87).

56 See Ellmann, *Identity*, 171–72. Tree and dying god signify essentially the same thing, as Yeats knew from Frazer. In *The Golden Bough* Frazer discusses the burning of trees thought to embody vegetation deities (853). He links this practice to the ritual slaying of gods in effigy to ensure their resurrection in a more youthful form (395). Recounting the rites of Attis and other vegetation deities, Frazer describes how these gods were often represented "in duplicate, both by the tree and by the effigy"—as in Yeats's poem (459, 853). No doubt Yeats would have been intrigued by Frazer's claim that the Celts systematically practiced such rites (855).

57 Lévi-Strauss, "Structural Study of Myth," 193.

58 Frazer, *Golden Bough*, 459–60; see also Ellmann, *Identity*, 171–72.

59 Alfred Nutt, *The Voyage of Bran*, ed. Kuno Meyer (London: David Nutt, 1897), 2:145.

60 "Ingratitude! thou marble-hearted fiend, / More hideous when thou show'st thee in a child / Than the sea-monster" (Shakespeare, *King Lear*, 1.4.259–61). The rhetoric and cadences of Yeats's lines suggest Lear's ensuing commands ("Hear . . . , Suspend . . .").

61 Freud, "Mourning and Melancholia," *SE*, 14:253.

62 Herbert, "The Forerunners," line 13; Shakespeare, *The Tempest*, 5.1.57.

63 Stevens, "As You Leave the Room," *Opus Posthumous*, ed. Samuel French Morse (1957; New York: Vintage-Random House, 1982), 117.

64 Bloom, *Yeats*, 458.

65 Nevertheless, we cannot understand the *Oisin* stanza by importing into it the story about Maud Gonne in the next stanza, unless, like Bloom, we try to read "starved for . . . his faery bride" as "starved for Maud Gonne," even though Yeats had not yet met Maud Gonne at the time of composing *Oisin*; see *Yeats*, 458. Daniel Albright observes that this is the first time Yeats "posited a strictly psychoanalytic explanation of one of his

created women" (*The Myth Against Myth: A Study of Yeats's Imagination in Old Age* [London: Oxford University Press, 1972], 160).

66 See Susan Gubar's discussion of Pygmalion and the blankness of women in men's texts: "'The Blank Page' and the Issues of Female Creativity," originally published in *Critical Inquiry*, rpt. in *Writing and Sexual Difference*, ed. Elizabeth Abel (Chicago: University of Chicago Press, 1982), 73–89.

67 For an analysis of the structure of the literary meditation, see Louis Martz, *The Poetry of Meditation*, 2d ed. (New Haven: Yale University Press, 1962), 32–39.

68 See Beaty, *Craft of Dying*, 16, and Ariès, *Hour*, 130–31.

69 See the prose draft transcribed by Stallworthy in his *Vision and Revision*, 60.

70 In addition to the works I have mentioned, the lines also evoke "Easter, 1916" and the related elegies, "Upon a House shaken by the Land Agitation," and "Sweet Dancer."

71 See Ariès, *Hour*, 105.

72 Wordsworth, "Intimations Ode," line 58.

73 For commentary on the relation between the "Rejoice" of "The Gyres" and this "rejoice?" see Whitaker, *Swan and Shadow*, 296, and Koch, *W. B. Yeats*, 115–16.

CODA

1 Burke, "Thanatopsis," 370.

2 Wilfred Owen, *The Poems of Wilfred Owen*, ed. Jon Stallworthy (New York: Norton, 1985), 137–38. For more on Yeats and Owen, see Jon Stallworthy, "W. B. Yeats and Wilfred Owen," *Critical Quarterly* 11 (1969): 199–214, and Stanfield, *Yeats and Politics*, 90–95.

3 See Owen's draft "Preface," rpt. in *Poems*, 192: "My subject is War, and the pity of War. The Poetry is in the pity."

4 Owen, "Anthem for Doomed Youth," *Poems*, 76.

5 Blanchot, *Space*, 122.

6 Owen, *Poems*, 145.

7 Wilde, "The Critic as Artist," *Critical Writings*, 380.

8 Herbert Marcuse, "The Ideology of Death," in *The Meaning of Death*, ed. Herman Feifel (1959; New York: McGraw-Hill, 1965), 64–76; Louis-Vincent Thomas, *Mort et pouvoir* (Paris: Payot, 1978).

INDEX

Abrams, M. H., 100
"Acre of Grass, An," 82, 140
Adorno, Theodor, 53, 60, 64, 166
Afterlife (reincarnation), 1– 3, 6–7, 8, 37, 150, 161–65, 179, 197, 207n.1, 226n.52, 233n.39
"All Souls' Night," 36–38, 65, 113
"Anima Mundi," 185
Apocalypse, 20, 79–80, 95, 104–5, 106, 112, 125–33, 135, 145, 202
"Apparitions, The," 151, 201
"Appointment, An," 103
Ariès, Philippe, 11
Aristotle, 83, 103
Arnold, Matthew, 52, 83
Ars moriendi, 9, 167, 176–77, 193
Ashbery, John, 153
"At Algeciras—a Meditation upon Death," 170
Auden, W. H., 9, 16, 60, 133, 136, 152, 196
Autobiographical lyric, 12, 21– 22, 137–40, 147–49
Autobiography, The (Autobiographies), 4–7, 32, 37. See also *Estrangement; Reveries over Childhood and Youth*

Bakhtin, Mikhail, 103–4
Baudelaire, Charles, 23
Beardsley, Mabel, 16, 27–32, 40, 94
"Beautiful Lofty Things," 45– 49, 63, 65, 200
Berryman, John, 17, 136
Binary oppositions, 108, 127– 28, 176–78, 181–83, 185–86, 234n.49
"Black Tower, The," 1
Blake, William, 24, 53, 80, 82, 95, 105, 109, 129, 154, 162, 168;

America, 130; *The Four Zoas,* 94–95, 106, 130–31
Blanchot, Maurice, 29, 62, 140, 203– 4, 213n.18
Bloom, Harold, 4, 80, 109, 129– 30, 178, 189, 224n.42, 233n.39
Bly, Robert, 59, 74–75
Bornstein, George, 100
Browning, Elizabeth Barrett, 27
Browning, Robert, 85, 152
Buddhism, 92, 139
Burke, Edmund, 7, 108–9, 113, 131
Burke, Kenneth, 10, 109, 201
Burns, Robert, 15
Byron, George Gordon, Lord, 82, 92
"Byzantium," 21, 152, 159–61

Calvary, 29
"Cap and Bells, The," 134
Carpe diem, 12, 80, 91–92, 155, 181
Castiglione, Baldassare, 104, 119, 224n.36
Castration, 11, 109, 118, 172, 183
Cathleen ni Houlihan, 63, 196
Celtic Twilight, The, 24, 97
"Certain Artists bring her Dolls and Drawings," 30
Chaucer, Geoffrey, 34, 187–88
Christ, 29, 55, 107, 128, 139
"Circus Animals' Desertion, The," 33, 136, 139–40, 143, 151, 163, 187– 93, 194, 206
"Coat, A," 137–40, 142, 149, 161, 190
"Cold Heaven, The," 114, 119
Coleridge, Samuel Taylor, 82, 117, 136, 169; "Dejection," 94–95, 98, 187

"Collar-bone of a Hare, The," 104
"Come Gather Round Me, Par-
    nellites," 75
"Conjunctions," 116
"Coole and Ballylee, 1931," 112, 120,
    147
"Coole Park, 1929," 50–51, 146
Cordelia, 88, 94, 182
Countess Cathleen, The, 189–91
"Crucifixion of the Outcast, The," 121
Cuchulain, 8
"Cuchulain Comforted," 194
Curse, 12, 76, 79, 102, 106–7, 112,
    121–26, 130, 145, 183

Daimon (daimonic), 83, 112–13
Dante, 18, 44, 162
Davis, Thomas, 52, 61, 146
"Death," 7, 150–51, 206
Decadent poets, 18, 134
Deictis, 51, 61, 88, 149
De Man, Paul, 12, 23, 134–35, 230n.9
"Demon and Beast," 154
Derrida, Jacques, 12, 112, 131,
    213n.16
"Dialogue of Self and Soul, A," 101–2,
    112–13, 117, 120, 136, 163, 175–
    81, 189
Dickinson, Emily, 1, 11, 136, 203
Donne, John, 54, 218n.60
Dowson, Ernest, 91
"Dream of Death, A" ("An Epitaph"),
    17, 19, 20–24, 26, 206
Dryden, John, 97
Du Bellay, Joachim, 92

"Easter, 1916," 2, 20, 33, 53, 59–66,
    67, 68, 69, 70, 71, 73, 75, 76, 88,
    96, 119; quoted, 12
Easter Rising, 16, 33, 52, 59– 67, 68,
    196
Ekphrasis, 12, 49–51, 92, 136, 152–
    61
Elegy: ambivalence and aggression in,
    12, 15–17, 18, 26–27, 33–38, 43–

44, 45, 49– 50, 54–59, 61, 66–67,
    69, 76– 77; coda of, 36, 50–51,
    73– 74; economic problem of, 40–
    45; group, 32–38, 41, 43–45, 45–
    51, 56; identification with the dead
    in, 16, 28, 33, 38, 45–46, 51, 57–
    59, 63–64, 66– 67, 72–73, 76–78;
    private, 17, 26–51, 68; public, 17,
    52– 78; satire in, 54–59, 68, 75–
    76; and tragic joy, 80–81, 93– 98,
    116
Eliot, T. S., 8, 57, 105, 128, 142
Ellmann, Richard, 80, 146, 207nn.1,2
Emerson, Ralph Waldo, 42, 98– 99,
    131
Emery, Florence Farr, 37
Emmet, Robert, 65, 75
"End of the Day, The," 29–30
"Ephemera," 81
Epitaph, 17, 20–22, 26, 35, 51. See
    also Self-epitaph
"Epitaph, An." See "Dream of Death,
    A"
Eros, 5, 22, 124, 177
Estrangement, 139, 165

"Fallen Majesty," 24–25
"Fascination of What's Difficult, The,"
    79, 123–24
Fascism, 75, 77, 89, 126, 128– 29,
    131–33, 223n.17
"Fergus and the Druid," 36
Ferguson, Sir Samuel, 52, 146
"Fish, The," 121
"Fisherman, The," 137, 140–42
Fitzgerald, Edward: Rubaiyat, 91
Flaubert, Gustave, 162
Frazer, Sir James, 18, 65, 96, 183
Freud, Sigmund, 11; and elegy, 16, 18,
    22, 38, 56, 65, 76; and self-elegy,
    163–64, 172, 177– 81, 185; and
    tragic joy and the sublime, 80, 96,
    101–2, 109, 118, 126, 129
"Friends That Have It . . . , The," 139
Frye, Northrop, 12–13
Full Moon in March, A, 118

Gadamer, Hans-Georg, 82
Gender: dead or absent women and
    creativity, 3, 17–26, 73, 144, 171–
    72, 191; effacement of women, 17–
    26, 31, 52, 68– 69, 93–94, 99,
    142–44, 171– 72, 183–84, 190–
    91, 229n.103; suppression of own
    "femininity," 93–94, 99, 111, 126,
    141–45, 161, 201–2
"General Introduction for my Work,
    A," 84, 208n.8
Genre. *See* individual genres
"Ghost of Roger Casement, The," 75
Goethe, Johann Wolfgang von, 56, 82
Gonne, Maud, 21–22, 25, 26, 47–48,
    61, 62, 144, 190
Gore-Booth, Eva, 67–68, 71–74
Gray, Thomas, 29, 32, 136
Greek Anthology, The, 152, 231n.18
Gregory, Lady Augusta, 4, 16, 47–48,
    50, 141, 153
Gregory, Robert, 16, 38–45, 57, 65,
    70
Grossman, Allen, 121
"Gyres, The," 3, 9, 79, 80, 81, 85, 89,
    93–102, 111, 118, 120, 121, 126,
    130, 131, 142, 150–51, 198, 201,
    202

Hamlet, 57, 82, 86–87, 88, 90, 145,
    169, 194, 204
Hanrahan, 4, 122–23, 124, 170– 72,
    190
Happy death, the, 91–92
"Happy Townland, The," 1
Hardy, Thomas, 16, 21, 32, 57
Hartman, Geoffrey, 121, 232n.25
Heaney, Seamus, 8, 10
Hegel, G. W. F., 201
Heidegger, Martin, 60, 76, 80; on
    one's own death, 11, 29, 85, 110,
    163–64, 179, 204; and the sublime,
    109–11, 114, 132
Hemingway, Ernest, 8
"He mourns for the Change . . . ," 20
Herbert, George, 177; "The Forerun-

ners," 138, 186, 187– 88;
    "Heaven," 194; "Jordan" (II), 138;
    The Temple, 194
"Her Courage," 31
"Her Courtesy," 28–29, 63
"He remembers forgotten Beauty," 29
"Her Friends bring her a Christmas
    Tree," 31–32
"Her Praise," 25
"Her Race," 28, 30
Hertz, Neil, 110, 112
"Her Vision in the Wood," 96
"He wishes his Beloved were Dead,"
    17, 22–24
Hill, Geoffrey, 8, 10, 59
Hitler, Adolf, 89
Hobbes, Thomas, 103
Homer, 109, 147, 156–57, 158, 172;
    Iliad, 100
Horace, 118, 158, 159
Horton, William, 37
Hour-Glass, The, 6, 139
Hulme, T. E., 105, 142
Huxley, Aldous, 8
Hynes, Mary, 24, 170

"I Became an Author," 46
"In Memory of Alfred Pollexfen," 20,
    34–36, 37, 45, 48, 70, 200; quoted,
    12
"In Memory of Eva Gore-Booth and
    Con Markievicz," 67–68, 71–74,
    75, 155
"In Memory of Major Robert Greg-
    ory," 3, 18, 34, 38, 40– 45, 48, 65,
    73, 218n.60
Inscription, 21, 140, 147–49, 152
"Introductory Rhymes," 33–34, 47
Invocation, 12, 136, 140–41, 147,
    187
Ireland, 10, 16, 49, 52, 57– 58, 62,
    154
"Irish Airman foresees his Death, An,"
    38, 84–85; alluded to, 92, 204

Jarrell, Randall, 152–53

Jeffares, A. Norman, 175
Johnson, Lionel, 41, 43, 65
Johnston, Laura, 21–22
Jonson, Ben, 16, 54, 65, 218n.60,
    228n.81
Joyce, James, 33, 81

Kant, Immanuel, 106, 108–9, 112–
    18, 126, 129, 132
Keats, John, 7, 32, 136, 159, 203; *Fall
    of Hyperion,* 160; "Ode on a Grecian
    Urn," 152– 53, 156–57; "To Au-
    tumn," 175; "When I have Fears
    that I may cease to be," 11
Kenner, Hugh, 121
Kermode, Frank, 21, 219n.64
King of the Great Clock Tower, The, 118,
    134
King's Threshold, The, 103–5, 132,
    202–3
Kugel, James, 125

Lacan, Jacques, 22, 108, 112, 216n.46
"Lamentation of the Old Pensioner,
    The," 4
Lane, Hugh, 56–57
"Lapis Lazuli," 2, 9, 79, 87– 91, 94,
    96, 98, 101, 107, 109, 110
    (quoted), 111, 120, 126, 142, 152–
    53, 155–57, 161, 195, 201, 202,
    206
Laughter, tragic, 8, 32, 80– 81, 99–
    101, 101–5, 110, 132
Lawrence, D. H., 136
Lear, King, 82, 88, 90, 110, 122, 123,
    124, 130, 182, 183, 194
"Leda and the Swan," 114, 120, 126
Lévi-Strauss, Claude, 127, 183,
    234n.49
Lewis, Wyndham, 82
"Lines Written in Dejection," 142–44
Longinus, 106–16, 119–20, 126, 129
Love poems, elegiac, 14, 17– 26, 31,
    39
"Lover mourns for the Loss of Love,
    The," 20

Lowell, Robert, 8, 17, 59, 136
Lucian, 105

Mabinogion, The, 183
Macleod, Fiona, 141
"Magi, The," 114, 115, 118, 119
Mallarmé, Stéphane, 134–35
"Man and the Echo," 2, 3, 63, 134,
    136, 163, 165, 167, 193– 99, 201
Mangan, James Clarence, 146
"Man who dreamed of Faeryland,
    The," 1
Marcuse, Herbert, 206
Markievicz, Constance, 67–74
Mask, 4, 6, 27, 29, 44–46, 54– 55,
    98–101, 104–5, 111, 118, 148
Mathers, MacGregor, 37
"Meditations in Time of Civil War,"
    87, 113, 124–25, 158
Medusa, 118
Melancholia, 5–6, 38, 55, 76, 101,
    168, 176, 183–85
Menippus, 105
"Meru," 92, 101, 120, 157–58;
    quoted, 127
Middle class (bourgeoisie), 10, 30, 47,
    53–58, 82, 103–4, 124, 166
Mill, John Stuart, 47
Miller, J. Hillis, 157
Milton, John, 27, 29, 52, 54, 109, 140,
    141, 159; "Avenge O Lord . . . ," 32;
    "Lycidas," 14, 28, 32, 35, 56, 72,
    76, 78, 81, 95, 136; *Paradise Lost,*
    141, 147, 174
More, Henry, 143
More, Sir Thomas, 92
"Mountain Tomb, The," 91, 93
"Mourn—And Then Onward!" 26,
    55–56, 65
"Municipal Gallery Re-visited, The,"
    12, 26, 38, 45–46, 49– 51, 65, 74,
    147–48, 152–54, 161
Murdoch, Iris, 106–7
Murphy, William Martin, 56
Mussolini, Benito, 89
"My Descendants," 124–25, 131

"My Table," 159

Names and naming, 24–25, 64– 67, 75, 77, 88, 148–49, 226n.52
Naoise, 8
Narcissus, 4, 191
Nashe, Thomas, 15, 214n.28
"News for the Delphic Oracle," 2
Niamh, 103, 190
Nietzsche, Friedrich, 16, 98, 142, 164, 204; on Apollonian and Dionysian, 85, 87, 90, 102, 105; on eternal recurrence and sublime, 117–18; on tragic joy, 8, 80, 85, 89–90, 99, 104–5, 130; on Zarathustra, 85, 95, 184
"Nineteen Hundred and Nineteen," 9, 85, 92, 113–14, 116–17, 118, 125, 129, 157– 58, 204
Nutt, Alfred, 183

Oates, Joyce Carol, 94
Occult, 8, 16, 36–37, 112–13, 162, 207n.1, 233n.39
Oedipus, 82, 107–8, 110, 111, 121, 122
Oedipus at Colonus, 107
O'Grady, Standish, 47
O'Higgins, Kevin, 77, 150
"Old Men admiring Themselves in the Water, The," 4
O'Leary, John, 47, 58
"On a Child's Death," 26, 65
"On a Political Prisoner," 68– 71
On Baile's Strand, 104–5, 189
On the Boiler, 121
Ophelia, 18, 88, 93–94
"O'Rahilly, The," 75
Ovid, 191
Owen, Wilfred, 9, 57, 126, 201– 5; "The Last Laugh," 204–5; "S.I.W.," 202–3
Oxford Book of Modern Verse, The, 202

Parnell, Charles Stewart, 16, 26, 52, 55–57, 65, 74–78

"Parnell's Funeral," 18, 55, 74–78, 84, 159
Pater, Walter, 8, 24, 85, 91, 97, 204
Per Amica Silentia Lunae, 2, 9, 89, 98
Perloff, Marjorie, 44
Peter, Saint, 56, 76
Petrarch, 18–19, 25
"Pity of Love, The," 19
Plath, Sylvia, 8, 17, 136, 203
Plato, 11–12, 169, 173
Poe, Edgar Allan, 1, 18, 23
"Politics," 193–94
Pollexfen, Alfred, 34–36
Pollexfen, George, 35, 41, 43– 44, 65
Pollexfen, John, 35
Pollexfen, William, 5, 34–35, 110
Pound, Ezra, 8, 57, 128, 142
"Prayer for my Daughter, A," 52, 87
Praz, Mario, 8
Pre-Raphaelites, 18
Proctor, Thomas, 177
Prometheus, 85–87, 105, 130
Prophecy, 12, 105–8, 125–28, 128– 33
Prosopopoeia, 147–49, 152
Pygmalion, 190–91

Quintilian, 83

Raftery, 24, 170–72
Raleigh, Sir Walter, 92, 136
"Red Hanrahan's Curse," 122–23
Reincarnation. See Afterlife
"Reprisals," 38, 57, 68, 204
Responsibilities, 138
Reveries over Childhood and Youth, 4–6, 110
Rilke, Rainer Maria, 1, 166, 207n.2, 233n.38
"Roger Casement," 75
Romanticism: and death, 7–8, 11, 166, 204; and ekphrasis, 152–54, 156–57, 160; and elegy, 53–55, 64, 69, 71, 74, 81, 95; and self-elegy, 7, 137– 38, 140, 142–43, 164, 166, 174, 175, 187, 194; and the sub-

Romanticism (*cont.*)
  lime, 105–6, 111, 129–32; and
    tragic joy, 80–83, 85–86, 91, 94–
    95, 100. *See also* individual authors
Ronsard, Pierre de, 25
"Rose Tree, The," 66–67
Rosicrucianism, 91
Rossetti, Christina, 7, 136
Rossetti, Dante Gabriel, 7, 21, 152
Ruddock, Margot, 196
Ruins tradition, 80, 91–92, 155, 159

Sacks, Peter, 39, 211n.4, 214n.24
"Sad Shepherd, The," 14
"Sailing to Byzantium," 152, 159–61
Sappho, 109, 113
Sato, 159, 178
Schiller, Friedrich von, 106, 108
Schopenhauer, Arthur, 6, 92, 106, 150
Seanchan, 8, 103–5, 132, 202–3
"Second Coming, The," 79, 85– 87,
    105, 111–12, 113, 114–15, 116,
    117, 118–19, 120, 128
"Secret Rose, The," 33, 47
Self-elegy: career narrative in, 137–45,
    146–48, 179, 181, 189–90; mor-
    tification in, 162, 167, 169, 174,
    176–79, 186, 198; recathexis and
    decathexis in, 163–64, 175, 179,
    181, 189, 193, 198; self-division in,
    137–42, 144–45, 147–49, 163,
    168, 175–78, 181–83, 185–86,
    188. *See also* Autobiographical lyric;
    Ekphrasis; Invocation; Self-epitaph;
    Transition, poems of
Self-epitaph, 93, 136–37, 145– 52,
    161, 173, 193, 198
"September 1913," 54, 57–59, 64, 65,
    71, 73, 75
Shadowy Waters, The, 103
Shakespeare, 2, 16, 83, 88, 92, 97–98,
    107, 155, 163, 204, 216n.42,
    219n.63; *Richard III,* 125, 195;
    quoted, 187
Shapiro, Gary, 131
Shelley, Percy Bysshe, 5, 29, 53, 54,

55, 80, 96–97, 105, 129–31, 136;
    Adonais, 7, 26, 32, 42, 52, 76; *Alas-
    tor,* 7; "Defense of Poetry," 126;
    Hellas, 92; "Mont Blanc," 131, 194;
    "Ode to the West Wind," 94–95,
    96–97, 98, 120; "Ozymandias,"
    153; *Prometheus Unbound,* 85–87,
    124, 129–30; "To Wordsworth,"
    68–69; *The Witch of Atlas,* 130, 145
"Shepherd and Goatherd," 38– 40, 45,
    65, 70
Sidhe, 4, 8
Simmel, Georg, 38, 56
"Sixteen Dead Men," 66–67
"Song of the Happy Shepherd, The,"
    81
"Sorrow of Love, The," 19
"Soul in Judgment, The," 161– 65,
    197
Spender, Stephen, 9, 128, 132– 33
Spenser, Edmund, 92; *Astrophel,* 26–
    27, 40, 214n.27; *The Faerie Queene,*
    103, 140, 176; "Mutability Cantos,"
    62; *The Shepheardes Calender,* 34
"Spur, The," 140–41
"Statues, The," 159
Stevens, Wallace, 46, 57, 80, 98, 111,
    134–35, 136, 166, 204; "As You
    Leave the Room," 187–88; "Of
    Mere Being," 159– 60; "The Poems
    of Our Climate," 152; "Sunday
    Morning," 8, 91, 175
Sublime, the, 12, 60, 79–80, 86, 104,
    105–33; affective structure of, 101,
    108–13; and elegy, 80–81, 116;
    and genre, 105–7; and the father,
    110– 11, 115, 118, 121–22, 126,
    128; politics of, 126, 128–33; pros-
    ody of, 119–20; and repetition,
    114–18, 119–20; and tragedy,
    106–8. *See also* Apocalypse; Curse;
    Prophecy
Supernatural Songs, 92
Surrey, Henry Howard, earl of, 66
Swift, Jonathan, 77–78, 136, 147
"Swift's Epitaph," 147

Swinburne, Algernon, 7, 27, 70
"Symbolism of Poetry, The," 15
Synge, John, 37, 41, 43–44, 50, 65, 153–54

Tate, Allen, 13
Tennyson, Alfred, Lord, 7, 29, 35, 82; *In Memoriam*, 27, 28, 40, 42, 60
Thanatos (death drive), 5, 121, 124, 128–29, 177, 194
Thomas, Louis-Vincent, 206
"Three Marching Songs," 75
"Three Songs to the Same Tune," 75, 126
Tibetan Book of the Dead, The, 162
Timon of Athens, 15, 82
"To a Friend whose Work has come to Nothing," 104
"To a Shade," 54–56, 57, 58, 59, 65, 68, 75
"To a Wealthy Man . . . ," 57
"To be carved on a Stone at Thoor Ballylee," 149–51
"To Ireland in the Coming Times," 113, 146–48, 216n.43
"Tom O'Roughly," 93
Tone, Wolfe, 65, 75
"Tower, The," 2–3, 19, 20, 134, 136, 140, 163, 167–75, 176, 181, 188, 189, 190, 196, 201
Tragedy (tragic), 11, 12, 76, 79–90, 98, 106–8; chorus, 82, 85–90, 105; and elegy, 80–81, 93–98; hero, 2, 5, 8–9, 30– 31, 81–91, 93–94, 96–98, 102–4, 107–8, 129, 163, 202–5; internalization of, 81–90; joy, 3, 8–9, 12, 28–29, 78, 79–105, 106–111, 121, 125, 130–31, 135, 142, 151, 181, 201–2; soliloquy, 84–85. *See also* Laughter, tragic
Transition, poems of, 137–45, 147, 161
Trilling, Lionel, 137
"Twisting of the Rope, The," 171
"Two Love Poems," 19
"Two Songs from a Play," 127– 28

Tyndall, John, 8

"Under Ben Bulben," 2–3, 11, 93, 101, 121, 129–30, 145–46, 148–49, 150–51, 159, 161, 193, 195, 198, 201, 206, 231n.20; quoted, 136
Unicorn from the Stars, The, 132
"Upon a Dying Lady," 26, 27– 32, 48, 65, 68, 94, 95, 200; quoted, 101
"Upon a House shaken by the Land Agitation," 86, 104

"Vacillation," 84, 92, 96, 101, 113, 136, 163, 181–87, 189
"Valley of the Black Pig, The," 79, 96, 113, 127–28
Vendler, Helen, 15, 134–35, 161, 217n.49
Verlaine, Paul, 134–35
"Veronica's Napkin," 116
Villiers de L'Isle Adam, 205
Virgil: *Aeneid*, 100, 140, 147; Fourth Eclogue, 140; tomb inscription, 147
Vision, A, 2, 6, 27, 29–30, 32, 36, 44, 54–55, 91, 99, 107–8, 128, 134, 152, 161–65, 198
Visual arts. *See* Ekphrasis

Wanderings of Oisin, The, 4, 14, 81, 92, 103, 189–90
War, 8–10, 85, 89–90, 92, 98, 100, 104–5, 126–29, 131, 136, 166, 202–5
Weiskel, Thomas, 110
"What Then?" 151
"When You Are Old," 25
Where There is Nothing, 105
Whitaker, Thomas, 76, 127, 227n.66
Whitman, Walt, 136
"Who goes with Fergus?" 81
Wilde, Oscar, 21, 54, 83, 98, 205
"Wild Swans at Coole, The," 116, 142, 144–45
Wilhelm II, Kaiser, 90
William of Orange, King, 90

Wind Among the Reeds, The, 22
Wittgenstein, Ludwig, 10
Wollheim, Richard, 12
Women. *See* Gender
"Words," 172
Wordsworth, William, 54–55, 68–69,
    82; "Elegiac Stanzas on Peele Cas-
    tle," 152–54, 156; "Intimations
    Ode," 71, 94–95, 137–38, 143,
168, 187, 197–98; Lucy poems, 7,
21; "Preface" to *Lyrical Ballads,* 138,
166; *The Prelude,* 5, 47–48, 83,
109, 153–54, 194; "Tintern Abbey," 143

Yeats, John Butler (father), 44, 47,
    142, 153–54
Young Ireland, 52–53, 55

DATE DUE

MAY 0 4 199	MAR 2 8 2007		
APR 2 9 '9	FEB 0 5 2010		
MAY 2 8 '9	FEB 1 6 2011		
DEC 0 2 '9			
MR 08 94			
15 Jul 94			
20 Jul 94			
8 Aug 94			
09 Aug RT			
10 Aug 94			
JUN 0 2 95			
JAN 3 1 9			
AUG 14 1997			
MAR 24 1999			
DEC 1 3 1999			
JUL 0 6 2000			
7/21/00			
MAY 0 1 03			
GAYLORD			PRINTED IN U.S.A.